THE
LINCOLNS
IN THE
WHITE HOUSE

—

THE

LINCOLNS

IN THE

WHITE HOUSE

Four Years That Shattered a Family

JERROLD M. PACKARD

St. Martin's Press
New York

www.stmartins.com

Title Page Illustration: Library of Congress, Prints and Photographs Division, #LC-US262-2046

Library of Congress Cataloging-in-Publication Data

Packard, Jerrold M.
    The Lincolns in the White House : four years that shattered a family / Jerrold M. Packard.—1st. ed.
       p. cm.
    Includes bibliographical references (p. 273) and index (p. 279).
    ISBN 0-312-31302-0
    EAN 978-0-312-31302-9
    1. Lincoln, Abraham, 1809–1865. 2. Lincoln, Abraham, 1809–1865—Family.
3. Presidents—United States—Family relationships—Case studies. 4. United States—History—Civil War, 1861–1865—Social aspects. 5. Washington (D.C.)—History—Civil War, 1861–1865—Social aspects. 6. Washington (D.C.)—Social life and customs—19th century. I. Title.

E457.25.P23 2005
973.7—dc22

                 2005044236

First Edition: September 2005

10 9 8 7 6 5 4 3 2 1

CONTENTS

ACKNOWLEDGMENTS   ix

ONE   March 4, 1861—Washington City   1

TWO   Settling In   31

THREE   Calamity in War, Calamity at Home   74

FOUR   Death in the White House   109

FIVE   Shadows Everywhere   136

SIX   Victories   171

SEVEN   An Unfinished Work   212

EPILOGUE   The Flying Dutchman   254

NOTES   267

BIBLIOGRAPHY   273

INDEX   279

THE WHITE HOUSE
DURING LINCOLN'S PRESIDENCY

1   Lincoln's office connected by a private passageway to Family Living Room

2   Reception Room

3   Part of West Hall

4   Office stairs

5   Bedroom for Nicolay and Hay

6   Hay's office

7   West Hall

8   Nicolay's office

9   Family Living Room

10   Mary Lincoln's bedroom

11–13   Lincoln's bedroom/dressing room suite

14   Grand stairs and landing

15   Tad's bedroom

16   Willie's (Prince of Wales) bedroom

17   Service stairs

18–20   Pair of bedrooms divided by a corridor from whose window Lincoln spoke

21   Central Hall for family's private living quarters

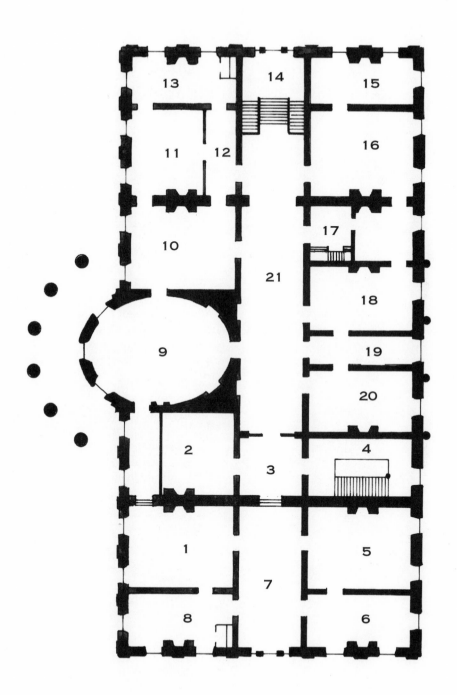

ACKNOWLEDGMENTS

M Y GRATITUDE FOR THEIR GENEROUS HELP WITH THIS book to my editor, Charles Spicer; to my literary agent, Natasha Kern; and to my partner, Merl Grossmeyer.

THE
LINCOLNS
IN THE
WHITE HOUSE

ONE

———

MARCH 4, 1861—WASHINGTON CITY

GRATEFUL TO BE FINISHED WITH THE DAY'S LONG AND tiring ceremony, Abraham and Mary Lincoln cheerfully crossed the threshold into the White House, escaping bleak skies and a cutting northwest wind that mirrored Washington's sense of unease. "Old Edward," head usher since anyone could remember, held the dilapidated door and bowed to the new president and first lady as they entered, both nearly blue from the cold.

Husband and wife felt markedly different about the dwelling that confronted them. What was to be the couple's home for the next four years looked more like a run-down plantation house than the head office of the American presidency. But the just inaugurated president took hardly any notice of the mansion's sad condition. His wife, Mary, on the other hand, triumphant in her new self-styled status as "Madam President," decided on the spot she was going to make this dismal place fit for its role as the chief executive's home. But what husband and wife did share was that neither had the first idea just how horrendous their new life in the White House was going to be.

Other, assuredly more important, concerns occupied Mr. Lincoln's thoughts. In America's eighty-five years of independence, the nation had never before found itself in a situation as dangerous as the one it faced on Lincoln's Inauguration Day. Lincoln's election as president fourteen weeks earlier had almost guaranteed that half of America would leave the Union. The new "Confederate" flag already flew above the legislative houses of seven Southern states that had formally abandoned the Union. Eight other states were considering secession. It was virtually certain that the loyal, Northern half of the nation would militarily challenge these secessions. After assuming the leadership of the still young Republican Party—many Southerners ridiculed it as the "Abolitionist Party"—Lincoln himself had signaled that the central government would never permit the breakup of the United States.

Though disagreements with the federal government over "states' rights" headed the South's list of grievances, the specific issue of slavery had counted above all else in the just concluded election. Slavery indeed overwhelmed every other public concern in America, nearly so much that other quarrels about politics and social differences mattered relatively little. A single unavoidable reality stood above this day's events: Abraham Lincoln would not now be stepping across the White House threshold if it weren't for slavery. He would instead have remained in Illinois, practicing law, spinning amusing tales, and playing doting father to his rambunctious—many of his neighbors would have said "insufferable"—sons. But Lincoln now symbolized the nation's overarching split. The officiant at this morning's inaugural ceremonies had been the cadaverous Roger Taney, octogenarian chief justice of the United States, who four years earlier in the court's *Dred Scott* decision had written that "Negroes had no rights the white man was bound to respect," his finding offending and polarizing a huge part of Northern opinion on the issue of racial justice. Taney's participation had drawn painful attention to the abyss that Lincoln was facing.

Only a few hours earlier, Lincoln had endured the ceremony that had elevated him from ordinary citizen to chief executive. Fortunately, the cold late-winter skies remained free from rain or snow during his swearing-in, but the near freezing air still penetrated the gabardine frock coat he chose to wear to be inaugurated as the sixteenth president of the United States. A tall, silken stovepipe hat combined with his extraordinary height ensured that he stood out in the crowd, making it possible for anyone, friend or foe, to easily see him. As he took the traditional drive down Pennsylvania Avenue from the White House to the Capitol with the outgoing president, James Buchanan, deep banks of onlookers lining the rough roadway nearly blocked their carriage. Lincoln was painfully aware that for the first time a heavy military presence had been mustered to keep an incoming president safe from would-be assassins. Both men must have been shaken by the symbolism of the rooftops lined with scores of troops, soldiers alert to any threat from the crowd. The seventy-five-year-old Winfield Scott, the federal army's commanding general, warned his men—most were members of the District of Columbia cavalry—to "watch the windows of the opposite side" and fire on anyone who looked to be pointing anything at the presidential carriage. In the Capitol itself, the largest structure in the country, guns protruded from every window while, just outside, dozens of musket-carrying soldiers surrounded the inaugural platform overlooking the building's east front.[1]

Lincoln had started writing his inaugural address long before he'd left his Springfield home. But changes both momentous and perfunctory to the critically important speech continued almost up to the moment he appeared before the crowd of thirty thousand expectant people standing below the Capitol's still-unfinished dome. An inelegant wooden stand cobbled together on top of the building's wide steps lent the setting the character of a construction site, but the little structure's small canopy at least provided the occupants with a bare minimum of protection against the weather. When Lincoln rose to speak, he realized his hat was still in his hands and quickly looked around for a place to put it. Stephen Douglas, once the new president's bitterest political enemy and a man who had decades earlier courted young Mary Todd, reached out and took the hat, graciously keeping it on his lap for the remainder of the ceremonies.

The heart of Lincoln's message was his steadfast determination to prevent the breakup of the nation, if necessary by armed force. But he extended an olive branch to the rebellious slave states in the speech's final paragraph. In his frontier cadences and high-pitched voice, Lincoln spoke words that would either thrill or dismay, leaving the nation's thirty-one million people frighteningly little ground for conciliation. "We are not enemies but friends," he pleaded hopefully. Speaking directly to the South's firebrands, he continued, "We must not be enemies . . . though passion may have strained, it must not break our bonds of affection. The mystic chords of memory, stretching from every battlefield and patriot grave, to every living heart and hearthstone, all over this broad land, will yet swell the chorus of the Union, when again touched, as surely they will be, by the better angels of our nature." Evidently agreeing with his rival's thinking, Douglas occasionally murmured "Good" and "Good again" as Lincoln spoke. The now ex-president Buchanan appeared to have slept through most of the proceedings.[2] In any case, few believed that Lincoln's words, however poetic and soothing, would be able to still the oncoming storm.

THE WHITE HOUSE

Though the White House was the most famous dwelling in America, Mary Lincoln knew next to nothing about the *home* she was entering. For the past four years the Executive Mansion's hostess had been Harriet Lane, the bachelor President Buchanan's high-spirited niece. Since the previous fall's election, Miss Lane had openly belittled the new occupants-to-be as unsophisticated yokels. Harriet had been told on what she believed to be good authority that Mrs. Lincoln in particular was "awfully western, loud & unrefined"[3] and conspicuously neglected to invite her successor to the White House for even a simple cup of tea and tour of the rooms. The Buchanan family's one thoughtful act was to order a meal to be ready for the new president and his family's party following the inaugural parade.

The capital's "traditions" in some measure explain the Buchanans' outwardly ungracious behavior. In antebellum Washington, old hands rarely lent much useful knowledge to the new family in the Executive Mansion, particularly regarding how to make the house function as a home. The departing occupants were never even expected to brief their successors on basic domestic matters. Furthermore, except for a doorkeeper, no real permanent White House administration existed, and nothing like a staff of civil servants was in place to get the place ready for the turnover. The Lincolns were to find no butlers or footmen who might render basic necessities to the family in their private quarters, nor even a domestic staff to sweep the floors or clear the dirty dishes from the departees' final, inauguration-morning breakfast. As matters stood, the Lincolns couldn't have been aware of the singularity of the meal laid on by Harriet Lane, a gift the new occupants were lucky to find waiting for them that first day.

The now ex-president Buchanan escorted his successor to the Executive Mansion and there bade the Lincoln family a relieved good-bye before leaving—doubtless ecstatic to be escaping—for his own Pennsylvania home. Exhausted from the whirlwind they had endured since dawn, the Lincolns knew these few hours of rest would be but a short respite before the afternoon public reception in the White House and the evening's inaugural ball at the City Hall that still awaited them. Having accompanied the first family to the White House, General Scott was enjoying his own sense of relief at having seen the Lincolns safely inside their new home and remarked in reference to the president's well-being, "Thank God, we now have a government."[4] Given the dangerous atmosphere in the capital, for the sake of security Scott had farsightedly ordered a detachment of soldiers to surround the Executive Mansion.

Assorted sisters, cousins, and nieces of the new first lady, altogether fifteen privileged family members, excitedly tagged along in the presidential party's wake, and all happily and gratefully sat down to Harriet Lane's ad hoc dinner. The meal ended just before the reception started, when a large waiting crowd was admitted into the north hall to shake President Lincoln's hand. For several hours extending into the early evening, the president and his first lady greeted what seemed like most of the plain, anonymous Americans who the prior November had voted the Lincolns into their new prominence. When ushers finally shut the doors on the good-natured and curious crowd, most of whom had been well-wishers rather than the office seekers who would soon enough descend upon the president, the family climbed the grand staircase to the mansion's second floor. There they found a gloomy region divided by a long central hallway into a clutch of closet-sized nooks, a few only slightly larger offices, several dismally small bedrooms, and one good-sized living room. Too tired to engage in any real exploring, everyone homed in on the first available bed on which to nap before undertaking the elaborate dressing required for the evening's inaugural ball, the climactic gala that was a part of every new president's entry into office.

For the ball, the planners had chosen a spot behind the City Hall and there threw together a huge but temporary plank pavilion, a muslin-draped affair the inaugural committee optimistically christened the Palace of Aladdin. Though the pavilion was outfitted with separate dancing and supper spaces, no one had thought it necessary to provide the rough facility with a cloakroom or toilets for the several thousand attendees expected; gentlemen's and ladies' facilities could only be reached by walking over to the adjoining City Hall, the men's toilets in its courtroom, the women's in the Common Council chamber.[5] Though the shoddiness of the setting in which she was making her debut as queen of Washington society disappointed the new first lady, she nonetheless was intent on looking and acting every bit the evening's sophisticated star.

For the occasion, Mary chose an immense blue silk crinoline, the great half-globe of her skirt draped with a French lace tunic. The new first lady further adorned herself with a matched set of pearl and solid-gold bracelets, earrings, brooch, and necklace; a blue-ostrich-feather-topped ornament crowned her head, the lavish confection trailing tendrils of sweet jasmine. Her glamor, if overelaborate by sophisticated Eastern standards, nonetheless belied any notion of frontier plainness.[6] Lincoln, wearing his new swallow-tailed coat and visibly exhausted by the day's trials, constantly tugged at the white kid evening gloves Mary insisted he wear for the sake of etiquette.

The president led off the opening quadrille, marching spiritedly arm in arm not with his wife but, as protocol demanded, with Washington's Mayor James G. Berret. The odd though traditional arrangement left Mary to find her own partner for the grandest dance of the evening, and she coquettishly chose Stephen Douglas, who had earlier in the day held her husband's hat just as many years before in her native Lexington he had held her hand as a suitor for her affections. To the sprightly and patriotic notes of "Hail Columbia," the company marched smartly from one end of the flame-lit ballroom to the other, the ensemble providing a stirring sight for the rest of the guests, few of whom were members of the city's oldest and most entrenched high society but who nonetheless shone brightly enough under the room's giant gasoliers. Lincoln departed an hour after midnight, but Mary and her cousins and sisters stayed on to dance until the new day's sun rose to brighten the city.

THE CAPITAL

Though Washington had been the nation's capital for six decades, the city was far from having yet taken its modern shape by the time of Lincoln's inauguration, with Pierre-Charles L'Enfant's majestic plan still only a small fraction completed. Anthony Trollope, the British novelist, who visited the capital in 1861, said that "of all the places that I know it is the most ungainly and most unsatisfactory: I fear I must also say the most presumptuous in its pretensions."[7] Countless Americans concurred in his assessment.

An almost endless list of factors made Washington the usually disagreeable place it was in which to live, do business, or conduct government. Foremost was weather. It was tropically hot and humid in the summer, bitterly cold, damp, and snowy in the winter, with only relatively short breaks of temperate pleasantness in between. Some of spring and autumn were admittedly appealing, but the rest of the year was routinely so bad that the British Foreign Office classified the American capital as an official hardship posting for Her Majesty's diplomatic representatives unfortunate enough to be stationed in it. In an age when summer heat was ameliorated only by fans and winter cold by fireplaces, Washington's extremes made for an exceedingly uncomfortable existence.

But more than just the weather gave the city its notable unpleasantness. Washington's water supply was not only dirty and polluted but represented in all its permutations a mortal threat to the health of the capital's inhabitants. The lowest parts of the city, which unfortunately included the White House and its precincts, rose mere inches above the sluggishly tidal Potomac River, some stretches of which were lined with swamps. As the stream coursed past the District, its most troubling habit was overflowing onto lower Pennsylvania Avenue.

If the effects of the uncontrolled Potomac weren't enough, smaller arteries of equally filthy water bisected the heart of the federal district. The Tiber Creek, formerly and less grandly named Goose Creek, emptied into the Potomac just below the White House; the canalized part of the stream flowed along what would one day become the Mall, crossed in front of the Capitol, and discharged into what was then known as the Eastern Branch, today called the Anacostia River. By 1860 the Tiber Creek and Canal were essentially sewers—filthy, dark, disease-carrying waterways, home to an inexhaustible supply of mosquitoes, the final resting place of numberless dead and bloated animals, the receiving culvert for a large part of the city's ordure, and chief creators of the foulest odors to be experienced anywhere on the Eastern seaboard. They were also breeding basins for every kind of human-threatening disease from typhoid and tuberculosis to malaria and dysentery. And, unfortunately, they were what lay at the bottom end of the White House's grounds.

What was more, dangerous humans represented nearly as much

a menace as did dangerous vermin. Only brave men and destitute women ventured alone onto the city's unlighted streets at night, when footpads and hoodlums freely ruled the darkness largely because the city's police force employed only fifty patrolmen.[8]

With its sixtysome thousand inhabitants, Washington was not small— at least when compared to America's other cities of the time. But it had little of the big-town liveliness or sophistication of New York or Philadelphia or New Orleans. Instead it lazed quietly, its "industry" be- ing the pen pushing and bean counting of government supplemented by a small but steady stream of cash-carrying sightseers who came to look at the building in which Congress made the nation's laws and the palace in which their president resided. It was, unmistakably, a Southern town, one that shut down when the afternoon sun got too hot, or—for a considerably longer period—when the Congress was in recess. Most no- tably, it was a slave city, sandwiched between the slave states of Mary- land and Virginia. The capital itself was thoroughly steeped in slave culture, the owning of black Africans perfectly lawful and accepted without demur by the District's white inhabitants.

The Washington the Lincolns would come to know most familiarly ran along the axis from their own residence to the Capitol, with Penn- sylvania Avenue the filament tying the two together. From the top of eighty-foot-high Jenkins Hill, on which the city's designer had placed the legislative house, middle Pennsylvania Avenue traced a mile-long chain of hotels, cheap saloons, and whorehouses bordering the top end of the street, while more respectable shops and the relatively imposing Willard Hotel—the town's best—continued westward. Just before the White House, the street reached the half-finished Treasury building, which, thanks to a whim on Andrew Jackson's part, was built squarely where it would block the president's view of the Capitol.

For this mile the town's life reached its highest peak of animation, the shops on the north side of the avenue lending the city the biggest dollop of mercantile class anywhere between Baltimore to the north and Charleston to the south. In 1861, a puny total of ten buildings represented the physical presence of the federal government; strewn between them were a few statues and the stub of the unfinished Washington Monument, squatting in the muck of the long and messy field—now the Mall—that spilled down the slope of Jenkins Hill from the Capitol to the Potomac. To the north of the White House, a few streets represented "downtown," where more shops, restaurants, hotels, and a couple of theaters pretty much completed what could be thought of as the "metropolis." Even Pennsylvania Avenue itself was really only half a street as far as pedestrians were concerned—slaughterhouses and wholesale markets occupied virtually its entire south side, all of which backed up to the fetid slit latrine and open sewer that was the Tiber Canal. What was more, when the town's only partly macadamized main boulevard wasn't flooded, it was just about always either muddy, dusty, or frozen over.

There *was* Quality in the city, mostly in the North End, roughly the blocks spread out in front of the White House's main entrance. That was where the well-to-do had built generously proportioned houses on choice sites, homes in the main still occupied by grandees such as the handful of rich senators and the (mostly) Southern ladies of high caste who controlled the capital's Society with resolute will and iron fists. But even these plutocrats lived on streets still unpaved and thus perpetually filthy—Pennsylvania Avenue was the only paved street in the entire city—and they shared the same miserable climate as everyone else, meaning that the well-off weren't all that much more comfortable than the poor during the execrable winters and summers. But these "cliff dwellers" always fell back on their assured belief that they were socially superior to the "transients," the first families that rotated through the White House every four or eight years. As Lincoln's Inauguration Day had approached, more and more of these sympathizers with most things Southern had ominously closed up their big houses, padlocked the doors, and moved south to await what they hoped might soon be a Washington that was capital of a new, *Southern* nation.

But, formally at least, the Executive Mansion—as it was still officially called—remained the lamp that lit social Washington. Most people had long since referred to the president's residence as the White House, the popular name implied by the color of the paint coating its sandstone exterior.[9] All visitors to the building passed a statue of Thomas Jefferson placed in the center of the front lawn, undoubtedly many noticing that the antique monument could have used a scrubbing to remove its coating of slimy green mold. When the Lincolns first entered the White House, the residence was almost as publicly accessible as any of the city's shops, hotels, or restaurants. A protective wrought-iron railing bordered the so-called Avenue Front, meaning the building's north side facing Lafayette Square and Pennsylvania Avenue. But the fence's pair of decorative gates remained open to anyone who cared to wander through them. No guard post impeded visitors, either friends or strangers, from walking straight up to the front door centered under the portico. The official doorkeeper stationed just inside the entrance existed more to hold open the door than to monitor who was coming through it. Though Lincoln could have exercised his authority to close the White House to visitors—certainly, at least, to casual, uninvited visitors—he quickly signaled his intention to allow virtually unlimited access rather than risk seeming aloof or undemocratic to the voters who had put him there.

Though few homes in America were larger than the president's residence, the part of the White House that served as the first family's private quarters amounted to only a small fraction of the building. No presidential "West Wing" then existed. Instead, the building's designer expected that the White House as conceived at the end of the eighteenth century would adequately fulfill its role as both home and office. What was more, today's third floor with its bedrooms and private quarters remained far in the future; the murky space squeezed in between the second floor's ceiling and the building's roof was then simply an empty attic. The large basement (today more elegantly known as the Ground Floor) was the preserve of domestic servants and cooks; the handful of such workers serving the Lincolns had mostly been Buchanan's staff, men and women who decided to remain after the inauguration and hoped to be kept on by the new occupants. This state of affairs produced far less comfort—let alone opulence—for the president and his family than many of the richest Americans took for granted in their own generously staffed mansions.

On the whole of the first floor, officially known as the State Floor, the Lincolns would enjoy only the Family Dining Room at their ordinary daily disposal. The five state chambers—the Red, Green, and Blue rooms (a disproportionately large part of the house's richness was concentrated in these three rooms), the State Dining Room (in which Mary would find that the White House's china "collection" was so inadequate that only ten diners could be served on matching dishes), and the East

Room (the largest in the building) were used for official receiving and entertaining, though the Lincolns would soon be adventurous enough to claim the Red Room in which to receive their private evening callers. This floor was, by any measure, the best maintained and decorated. But its elegant, heavy furnishings and accessories had been installed decades earlier—many during the administrations of Madison and Monroe—and had become noticeably well-worn, in some cases even shabby. Furthermore, an absence of paintings or hangings on the high white walls gave the house a sterile feeling. But Mary quickly took heart, having deduced from a book called *Lives of the Queens of England* that British royalty derived much of its authority from the pomp and majesty it so successfully projected. She determined to follow this same formula in at least these public parts of her own new home.[10]

Presidential families had always lived their private hours together on the mansion's second floor. But even there privacy meant something considerably different from how the couple would have defined it back in Springfield. The eastern end of the floor—the part directly above the great East Room one floor down—had long been given over to the offices of the presidency. In 1861 this area would be divided between a room for the president, two rooms for his two secretaries, a bedroom shared by said secretaries, and a handful of anterooms in which to hold visitors and supplicants, a daily swarm of whom, Lincoln would soon learn, regarded it as their birthright to be allowed to personally meet face-to-face with the president. Pocket doors divided this office area from the family's living quarters down the central corridor to the west, though nothing prevented anyone, including total strangers, from opening those doors and wandering at will into the "private" area beyond.

On its south side, the center of the second floor held the presidential family's "living room," a large oval room corresponding to the elliptical Blue Room below. Bedrooms completed the western end of the floor, all opening onto the central corridor, along which the wandering curious could and often did pass within inches of the doors to these family sleeping chambers. During their White House years Mary and Abraham Lincoln would sleep in separate but adjoining bedrooms on the south side of this passage, just as they had slept in separate rooms during their life together in Springfield. The family bedrooms had recently been fitted out with sinks and running water, the water piped in straight from

the sewage-laden Potomac; the disastrous consequences of these plumb-
ing arrangements quickly hit the family with the force of a bomb. In
addition, off the west end of the first floor stood a large working conservatory, a well-appointed gardening center of which Mary would soon
make extensive though frequently controversial use. For the entire second floor, there were two toilets, although countless chamber pots were
strewn about, as were many well-used spittoons.

Though most people likely regarded the White House as palatial,
which it was when compared with the vast dreary bulk of the city's
dwellings, this cold and unhomelike house seemed less like a place
where normal people actually lived than what one observer likened to
an "old and unsuccessful hotel."[11] But on the Lincolns' inaugural night,
with the late-winter winds sweeping the streets of the agitated capital,
inside the building's thick walls the first family and their tribe settled
down thankfully for their first night.

Elsewhere around town, less affluent visitors lodged themselves into
whichever they could find of the city's available nooks to pass the night
before returning to the towns and farms whence they'd come. At least
on this opening night of the new presidency, America remained a nation
at peace, but a condition few assumed was going to last much longer.

THE LINCOLNS' FIRST DAYS

Awakening at dawn on his first full day as president, the new commander in chief found himself staring straight at the revolutionary reality of a broken Union. Seven Southern legislatures had already declared
that their states were no longer part of the United States, all making
clear that they would go to war with the federal government to sustain
their decisions. Lincoln's immediate crisis had condensed to a single
flashpoint, a standoff between federal authority and the new union of
Southern states that called itself a confederacy. At the emergency's center was a highly visible and enormously symbolic army fort on an island
in the harbor of Charleston, South Carolina. In the inaugural address
that he had delivered to the nation just twenty-four hours earlier, Lincoln had expressly pledged to "hold, occupy, and possess the property
and the places belonging to the government." It now appeared certain
that Charleston's Fort Sumter was going to be a test of that pledge.
South Carolina had conspicuously stood at the head of the exit line of

states leaving the Union, and its leaders were now determined to wrest control of that fort from the federals.

As president and protector of the nation's peace, Lincoln was equally determined to avoid firing the first shot in any civil conflict between the country's two sections. But Sumter's garrison was facing starvation, its provisions due to run out in six weeks in the judgment of its command-ing officer, Major Robert Anderson. Lincoln knew the South Carolina state militia's guns that were trained on the island fortress could and would prevent food from arriving. Both of the president's alternatives—either attempting to supply Anderson and his garrison or abandoning Sumter to rebel occupation—would, he understood without question, end disastrously for the United States.

Not only was the new president confronted with the near certainty of a military and political catastrophe, Lincoln still possessed only scant knowledge of how to make his government do what he wanted it to do. The executive branch then possessed nothing like today's "transition teams," and the minuscule office of the presidency consisted of himself and his two secretaries, the latter as untutored as their boss in the work-ings of executive governance. John Nicolay, the senior of the two private secretaries Lincoln had brought with him from Illinois, would act as something like a chief of staff in modern terms. Only a few days before the inauguration Nicolay had visited the White House to attempt to ori-ent himself to the physical spaces in which he would work. He also called in at the State Department to get information on the social cus-toms and usages the new president would have to follow to ensure that the fledgling administration got off the ground.

In 1861 there were no press staff, no speechwriters, and certainly no "councilors to the president." Civil servants ready to translate the chief executive's wishes into coherent commands were found nowhere in the White House. Even such tactical essentials to military planning as ade-quate maps were missing, except for the handful of old varnished charts that Buchanan had left hanging on the walls of his office. Nor was the cabinet—the group of men heading the federal departments—yet com-plete; on Lincoln's second day, he sent to the Senate for confirmation only a partial list of names of the eventual eight men who would lead the federal bureaucracy as well as serve as the president's principal sounding board. Most troubling, his critical choices for State and Trea-sury hadn't even yet formally accepted his invitations to serve. Crucial to the about-to-explode Sumter stalemate was Lincoln's top military adviser, Commander of the Army General Winfield Scott. Though the superannuated Scott was a loyal officer and eager to help his new chief untangle the Sumter crisis, the general had not yet worked out a serious plan to resolve the military issues facing Lincoln's new government, which this morning most critically meant the storm about to break in Charleston harbor.

MARY

While her husband grappled with the issues of war and peace, Mary Lincoln's hardworking mind was filled with entirely different concerns on her first morning as mistress of the mansion. With her customary high energy and despite her late night before, she had arisen early to join all her female relatives at breakfast. The maid had laid out the meal on a sideboard in the second-floor Oval Room, a meal probably consisting of little more than eggs, toast, and coffee, given the kitchen's still un-stocked state. Away from gawking outsiders, the women felt free to re-main in their light wrappers and dressing gowns instead of donning crinoline dresses and the cumbersome steel hoops meant to keep their skirts fashionably bulbous. Mrs. Lincoln herself was dressed in an ele-gant cashmere robe decorated with fancy quilting on the front—and rarely without some kind of head covering, this morning Mary had done up her hair with a lace cap neatly pinned on top of it.

The single invariable job a president's wife performed in the nine-teenth century was to attractively complement her husband while the White House's social functions were carried out. The first lady was meant to greet visitors, chat politely with guests, serve tea to the wives of the men who ran the government, and all the while look as fashion-ably presentable as her own natural assets and dressmaker's skills made possible. She should, so theory and tradition had it, be heard and heard of as little as possible and then only in ways appropriate to her role as at-tentive and dutiful wife. If circumstances dictated, she would, of course, serve as nurturing mother to the president's children, though in the mid-nineteenth century presidential children were, before the Lincoln boys arrived, already adults themselves. Importantly, she would not offer nondomestic advice except possibly over the pillow and then only if her husband solicited such counsel. She would not, in short, be anyone of substance except a helpmeet, and certainly not a woman bringing attention to anything but her own gracious quiet and decorum. The country was about to find these nearly universally accepted guidelines of the era fundamentally changed by the wife for the past eighteen years of Abraham Lincoln.

Mary Lincoln—she did not, incidentally, call herself Mary *Todd* Lincoln, a common formulation used for her after her death—was a Westerner and a woman long accustomed to hard work, but she was not a frontier naïf in the way that her husband was widely caricatured. Though not the submissive wife in the manner expected of women of her time, neither was Mary any kind of early feminist. She believed, traditionally, that she belonged principally in the role of homemaker and mother, but far less traditionally, she expected that she should not be disregarded. She in fact demanded that she be listened to, paid attention to.

Mary was born in 1818 into a family of only middling wealth but of a well-established name and reputation, a clan that claimed and was accorded high social position among the proud gentlefolk of Lexington, Kentucky. The Todds were a self-confident family of high expectations—although one that too close intermarriage had occasionally brought low.[12] Because they lived in a state in which slavery was legal, it was in no way extraordinary that a black servant woman had attended to most of the hard work of actually raising Mary.

The Todd family nanny was named Sally. She was the legal property of Mary's father, as were the other black men, women, and children in the Todd household, all of whom together made life flow smoothly and pleasantly for the white inhabitants of this privileged world. As a girl, Mary believed, likely only wishfully, that Kentucky's slaves fared better than those in any other state. For example, educating blacks wasn't outlawed there as it was elsewhere in the South, although little enough black education existed even in Kentucky. Wherever the institution of slavery existed, though, its reality meant that black newborns became their white owner's property. It meant that the black family could be destroyed when the owner sold its members separately, and it meant that slaves could be and often were flogged for whatever actions their owners found objectionable, and that "catchers" could legally kill slaves attempting to escape. Such realities represented the underside of Mary's childhood experience with slavery, however much the Todd family's own relative kindness at home alleviated the institution's worst horrors.

The combined effects of her mother's death and her father's hasty remarriage represented the first significant upset in Mary's life. Mary was the second youngest of Robert Todd's six children from his first marriage. The second Mrs. Todd gave her husband seven more children, which meant an astonishing twenty-eight years separated Robert's first child by his first wife from his last child by his second wife. Lost in a crowded field of a dozen siblings and half siblings, by the time she was an adolescent Mary wanted nothing so much as to escape her crowded home and an uncongenial stepmother, whose principal interest lay in her own children. Moreover, a girl who craved paternal attention now found herself faced with a father whose concerns had turned almost wholly to his new wife.

From her earliest childhood, Mary suffered from the combined effects of a volatile temper, a moody disposition, and an inability to silence her too-often-barbed tongue, all traits running counter to the prevailing ethos of the day that young people should be little heard and not much more seen. But as a Todd, she would at least be well educated by the virtually universal standards of her day for females. She even became skilled at French, thanks to the efforts of Madame Charlotte Mentelle, the headmistress at the boarding academy on the outskirts of Lexington to which Robert Todd sent her. Her ultimate rescuer from Lexington was one of her elder sisters, Elizabeth Edwards, who had married well in far-off Springfield, Illinois, and who sympathized with the younger girl's feelings of suffocation in the crowded Todd household. The generous Elizabeth invited Mary to come to the still raw Illinois frontier to live with her and her husband. Mrs. Edwards's hope, of course, was that Mary would find, court, and marry a well-situated man, a standard series of tasks not expected by either sister to take too much time *or* effort.

Over the next decades, many trials would all but demolish the shaky structure of Mary Todd's life. But none among them was so damaging to her as her own thorny personality. From her teens there was hardly a time when she wasn't dismaying someone or exhibiting inexplicable and sometimes self-destructive behavior, the latter often manifested by the cutting edge of her tongue. She was not then, though, mentally ill, at least not *continually,* or beyond a safe return to normal conduct. Where she could easily lose forbearance with someone or something, and thereby cause lasting pain in expressing her anger or impatience, she could and would also turn on a dime, resuming a seemingly lighthearted kindness—though the object of her scorn would rarely forget Mary's stings. In short, Mary was alternately kind and sarcastic, generous and unforgiving, and most of her new friends in Springfield would agree with a comment made about the twenty-one-year-old: "She was either in the garret or the cellar"[13]—a telling parallel of a modern manic-depressive diagnosis.

In his sympathetic 1932 study of Mary's personality, Dr. W. A. Evans, a psychiatrist, wrote that "the peculiarities of [Mary's] behavior resulted from her emotions rather than from her thinking." He noted that her conduct was "determined by an insanity of her emotions rather than of her mind."[14] What many perceived as colorful and intriguing in the child—her high-strung quickness and an eagerness to laugh derisively at others' foibles and shortcomings—became far less benign traits in the mature woman. History entered the picture when this quicksilver young woman fascinated and captured Abraham Lincoln's attention as a possible wife. But Lincoln eventually came to perceive her as others did and recognized that her personality might well represent a heavy burden on any life they would make together. But after vacillating, he evidently decided to ignore the dangers, instead comparing Mary favorably to the other proper but tongue-tied and ill-educated belles of Springfield's upper-middle class. To Lincoln—and to many other young men—Mary must have seemed a highly desirable firecracker; as Elizabeth's husband depicted his future sister-in-law's charm, "she could make a bishop forget his prayers."[15] Attractive, outspoken, and usually the center of attention, Mary could choose from a large field of eager suitors. Lincoln knew this, and it made him want her all the more.

Almost without exception, Mary's relatives tried to dissuade her from an alliance with a largely untested lawyer, an awkward newcomer to the social graces, whose financial state could most optimistically be described as low—though not entirely without promise. Mary saw a man with a future far more auspicious than those of her two brothers-in-law. In her budding young womanhood she probably did possess the necessary characteristics to marry a more obviously suitable young Springfield gentleman. But some quality in Lincoln's brooding mix of intellect and gravitas led Mary to bet her own happiness and future on what she, and she nearly alone in her family, envisioned him someday achieving. As it happened, within three years of their wedding Abraham Lincoln would enter Congress as the representative from the Eighth District of Illinois, a distinction in itself greater than most men achieve in a lifetime.

The early years of marriage did bring Mary satisfaction and evidence that her optimism about the soft-spoken lawyer had paid off. Even her family soon began to acknowledge the extraordinary worth in Lincoln. In their early days the couple paid four dollars a week for room and board in a Springfield combined tavern and inn, a threadbare affair called the Globe. There in 1843, the year after their wedding, their first child was born, a son they named Robert, for Mary's father. Their modest living arrangements soon graduated with the purchase of a small but pleasant house in a respectable part of Springfield. Lawyer Lincoln's fees now began to provide modest comforts, such as servants as well as a degree of financial safety, the latter undoubtedly gratifying for Lincoln but absolutely indispensable to his insecure wife. Before long Lincoln's rising renown as a serious thinker about serious issues brought him his single two-year term in the U.S. House of Representatives, giving Mary the opportunity to live in Washington and allowing both to visit the sophisticated cities of the Northeast and New England.

The first great lasting wound to Mary's mental health struck in her eighth year of marriage. Three years after Robert's birth, Mary delivered a second child, another boy, on March 10, 1846. Edward Baker Lincoln was born in the family's home at Eighth and Jackson streets. His parents named him for Edward Dickinson Baker, a local Whig lawyer and an old and intimate friend of the baby's father's. For much of Eddie's short life Lincoln was away from home, living in Washington as a congressman or crisscrossing Illinois as a roving lawyer. But he remained a genuinely loving father, generous with gifts for the boy, and happy to carry him around on his shoulders. In his wife's unsentimental opinion, he very much spoiled his new son, one he habitually referred to as a "blessed child," or as his "dear codger."[16] But even a father's love acted as no barrier to the little understood plagues of the nineteenth century, illnesses that invaded the neat frame house on Springfield's Eighth Street just as lethally as they did countless other homes across the country.

Shortly before Christmas 1849, the now three-year-old Eddie got sick with the disease that would end his life. Mary's father had died of cholera only a few months earlier in Lexington, and that loss, combined with the death of a close friend's child soon thereafter, caused her to be especially fearful for the health of the always frail Eddie. It would be exactly fifty-two days from the time the boy's parents first noticed the signs of sickness until his death. Medical authorities later speculated Eddie had contracted diphtheria, though there is no certainty of the diagnosis; that illness generally runs its course in a far shorter time, and some modern historians speculate that pulmonary tuberculosis was the likely cause.[17] Whatever sickened and finally killed the boy, the medicine of the time was powerless against it. For nearly two months Eddie's parents could do little more than stand by helplessly as their child grew weaker and sicker by the day.

On January 31, 1850, the doctor starkly described Eddie as "desperately ill." With hope for recovery finally all but abandoned, he succumbed a few hours later, on the first day of February. The neighbors who arrived to sit with the Lincolns beside the body, the custom of the time, were the first to see the young mother and wife almost out of her mind with grief. For the first time in Mary's life, her pain was such that no one could even help ease it, let alone make it go away, and for weeks she gave herself over to what seemed like a sorrow that would kill her. Neighbors and family experienced a woman refusing food and lying prostrate on her bed, unable to arise or even acknowledge the kind friends who tried to comfort her. Her husband, himself understandably distraught over the loss of a son, was shaken by Mary's reaction to Eddie's death, pleading with her, "Eat, Mary, for we must live."[18] In a time when the loss of young children to diseases was almost expected, Mary's prolonged loss of self-control looked ominous in terms of her future ability to bear trauma.

Even the miracle of Robert being spared the illness that killed Eddie seemed not to have lifted Mary during her weeks of suffering. Bob, as his family called him, was turning out to be an anomaly, a slightly perplexing mystery to both his mother and, especially, his father. The boy's personality created an often unbridgeable space between himself and his parents. Robert's inherent makeup seemed markedly different from those of the brothers who came after him. And it wasn't temporary. For the remainder of his life, Robert Todd Lincoln stood apart from his living parents and, after his own death, even from his parents' legacies.

History's often repeated explanation that Robert was "entirely Todd" implied he wasn't at all like his father, that his makeup was instead like that of the aristocratic Todds of Lexington. Such may explain some or even the major part of the gulf distancing him from his father. But his father's absence on legal travels during Robert's formative years might explain more. And the similar but conflicting personalities shared by mother and son throw more light on the family breach. But during the years Abraham and Mary Lincoln and their children lived together as a family, Robert was, in many ways, the odd member out.

Because of concern for Mary's mental stability in the wake of Eddie's death, Lincoln likely began to reason that turning her attention and love to a new child was the best way to restore his wife's well-being. Thus in just under eleven months, a third child was born at Eighth and Jackson. Entering the world on December 21, 1850, the husky boy was named William Wallace Lincoln—his first two names honoring the physician husband of Mary's sister Frances. A seemingly perfect child, the son the Lincolns immediately began to call Willie did appear to bring Mary out of her depression. And likely regretting the gulf that had distanced him from Robert, Lincoln fell into an unalloyed love with Willie from the moment he was born, a love that would greatly ease the political pounding inflicted on him in his first year in the White House.

Mary reacted just as her husband had. From the beginning, she, too, gave Willie a vast and undemanding love. Whatever faults she may have had as a wife or friend, her devotion to her sons in their childhoods never for an instant wavered. From Lincoln she expected husbandly obedience to the solemn and unyielding social norms of the times. But she allowed her children broad leeway, permitting them almost any mischief or wildness or adventures they might devise. Mary was capable of harshly disciplining her sons if they crossed forbidden boundaries, though their father almost never raised a hand or even his voice against them. Though Robert's persona was in Springfield already settling into the reserve that would mark his entire life, Willie's nature and capabilities flew spectacularly high with such wide freedom from parental constraint or disapproval.

The family's missing part was a daughter. We don't know how much the absence of a girl child bothered Lincoln—though in 1860 he somberly wrote, "I regret the necessity of saying I have no daughter"[19]—but Mary's delight in girls suggests that she deeply wanted a daughter, one who would grow up sharing her woman's world, then a sphere dramatically separate from that of men. She became pregnant only one more time. On April 4, 1853, her fourth son was born (the delivery was medically difficult, likely the main reason the Lincolns didn't attempt to try again with a girl in mind). Thomas Lincoln, named for his father's father, was from birth called Tad, or Taddie. The nickname supposedly referred to his large head and its relationship to a small body, meaning that the baby must have resembled, at least in his father's estimation, a tadpole. Tad was born with what was probably a harelip and, possibly, a partially cleft palate, and understanding his speech would be difficult throughout his entire life. To Lincoln, however, other people's views of his youngest son's problems were inconsequential, and from the child's birth the father lodged Tad in the same safe and secure place that Willie occupied in his affections.

With undeniable irony, part of Mary's difficult personality became an agent that greatly raised Lincoln's presidential prospects. Lincoln must have borne the requisite intellect in the inner workings of his mind to eventually become the greatest president in American history. But to achieve that future, he was missing one critical quality. To reach the top requires an unquenchable drive, and Lincoln's own reservoir of it was probably a degree short. Mary gave him the missing component. After their marriage, his wife drove him ahead, sometimes subtly, sometimes relentlessly. She urged Lincoln to continue taking successive steps forward, to push himself harder, to reach out for the next prize. As with many couples, in the first years of marriage this husband and wife each clearly established the measure of the other. Lincoln learned of Mary's extensive emotional fragility, particularly her inability to control her moods and passions. What Mary miraculously measured correctly was Lincoln's brilliance—a quality that eventually dazzled an enormous segment of the nation's intelligentsia. But his mind needed her encouragement to push it forward, and on the road to the White House, Mary's prodding proved a critical key to Lincoln's success. Yet in the end, no amount of understanding or introspection on either partner's part would ever completely carry Mary Lincoln around the demons that bedeviled her.

THE FIRST LADY AND THE BLACK SEAMSTRESS

From the first day of Lincoln's presidency, scores of people walked up the curved driveway to the north entrance of the White House every day, but only a few did so in response to the first lady's bidding. And almost none of those so bidden were black. But on the day after the inauguration, a purposeful-looking, well-dressed African-American woman arrived in response to Mary Lincoln's request.

In 1861, the elements of Elizabeth Keckly's life would have been regarded as highly unusual anywhere in America. Born a slave, at the age of thirty-eight she had bought her freedom from her owner and, in her hometown of St. Louis, made a comfortable life for herself as a seamstress, her extraordinary skills bringing her substantial business and even greater repute. In 1860 she moved to Washington, where her now prodigious talents in dress design and high-quality sewing quickly attracted the attention of the most influential women in the capital. Her core business was not the making of ordinary dresses, but rather of couturier clothes: She designed and sewed by hand what were considered by wealthy Washingtonians the city's most opulent and fashionable gowns. By early 1861, Lizzy—the name by which her customers knew her—had become a flourishing, unquestionably competent businesswoman who was hired as dressmaker by many of the capital's best-known women, including the strikingly handsome Varina Davis, wife of Alabama's Senator Jefferson Davis. That renown predictably brought her to the new first lady's attention. Mary Lincoln stood at the beginning of her life at the epicenter of the nation's brightest spotlight, and she was in urgent need of dresses of the style and excellence that Mrs. Keckly could provide. A lady's reputation was strongly tied to the quality and breadth of her wardrobe, and no woman's reputation was more important, or more subject to criticism, than the first lady's.

The Executive Mansion's doorkeeper admitted the statuesque Mrs. Keckly to the vestibule. As the businesswoman waited, upstairs in the second-floor oval sitting room Mary Lincoln and her sister Elizabeth Edwards were busy interviewing a number of other dressmakers, women who had been arriving at precisely timed intervals since the first lady and her guests had finished breakfast. The African-American couturier's appointment was Mrs. Lincoln's last. When summoned, Lizzy

Keckly climbed the main staircase and made her way past hordes of office seekers clamoring to see the president, Lincoln's first full day in office already plagued by what he would quickly come to realize was one of the worst tasks inherent in the presidency. Mrs. Keckly walked around the mob and through an open door into the oval chamber. There she found Mrs. Lincoln in animated conversation. Mary warmly and respectfully welcomed her caller, a kindness that in 1861 was hardly a typical recognition from a white lady of prominence to a onetime slave.

Sheer force of will was the dominating feature on the face of the woman greeting Lizzy Keckly. The combination of Mary Todd Lincoln's genes and her new position as the wife of the president lent the small and fleshy woman a magnetic aura, her countenance this morning almost vibrating with purpose. Unkindly described as "dumpy" by many, Mary's appearance now at forty-two had modulated in the two decades since her marriage from that of a sparkly young woman, one whose attractiveness sprang principally from her vivacity, to that of a middle-aged housewife long bereft of any sexual beauty. She stood five feet three inches tall and weighed 130 pounds. In her middle years those proportions could have been turned into at least a poised gracefulness. But while Mary's appearance was still often striking when her mood was buoyant, she no longer bore any of the physical fairness of her youth. The doll-like cheeks, round face, and small mouth with thin lips were not helped by the ugly but at the time nearly universal female coiffure in which her hair was sharply parted in the center and pulled securely around the head into a kind of smooth, no-nonsense helmet. The first lady's eyes even lacked any kind of natural friendliness, instead too often looking as though they were taking frank stock of whomever or whatever they settled on. Notwithstanding all this, Mary's perky animation often managed to bring a glow to her features, a luster that many who met her long after remembered.

Unknown to Lizzy Keckly, before the seamstress had even entered the room Mary was already clearly determined on choosing the mulatto (a term designating a person with mixed European and African heritage) as her dressmaker. That the famously beautiful and genteel Varina Davis relied on Keckly was commendation enough for Mary; the first lady greatly admired, as did many in Washington, the courtly Mississippi senator's stunning wife. What was left for the women to negotiate were only the financial details. In Mary's down-to-earth, not to say abrupt,

Midwestern manner, she climaxed the interview by laying out her cards. "I trust your terms are reasonable," she said to Mrs. Keckly without a hint of haggling, adding, "I cannot afford to be extravagant . . . we are poor . . . if you do not charge too much, I shall be able to give you all my work." For good measure, Mary then once more drove home her central point: "I can't afford to pay big prices, so I frankly tell you so in the beginning."[20] Mrs. Keckly nodded her agreement, wisely avoiding any hint of negotiating: The practiced businesswoman well understood she had just gained a patron who firmly secured her future in Washington. The initial commission—a dress for the opening postinaugural reception in the White House—would be one of Mary's old gowns that she wanted her new couturier to remake. Business dealings thus completed, the first lady spent the rest of the day accompanied by her female relatives in a meticulous, room-by-room inspection of her new home.

BUSINESS AT THE OTHER END OF THE HALL

While Mary was enjoying a good look through the White House, her husband was deeply involved in figuring out the mechanics of the presidency. Luckily, he had resourceful help. More than anyone else, the two young secretaries Lincoln had brought with him to Washington bore the responsibility for seeing that their boss learned, as quickly as possible, the basic workings of power in the executive branch.

Happily for the presidency, the personalities of John Nicolay and John Hay meshed perfectly where Abraham Lincoln's needs were concerned, even though the pair's styles and strengths remained distinctly different. The men formed a combination that would, in political terms, magnificently serve the president for the next four years. It would also equally agreeably serve the pair's long lifetime of friendship, culminating in a jointly written encyclopedic memoir of the Lincoln administration that would be published twenty years after the president's death.

Thirty-year-old John Nicolay was the first of the two men to enter Lincoln's life. Nicolay was born in Bavaria, then an independent kingdom in a politically fragmented Germany. His parents brought him to the United States when he was still a young boy. Reared in Illinois, for the rest of his life he nonetheless retained more than a trace of a German accent, though in adulthood it only seemed to add to his air of efficiency and high intellect. A small-town newspaperman in his early career,

Nicolay first earned Lincoln's friendship while working as a law clerk in the older man's Springfield office during the political campaigns leading up to the 1860 election. It was an easy call for Lincoln as the new president-elect to invite the closemouthed Nicolay to accompany him to Washington and serve as his private secretary. The tall and thin Nicolay, who revealed little humor on his saturnine face, wore a muzzlelike goatee and heavy mustache, his long, stringy hair prematurely receding several inches from a broad forehead. Lincoln already regarded his young secretary with great affection, warmth Nicolay would repay in unshakable loyalty to his boss. Often acting as an éminence grise as if to a French monarch, throughout the administration's tenure Nicolay would serve Lincoln by personally conveying messages and instructions too sensitive to be committed to paper, often doing so secretly and over considerable distances.

Fully as dedicated and loyal to the president as Nicolay, John Hay represented the younger half of Lincoln's office staff. Though Hay was always the junior in official rank as well as in duties (he generally took care of the president's personal correspondence, while Nicolay attended to official letters received at the White House), he would make himself indispensable to the president both in his performance and through a vibrant personality that often relieved Lincoln's depression and helped him to endure some of the most terrible times of the presidency. Hay, like Nicolay, sprang from Illinois and was the son of a physician, Dr. Charles Hay, who bequeathed him his abhorrence of slavery, with the younger man becoming a convinced abolitionist.

After an undergraduate education at Brown University, followed by law school (gaining a very different grounding in the law from Nicolay's then common but less structured apprenticeship in the discipline), Nicolay recruited Hay to work in the 1860 Republican campaign, the latter focused on canvassing and helping to write the candidate's speeches.[21] When Lincoln chose Nicolay to serve as his private secretary, the latter suggested Hay be brought along to the White House as well. Thus at twenty-two, the smart but green young lawyer found himself half of the new president's executive staff. Hay was short but youthfully handsome, and he possessed a sharp mind, though one prone, like the president's, to deep depressions. His mouth was often flippant and habitually sarcastic, but Lincoln appreciated the mordant humor that afforded laughter in a White House besieged by tragedy. Though egalitarian in spirit, Hay possessed a brilliant mind and a sharp pen, and he rarely tolerated ignorance or ignorant people for long. His boss called him John, making him one of the few people Lincoln addressed by first name; even Nicolay was addressed by his last name by the president. Noah Brooks, a journalist and Lincoln family friend, described the relationship between the president and Hay: "Lincoln treated Hay with the affection of a father, only with more than a father's freedom. If he waked at night, he aroused Hay, and they read together; in summer they rode in the afternoons, and dined in the evenings. . . . In public matters the older man reposed in the younger's unlimited confidence."[22]

To serve as their living quarters in Washington, the president gave the two young men the northeast corner room of the White House's second floor, directly across the center hall from his own office. The high-ceilinged chamber performed double duty as the pair's sitting room and bedroom for four years. Lincoln himself often found refuge there from office seekers and other importuners, and even sometimes from his insistent wife. Hay at first tried with moderate success to maintain a cordial relationship with Mary, but Nicolay's relations with the boss's wife started out badly and soon became significantly worse. Lincoln realized his wife didn't possess the knowledge or the temperament to adequately manage the Executive Mansion's social life, and he turned over most of that responsibility to Nicolay. Nicolay took up the task with professional zeal, sometimes overriding Mrs. Lincoln when she attempted to inappropriately interfere or to express a problematical preference for certain dinner guests. Unsurprisingly, Mary deeply resented Nicolay for what she saw as his interference. And Nicolay's almost conspiratorial connection to Hay meant that her animosity to the elder of the pair eventually spilled over to the younger. Soon the two men developed disrespectful nicknames for the first lady, "hellcat" and "La Reine" being two of the milder ones.[23] Mary thus wielded relatively little managerial control in her own home, all but guaranteeing that the atmosphere between herself and her husband's most important aides was deeply damaged from the first weeks they all shared the mansion together.

The pair's workload started off heavy and quickly got heavier. Before long the daily avalanche of mail directed to the White House became too much for Nicolay and Hay to handle, even when they passed off as much of it as possible to appropriate government departments for action. To help with the office tasks, the president "borrowed" a young man named William O. Stoddard, a land-patent clerk at the Interior Department. Stoddard remained officially employed at Interior, but because relatively little issuing of land patents occurred during the war, Lincoln decided that his new helper could fulfill his nominal duties just as well in the White House, meanwhile using his "extra" time to assist the two private secretaries. The president eventually asked the good-natured and good-looking Stoddard, given a desk in Hay's office, to help the first lady with her social needs, a task the diplomatic young clerk fulfilled with far greater tact than did either Nicolay or Hay. Mary called him Stod and prized that he opened and attended to all her mail, even her private family letters, while at the same time never betraying the trust she placed in him.

Presidential secretaries had lived as part of the first family in many administrations, such assistants often having been related to the chief executive. Though Nicolay and Hay were to live throughout the entire term in extremely close proximity to the Lincoln family, during which time the eldest Lincoln son became exceptionally close to Hay, the president nonetheless made sure an appropriate social distance was maintained. His likely reason was simply because he wished to appease Mary's abiding jealousy of the men; left to Lincoln's own preferences, the three men would probably have joined each other at most meals so as not to waste hours that could be spent working. Consequently, Nicolay and Hay left the White House three times each day to walk the few blocks down Pennsylvania Avenue to eat in the luxurious Willard Hotel, the best in the city and the residence of many of the wealthier Northern congressman and senators. Its dining room served what was probably the finest food in Washington. This arrangement held even on holidays. On Christmas Day, 1861, Nicolay wrote to his fiancée, Therena, loyally waiting for him back in Illinois: "John and I are moping our day away here in our offices like a couple of great owls, and expect in an hour or two to go down to Willards and get our 'daily bread' just as we do on each of the other three hundred and sixty-four days of the year."[24] Stoddard later wrote admiringly of Nicolay's tremendous responsibilities in the war years; Nicolay had, he recorded, "vast power for good or evil which is placed in the hands of a man constantly in the President's confidence, able at any time to 'obtain his ear,' sure to be listened to without suspicion or prejudice, and always in possession of current State secrets."[25]

THE FIRST LEVEE

Four days into their occupancy of the White House, the Lincolns hosted the administration's first party. Called an evening levee, this long-since-discontinued form of hospitality was most notable for its juiceless formality. No food was served and no dancing was allowed, which might have lent these affairs a bit of merriment. All a levee really amounted to was a kind of open house, one in which large numbers of the well-placed or well-connected public eager to observe the new president and his lady up close could do just that.

Washington had for weeks been breathlessly waiting to see how a president born in a log cabin would deal with his exalted office's social responsibilities. Because Lincoln was presumed to be unlettered in the ironclad rules and traditions of official Washington, the State Department sent him a lengthy advisory memorandum, one largely written by the State Department and meant to help steer the first couple through what the department assumed would be terra incognita for them. William Seward, the brand-new secretary, viewed himself as the president's chief adviser in all matters related to the White House's hospitality and how the president and his wife should dispense that hospitality. Persons who mattered in the official, protocol-driven sense were obligated to be treated according to well-established rules, which is to say in accord with their precise place in the capital's official social ranking. If such status was ignored or miscalculated, Seward knew that resulting injuries to pride could be deep and cause the administration long-lasting damage. Since neither the president nor his wife were anything like competent judges of such matters at the beginning of their White House tenure, Lincoln accepted Seward's instructions without alteration.

But calamity of a surprising kind almost overtook the couple before their introduction to social Washington could even get under way. Lizzy Keckly, painstakingly finishing the complicated changes to the first lady's reworked gown, was late in delivering the garment and got it to the White House only minutes before the guests were due to arrive. There she found a first lady twisting in rage. Evidently convinced Keckly wouldn't arrive, Mary had agitatedly been informing her female relatives—several were staying on at the White House for extended visits before returning to their Midwest homes—that she "could not go down" to the party because she had "nothing to wear." She petulantly added that "Mr. Lincoln can go down with the other ladies."

When Lizzy and the dress showed up, Mary's sister Elizabeth Edwards and cousin Elizabeth Grimsley gently coaxed the first lady into allowing the dressmaker to get her into the enormous and complicated costume. When the skirt was finally fluffed and smoothed, Mary's pearl earrings, necklace, and bracelets adjusted, and fresh roses carefully placed in her shiny, tightly pulled-back hair, someone handed her a mirror so she could observe herself in all her splendor. Finally a smile began to relax Mary's tight face back into its standard edgy but acceptably pleasant state. Cunningly, Lizzy Keckly had trimmed the dress to expose as much as was decently permissible of Mary's creamy chest and arms, features that their owner believed to be her finest and which she wished to show to advantage in society. When the president came into the room to lead the family group downstairs, his remark to his wife cut through the tension. "I declare, you look charming in that dress," he said. "Mrs. Keckly has met with success." Lincoln's ability to manage Mary's moods was remarkable, though even he was not always able to smother some of the most severe outbursts of her childlike anger. Mrs. Keckly's duties after this early trial with Mrs. Lincoln's difficult personality expanded into something like those of a lady's maid and, eventually, into genuine friendship. But the bedroom scene that evening had been an ominous portent of the behavior that would eventually overtake Mary, though its most noticeable effect this time was to simply embarrass those witnessing it.

With Mrs. Lincoln's threatened refusal to attend fortunately avoided, the president's first levee was acclaimed a "monstrous success" by the guests.[26] And in a generous vote of confidence for the infant administration's first effort, Old Washingtonians hyperbolically hailed the evening's gathering as the White House's "most successful party ever."[27] Mary did look suitably grand in Mrs. Keckly's creation. But her distracted husband, again wearing his new inauguration suit, shook so many hands over the two and a half hours of the affair that he was occasionally compelled to switch to his left hand. Unfortunately, the tightly packed throng crushed many a crinoline dress, the hoops and straps maintaining these outfits' gigantic tentlike silhouettes dented into scrap steel and tangled canvas.

———

After the evening's social obligations were fulfilled, Lincoln snatched but a few hours' sleep before facing the next morning's reality, when he again found himself confronted with the responsibility for managing the nation's looming military crisis, a predicament now unalterably his alone to resolve. Only a short prebreakfast horseback ride around the city gave him a few minutes of peace before meeting with his new cabinet to try to find a way to chase away the tempests of war that were bearing down on them all.

TWO

SETTLING IN

FOR THE REMAINDER OF HIS PRESIDENCY, LINCOLN would have two families. Though his wife and sons gave him more than the occasional headache, this pain generally paled compared to that from the seven men—his cabinet—who would become his brothers-in-arms, his official body of advisers, and, as often as not, his most critical antagonists.

In 1861, the concept of cabinet power as a body still meant something beyond the ritual gatherings of obedient executive-department heads that had by late in the next century become the norm. In Lincoln's day the cabinet served as the president's only official advisory and counseling body, that in a time before the establishment of the multilayered structure of executive-branch bureaucracies that now serves the chief executive. From the moment Lincoln knew he had captured the presidency, his main concern became selecting the heads of the federal departments—State, Treasury, War, Navy, Justice, Interior, and Post Office. Because of their overall advisory function to Lincoln regarding the war everyone knew was coming, these men were magnified by the nation as more important in their totality than merely in the sum of their individual responsibilities.

Lincoln entered office with highly suspect executive skills, at least in terms of his widely assumed inability to actually run the country and prevent a split over slavery. The strength of his positions on states'

rights, union, secession, sectionalism, and, most important, slavery was
what had put him in the White House. Had the people of the slave
states and like-minded Northerners combined their electoral strength
behind a single candidate, Lincoln would have lost the election. Instead, his opposition splintered into three factions, splitting the pro-
slavery vote and handing the presidency to a candidate whose policies
everyone *knew*—or believed they knew—meant the *eventual* end of slavery and thus the beggaring of the South by destroying the mainstay of its
economy.

In the view of a substantial part of the electorate, this minority president was in the White House largely by fluke, a man dismally untutored in national politics except for his two unremarkable years in
Congress a decade and a half earlier. Moreover, his party, of whom he
was the first member to be elected president and which hadn't even
existed four years earlier, was an unknown quantity except for its commitment to stop the spread of slavery and otherwise (presumably) follow in the basic old blueprint of the Whig Party, a pattern that stood
for little other than opposition to "executive tyranny" and whatever
the Democrats were doing. Even Lincoln's home state was far removed from the Eastern power centers that had always run the country. And there were personal issues: Lincoln's ungainliness, his
Western folksiness, his high and piping voice strongly accented with
the sounds, rhythms, and vulgarisms of the frontier, and, not least, the
unusual and worrisome quality of his wife. It wasn't surprising that
nearly every one of the candidates for membership in his cabinet
believed he could manage the country better than Lincoln could,
that most thought of themselves as a better potential president than the
man who had actually been elected, and that all made their outlook in
regard to these matters clear to Lincoln. Contributing enormously to
Lincoln's exceptionality was that he knew all this and furthermore
believed there was much justice in it. Yet not for an instant did he
capitulate to any of it.

THE VICE PRESIDENT

In constitutional terms, one man stood with Lincoln ahead of the cabinet. Yet he would remain not much more than a cipher for the next

four years, even while filling a role of immense *potential* in the Lincoln presidency and the history of the Civil War. Hardly remembered today, Hannibal Hamlin was Lincoln's vice president, his successor in the event of the chief executive's death in office. If Lincoln hadn't allowed Hamlin to slip off the ticket in 1864, this unknown man would, by directing the nation through the critical postwar reconstruction period, have become a giant in the American story, though admittedly a giant of unknowable quality. Americans today have little idea how near Hamlin came to ending up in the large print rather than buried in the footnotes.

Hamlin's unusual given name came indirectly to him from a grandfather fascinated by the great generals of antiquity and who extended his interest by calling his three sons Scipio Africanus, Cyrus, and Hannibal. A generation later, the middle son, Cyrus, named his own son after his brother Hannibal. This younger Hannibal grew up near Lewiston, Maine, in a hamlet called Paris Hill. He became a lawyer by vocation and soon after an outspokenly abolitionist politician by avocation. Though a Democrat, he hewed to the antislavery wing of the party and served with distinction in both the U.S. House of Representatives and Senate. In the latter body, his political views on slavery, the issue that dominated all others on the national scene, drew him into passionate floor fights with the likes of Mississippi's arch-anti-abolitionist Senator Jefferson Davis. The animosity this earned Hamlin grew so great that he began to carry a pistol for self-protection every time he set foot in the Capitol.

Eventually, the leaders of the new Republican Party persuaded the Maine senator to abandon the Democrats, of which party so many members held pro-slavery positions. Accordingly, in 1857, Hamlin reentered the Senate as a Republican, gaining significant recognition for the important voice he lent his party against President Buchanan's pro-Southern appeasement on the issue of slavery and, most contentiously, the institution's spread into the Western territories. All of this led to his name coming up when in 1860 his new party was considering a vice-presidential candidate for its national ticket. Though he would far rather have remained in the Senate than give up his authoritative legislative voice for the near powerless vice presidency, Republican leaders persuaded him to accept on a point of honor, namely that were he to refuse, the Democrats could then convincingly besmirch Lincoln by charging that Hamlin was reluctant to risk his career by running on a ticket that was likely to lose. Hamlin wrote his wife, explaining that "I neither expected it [the nomination] nor desired it, but . . . as a faithful man to the cause, it leaves me no alternative but to accept it."[1] Hamlin won the convention's nomination on the second ballot. In keeping with the racial maliciousness of the era, during the fall campaign a Southern newspaper editor ran a story insinuating that the dark-complexioned Hamlin was a "mulatto," his "evidence" probably having less to do with Hamlin's appearance than with the observation that the vice-presidential candidate's uncle had borne the name Scipio Africanus.

As to the powerlessness of his new job, the vice president turned out to be right. Hamlin told a reporter soon after coming into office, "There is a popular impression that the Vice President is in reality the second officer of the government not only in rank but in power and influence. That is a mistake." Though Lincoln seems to have had no specific grievance against Hamlin and treated him from the beginning with courtesy, that is about the best that could be said of the relationship. The chief executive rarely included his vice president among his closest sources of advice, and just as rarely invited him to cabinet meetings (which relationship, in fairness, had in that era been standard between presidents and vice presidents). In short, Lincoln all but ignored Hamlin. What the vice president actually did for four years was serve as president of the Senate, in which capacity he would, if needed, cast a tie-breaking vote, just as the Constitution provides. Probably in an attempt to keep his humor, he laughingly told his friends that he considered himself no more than the "fifth wheel of a coach."

THE CABINET

On the day after his administration's socially successful levee, Lincoln spent part of the early-morning hours writing to General Scott about the president's most pressing issue, namely how to handle the crisis fermenting in Charleston harbor. In brief, Lincoln wanted a detailed plan for supplying and reinforcing the strategically critical island fortress.

Once he had completed that critical task, the minutiae of the presidency filled most of the rest of that Saturday: meeting with a delegation from the brand-new state of Oregon, greeting well-wishers, spending a half hour getting to know his new Navy secretary. But the major event on the president's schedule came that night, when the entire cabinet gathered in Lincoln's second-floor office to thrash out their views on Fort Sumter. Every one of the seven cabinet officers expressed outrage over the secessionists' actions, characterizing the rebels as hotheaded Carolinians determined to starve the federal post into surrender. Yet other than the Southern states declaring themselves as seceded, the Southerners still hadn't turned to overt military action against federal authority. But it remained plain to every man in the room that if federal authorities did attempt to enforce their rights over the beleaguered fort, the so far "merely" illegal acts of a few Southern legislatures would instantly be upgraded into a real war with real shots being fired against the government of the United States.

The seven men making up the cabinet were not the president's friends, nor even his former associates or colleagues. Whether any of them would prove to be personally congenial with Lincoln had not been a factor in their selections. In the choice of his top two lieutenants—those representing State and Treasury—the president named outsize personalities but courageously put aside any fears he might have had of appearing weak in comparison, instead regarding the needs of the country higher than any personal vanity. The men were chosen, largely if not entirely, on how Lincoln assessed their abilities to do their prospective jobs and whether their advice to him would be smart and helpful,[2] though reality did dictate that political promises (especially those made at the convention) as well as geographical balancing be considered, especially for the men below the level of secretaries of state and treasury. His friend Leonard Swett described Lincoln's awe-inspiring ability to discard personal prejudice in his assessment of political choices: "He never judged men by his like or dislike for them. If any given act was to be performed, he could understand that his enemy could do it just as well as anyone."[3]

The chosen seven came from both sides of the political Whig-Democrat divide. The old-line Whigs, men from the party that had remade itself into the Republican Party, included Secretary of State William Seward,

Attorney General Edward Bates, and Secretary of the Interior Caleb B. Smith. The four Democrats were Secretary of the Treasury Salmon P. Chase, Secretary of War Simon Cameron, Secretary of the Navy Gideon Welles, and Postmaster General Montgomery Blair. None was a faultless choice either for the department he would represent or for his ability to mesh with Lincoln. But they were the best the president believed he could collect from a wrangling political class a large part of whose members had already abandoned or were on the verge of abandoning both the idea and the reality of the Union.

Lincoln's most serious competitor for the Republican nomination in the summer of 1860 had been Senator William Seward of New York. Seward had been so confident he would be the convention's choice that a loaded cannon stood at the gate of his Auburn home ready to be fired in celebration of his selection.[4] Neither the public speaker nor the profound thinker in Lincoln's unique mold, Seward was nonetheless a highly practiced and polished legislator, the widely presumed leader of the Republican Party, and a man who would unhumbly have defined himself first as a statesman and only second as a politician. At sixty, he was eight years older than Lincoln and over a lengthy career had been involved in many of the great issues of state—tariffs, transcontinental transportation, finance both national and international—and had long, honorably, and successfully served his state as both governor and senator. As to slavery, he was a procrastinator rather than the firebrand many thought him to be, a man willing, if necessary, to appease the South in the name of national unity. Indeed, his earliest advice to Lincoln had been to change the national debate from one over slavery, as he believed Lincoln had so framed the issues leading to secession, to the more widely palatable alternative (in the North) of "union or disunion."

Seward was capable of great warmth and kindness and was generally unpretentious, though he was, understandably, astonished at having lost the Republican nomination to "a little Illinois lawyer."[5] He was handsome, notwithstanding a sallow complexion and a nose the shape and approaching the size of a schooner's keel. He was also conceited (mostly about his high intelligence but also about his stately looks), sarcastic, overweening, persnickety, and fully capable of telling Lincoln exactly how little he thought of the president's policies and ideas. In fact,

Seward's incivility to his boss in the administration's early days could reach astonishing heights, as we shall shortly see. The delicate dithering back and forth between himself and the president over his appointment nearly killed his selection until, on Inauguration Day, it finally became a done deal.

Not unexpectedly, Mary Lincoln despised Seward, largely because she knew he wholeheartedly believed (and rarely kept to himself) that he would have made a better president than the man presently occupying the White House. Her animosity grew worse when she found out he, instead of she, would be in official charge of state entertaining at the White House, and that he meant to see that it stayed that way. Moreover, the Southern-born first lady found his abolitionist "extremism" distasteful, views that also underlay the South's universal contempt for him. Ironically, both Mary Lincoln and the Southern masses had to a degree misread Seward in this regard, given his efforts to appease the South over the issue. But what counted, of course, was that Lincoln liked him very much, a liking that would radically increase over the next four years.

Seward lived on Lafayette Square, across the street from the Executive Mansion, in a smart town house he rented for $1,800 a year (his melancholic and virtually estranged wife, Frances, stayed home in Auburn, never visiting him in Washington during his secretaryship; his daughter and daughter-in-law acted as his hostesses in Washington), and it was therefore a simple matter for Lincoln to drop in on his adviser. These visits served the secondary but highly restorative function of allowing the president to get away from both his wife and the pesky office seekers who continually overran the White House. Incidentally, only six years after his appointment, Seward would be responsible for one of the most massive land purchases—as well as the greatest financial coup for the buyer—in the history of not only the United States but the world.

The man who had run closest behind Seward for the nomination was now, in constitutional terms, the second-ranking member of the cabinet, the handsome, ambitious (mainly to be president) but platitudinous Secretary of the Treasury Salmon P. Chase. Physically, he bore an artless face that formed an almost perfect square, one topped by baldness that went halfway back on the crown, from where a cascade of

neck-length hair fell on his collar. His view of his high intellectual abilities ranked fully on a par with Seward's elevated self-image. Lincoln
had had to cajole Chase into accepting the Treasury office: As a powerful senator, the Ohioan not only disliked giving up his own power base
but also resented serving a president he, like Seward, thought should
still be in Illinois practicing law. Carl Sandburg recorded that Chase
liked to look into mirrors, bowing and murmuring to himself, "President Chase."[6] Unlike Seward's increasingly ebbing enthusiasm for
forcibly ending slavery, Chase's abolitionist sentiments were unshakable, his antislavery credentials the most concrete in the cabinet: As an
Ohio lawyer, he had helped scores of runaway slaves stay out of their
owners' clutches.

Aside from his vanity and his intellect, the treasury secretary's chief
possession was his daughter Kate. Probably Chase's strangest peculiarity
was that he ran just about neck and neck with his daughter when it came
to national attention. The young, dazzlingly red-haired Kate Chase considered herself her father's head booster in his quest for the presidency.
After she installed herself with him in their Lafayette Square mansion,
Kate comported herself for all of Washington society that mattered as
though she were the capital's true first lady. Mary Lincoln knew all
about Miss Chase's ambitions and pretensions and knew equally that
the younger woman ridiculed her as a hopeless hick from the Wild West.
In return, through the entirety of Mary's years in Washington she directed a huge part of her always abundant supply of rancor squarely at
the treasury secretary's daughter.

As for Kate's father, Chase's yawning presidential ambitions during
Lincoln's first term would eventually reach a level of almost open rebellion against the president. Almost as bad, his relations with most of
his fellow cabinet members were often abysmal; throughout his service
in Lincoln's cabinet, Chase's undisguised loathing for his old rival
Seward would cause their boss substantial trouble. But Chase did master the duties of a competent treasury secretary—the introduction of
paper money ("greenbacks") and its critical importance to the Union's
capacity to finance the war was his most famous contribution—and
thereby made himself useful to a chief executive who miraculously
never quit judging men by their worth rather than by their ambitious-
ness or belligerence.

Until Edwin Stanton joined the cabinet a year after the inauguration,

Seward and Chase were by a long measure Lincoln's most important executive heads, the other five members of the cabinet as originally organ-
ized never approaching these two genuine intellectuals in importance to
their president. Simon Cameron, the new war secretary, had become
both controversial and enormously rich on transportation and banking
earnings, and as a Pennsylvania politician was known as that state's
"czar" thanks to his ability to pass out generous helpings of largesse to
his political allies *and* to mete out ruthless punishments to his enemies.
He was described as a man who "reeked with the stench of a thousand
political bargains,"[7] this the kind of blunt insult common in nineteenth-
century politics and that added so vibrantly to the era's political color.
Cameron's success in business and his support from the convention's
important Pennsylvania delegation were probably the main reasons Lincoln put him in a position that the chief executive knew a war was soon
going to make extremely important. Sadly, Cameron would quickly become an impediment to Lincoln because of a penchant for putting his
friends' financial interests ahead of the good of the army. The president
eventually realized that his own popular nickname of Honest Abe would
likely suffer if Cameron were allowed to continue greasing old friends'
palms.

Cameron's counterpart in the Navy Department (nearly a century
would pass before the two were joined as the Defense Department)
was Gideon Welles of Connecticut. Welles had left the Democratic
Party over the slavery issue, and though he knew little about naval
affairs—he had never even been on a ship that was actually at sea—he
had long shown skill as an administrator, and he rapidly became a loyal
lieutenant to the president. Welles's personal appearance was the
strangest of the lot. On top of his short, fat body sat a big head made even
bigger by the addition of a great woolly wig and a biblike white beard
that reached down to his breastbone. From the beginning, Welles held
that his own service was fully as important to the prosecution of war as
was that of his army counterpart, a misjudgment that would come to ad-
versely affect the needed coordination between the War and Navy bureaucracies.

Sixty-eight-year-old Edward Bates—his bearded face was almost as
Mosaic as Welles's—took over the Justice Department as attorney general. His executive experience came from serving as Missouri's attorney general and his broader grasp of currents events from a later career

spent in the U.S. House of Representatives. Though a onetime slave-holder (paradoxically, one who had spoken out against the institution), Bates's appeal to Lincoln was founded on his scholarly honesty and his strong Union voice from a slave state, the latter making the Missourian a valuable geographic addition to the cabinet. Furthermore, Bates was also in tune with Lincoln's strict-constructionist approach to the Constitution, which went far in recommending him to the new president. Interior Secretary Caleb Smith's attractiveness to Lincoln sprang from his being from powerful Indiana. Probably more to the point, though, the post had been promised Smith at the Chicago convention by Judge David Davis, one of Lincoln's most powerful political operatives. The expected quid pro quo would, of course, be Smith's cooperation in Lincoln's nomination, which was duly received at the convention. The new secretary remained one of Lincoln's most loyal, if least publicly known, cabinet colleagues. Montgomery Blair filled the final seat in the president's inner council. Many today regard the position of postmaster general as more technocratic than political because of the semiprivatization of that department. But in Lincoln's time the post's holder was important simply for belonging to the cabinet and thus providing a presence in the administration's inner council. The whole Blair family had long been involved in Washington politics, and as Blair was a member of a border-state clan—he moved from border-state Missouri to border-state Maryland—Lincoln anticipated that he would have a crucial strategic need of the new postmaster's voice in keeping the not-yet-seceded Maryland and Missouri from attempting to eventually do so.

SUMTER

Lincoln had first met with his cabinet the day after the inauguration, but that session had merely been formal. The gathering this Saturday evening—the first weekend of his presidency—involved hard business. Portentously labeled "A Meeting upon the State of the Country," it entailed deliberations going far beyond formality. If a solution to the immediate Sumter crisis weren't quickly found, and no one present believed a genuine "solution" existed, a civil war over slavery and the Southern states' right to secede to preserve that institution loomed as a dead-sure inevitability.

Major Robert Anderson, the highly competent garrison commander at Fort Sumter, had graduated from West Point, but as a Kentuckian was proud of his Southern origins. And though sympathetic to his native region's resentments against the North, he nonetheless remained a Union loyalist. Now he was able to do little other than watch as the surrounding secessionist forces outmaneuvered him. The South Carolina rebels made it plain to Anderson that they would not permit the resupplying of the 135-gun post. With food and medicines nearly exhausted—the commander estimated his last remaining scraps of flour and bacon would be consumed by April 15—the Union forces would be obliged to fight or else surrender the fort in the face of unassailable opponents already determined to take the island and its fortress from federal control.

The essence of Lincoln's dilemma lay in his strategy that the Union not be driven into firing the first shot of a plainly imminent war. He would, though, do whatever was required to fulfill his inaugural pledge that the government preserve its own property, meaning the president believed himself honor-bound not to merely surrender or evacuate the fort. He knew that any action to preserve the federal presence would provoke fire from the rebel batteries, posts under the command of General P. G. T. Beauregard and whose guns nearly encircled the island. The assessment Lincoln received from General Scott, his top military commander, was that a military action to successfully defend Sumter would require a minimum federal force of twenty-five thousand men, a number short of what the president then possessed. Thus Lincoln sent his cabinet away that evening charged with trying to envision any other conceivably workable solution. When America went to bed that spring night, the burning fuse about to ignite war was represented by one highly symbolic federal fortress sitting in Charleston harbor that both North and South viewed as a crucial symbol of their causes.

Two days later the cabinet regathered, and its straightforward advice to the president was what he surely expected it to be, namely that he withdraw all federal troops from Sumter. Yet still seeking another course of action, four days later—March 15—Lincoln asked all members to give him their specific views on the simple reprovisioning of the fort, by which he meant attempting to provide Sumter with medicine and food but no armaments. Seward and Cameron were against the idea, while Chase equivocated. The decision was, of course, Lincoln's alone to make. He held off for as long as he could, probably not in the hope that anything would resolve the crisis but presumably because he was still looking for some yet unseen answer short of the extremes of war or federal surrender. Envoys sent to Charleston by the president charged with evaluating the secessionists' resolve returned to the White House convinced that the South Carolinians were beyond any conceivable accommodation with the federal government, and that they in fact now considered their state part of a separate nation no longer bound to the dictates of the United States of America. At this point the most influential Northern newspaper, the *New York Tribune*, unhelpfully editorialized that Lincoln should allow the seceding states to "go in peace"—a stance that amounted to a clear acceptance of federal impotence.

Finally having passed the limit of further equivocation, Lincoln acted. He understood that no military answer to the Sumter crisis existed that would result in Union victory. He further knew that the just constituted Confederate government was, from its capital in Montgomery, Alabama, urging South Carolina's governor to speedily resolve the standoff on which was focused much of the world's attention. Moreover, Jefferson Davis, the Confederate "president," wanted the fortress attacked and taken under Southern control. And finally, Lincoln accepted that even an attempt to bring only food and nonmilitary supplies to Anderson and his men would almost certainly provoke Southern fire.

But this last scenario gave Lincoln a glimmering hope of gaining some advantage. Lincoln judged that many in the North would view return fire from the island as a self-defense measure on the federals' part, that scenario being the most the president could get out of the deadlock that might salvage federal honor. Put simply, he hoped the onset of fighting and thus of the war itself would be blamed on the secessionists and not on the federal government—by no means a negligible factor in the protocol of making war. There was little doubt the South Carolinian incendiaries, men proud of their state's status as the cradle of the secessionist movement, would fling themselves headlong into their dream of glory, a dream still unruffled by the horrific reality of war's consequences. In one of the last acts of his presidency, James Buchanan had tried to send a supply ship—the *Star of the West*—to the beleaguered fortress, only to have the Carolinians fire on it and force its withdrawal in the first overt sparring of the war. Lincoln could have had little doubt that the same fate would meet another Union ship attempting the same maneuver.

These first six days of his presidency had been agonizing for Lincoln. He faced the certainty that no alternative to war existed if he was to fulfill his pledge to keep the Union intact. Conflicting views and advice were battering him from all sides: defiant Northern voices counseling that it was time Southern treason be met with Northern steel, Northern appeasers pleading to let the slave states go, Southern hotheads impugning him for his denying their region's wish to leave the Union, his military advisers' warnings that the federal army was woefully unprepared for war, abolitionists crying to free the South's four million slaves from their bondage—even Seward and his extraordinarily impertinent threat that Lincoln make *some* kind of policy for the Union to follow or Seward would be pleased to step in and do it for him. As for the latter, Lincoln told his secretary of state that the nation *did* have a policy, that policy being that the Union be preserved against any threat whatsoever.

In the early hours of April 12, a Union fleet settled off the entrance to Charleston harbor. Lincoln had sent word to the governor of South Carolina that the ships were not bringing military supplies but simply delivering food and medicine. But the fomenters of war had made up their minds. Certain that their newborn nation's only path to independence lay in the sword, the Confederate hawks fired on the fatally weakened fort and its federal garrison. After a steady thirty-three-hour-long hurricane of cannon balls and shells thrown on the island from the rebel batteries ringing his doomed position, Major Anderson surrendered. The victorious insurgents generously allowed Anderson's blue-uniformed soldiers to board unhindered a waiting Union supply ship, which then sailed away without further harassment. The courtesy represented one of the last chivalrous acts of a war in which ferocity would soon become both sides' tactic of choice.

WAR

In the days immediately after the onset of physical hostilities, a sense of emergency descended over Washington. Though it would take a while longer for the reality of the city's isolation to sink in with the general population, the president knew that Washington now faced deadly peril. And beyond that certainty, whatever steps he would take to secure the capital and the government against an attack had to be calculated to try to persuade the as-yet-unseceded slave states from joining the rebellion.

Ominously, any hope that Virginia would resist the secessionist siren was dashed within a few days of the loss of Fort Sumter. Lincoln called upon the states to send militias to defend the government against a rebel invasion, a plea all the upper-South state legislatures unsurprisingly regarded as a declaration of war not only against the already seceded states but against themselves as well. Within a short time North Carolina, Arkansas, and Tennessee joined the rebellion, as did—disastrously—Virginia. The latter defection actually brought the enemy within sight of the Executive Mansion, the first family now able to see rebel territory simply by looking out the White House's south windows at the hills of Virginia's Fairfax and Arlington counties. To secure the capital itself from attack, Lincoln quickly ordered the occupation of the city of Alexandria and Arlington Heights, the latter encompassing Robert E. Lee's majestic and just evacuated home on the high ground and which took in a panorama of Washington from the White House to the Capitol.

No immediate danger weighed heavier on Lincoln than did the prospect of Maryland joining the new Confederacy. With no substantive Union army yet marshaled, a Maryland intent on secession might well be impossible to hold, even if the entire forces currently at Lincoln's command were put to the task. And if Maryland went over to the enemy, Washington would be surrounded by secessionist states and thus face the strong possibility of having to at least temporarily abandon its position as seat of the federal government. In light of this imminent threat of a Confederate Maryland, Lincoln took the stunning step of ordering the suspension of the Constitution's writ of habeas corpus, a move that would permit federal authorities to take suspects into custody without having to demonstrate cause for such arrests. Chief Justice Roger Taney, a Marylander, swiftly ruled Lincoln's action unconstitutional, insisting the crisis at hand did not merit this unprecedented action. Lincoln essentially ignored Taney. Moreover, presidential concern about further state defections didn't end with Maryland. Lincoln judged that Delaware, the smallest of the slave states, could probably forcibly be kept in the Union, but if slave-holding Kentucky were to leave, the Northern situation would, he knew, descend to a state of emergency almost beyond contemplation.

In the first days of war, Washington became a city that in some ways already seemed to be under siege. Public access to government buildings was blocked. The so-called Frontier Guard, some of whose members were serving senators and congressmen and which was commanded by Kansas senator James Lane, protected the most important and sensitive sites in the District. With its own surrounding contingent of troops, the White House itself assumed the appearance of a fortress. The army hurriedly drafted plans for the evacuation of the first family: In an emergency, the Lincolns would be taken to safety in the huge and, it was hoped, impregnable Treasury building across the street to the east of the president's residence.

In late April, the first sharp clap of personal misfortune struck the White House, when the war-caused fragmentation of the Lexington Todds eerily mirrored the larger hostilities between North and South. Of Mary's full brothers, the elder, Levi, remained loyal to the Union, but the younger, George, joined the Confederate army; of her half brothers, all three—Samuel, David, and Alexander—went South into Jefferson Davis's army. What was more, the husbands of her half sisters Martha White, Elodie Dawson, and Emilie Helm were also Confederate officers.

The loss that was the hardest for Mary to bear, and which represented the deepest personal wound, was that of her youngest half sister, Emilie. Years before in Springfield the Lincolns had warmly hosted Ben and Emilie Helm, happily taking the young couple into the closest possible embrace of their own family. An ardent friendship grew between Lincoln and Ben, the latter a West Point graduate and son of a slave-owning Kentucky governor. The Lincolns' love for Emilie—many years Mary's junior—was almost parental in nature; Lincoln affectionately called the pretty and fresh-faced Emilie "Little Sister." When Mary left Illinois for Washington in 1861, she had looked forward to having a great deal of Emilie's companionship in the White House to help her through what she knew was going to be a daunting experience, particularly the loneliness she was bearing for the Todd relatives left behind in Springfield.

When the war began, Lincoln undoubtedly anticipated Ben Helm throwing in his lot with the Confederacy and his now home state of Mississippi. Southerners who saw themselves as besieged by bellicose Northerners generally bore state loyalties immeasurably stronger than any ties to the United States as a nation. Even so, Lincoln held a faint hope for a different outcome with young Helm. Respectful of his brother-in-law's professional military education and conscious that Emilie's disappearance into the Confederacy would come as a severe shock to his acutely family-oriented wife, the president invited Helm to the White House, there to offer the young man the substantial position of paymaster in the Union army, and along with it the rank of major. Handing his brother-in-law the terms enclosed in a sealed envelope, Lincoln said (according to Emilie's memory of the event), "Ben, here is something for you. Think it over by yourself and let me know what you will do."[8] The sweet-faced, young Kentuckian was at that moment evidently still undecided as to which course he would take.

Leaving Emilie with her sister and the president at the White House, Helm immediately took a train back to his Kentucky home, where he found most of his military friends preparing to go south. The contest in his mind came down to greater loyalty: whether he owed his principal alliance to his friends and fellow Southerners or to a nation he no longer considered his own. His wife would later say that in the end he simply could not abide the specter of "striking against his own people."[9] Accordingly, on April 27, 1861, Helm wrote to his august brother-in-law to decline the offer made him in the White House, portraying his decision as the most painful of his life. A little over two years later, Confederate general Ben Hardin Helm would fall, mortally wounded, in a battle south of Chattanooga.

Ben and Emilie weren't the Lincolns' only personal loss in the war's early days. Even closer to the president than Ben Helm was Elmer Ephraim Ellsworth. Ellsworth was a handsome man, short but blessed with a strong physique and an ebullient personality. Shortly after being elected president, Lincoln had invited Ellsworth—Nicolay and Hay had only shortly before introduced him—into his Springfield firm to get a start at reading the law, then still the most common way for an aspiring lawyer to learn the craft. Earlier the energetic twenty-four-year-old had formed and become "colonel" of his own self-styled "Zouave" regiment, one that traveled around the country staging exciting shows of military drill expertise and in which each member was outfitted in red, baggy-pants uniforms modeled after the dashing French colonial outfits worn in Algeria. In the summer of 1860 the troop of blood-stirring young hearties performed on the White House lawn, holding the rapt attention of President Buchanan and niece Harriet. Ellsworth's long hair captured almost everyone who encountered him, and his striking mustache further lent him the flair of a romantic heartbreaker and helped make him enormously popular wherever he performed. In fact, the public so admired his soldiers that a Zouave craze swept the North, prompting imitators to adopt the uniform, outfits that would remain a colorful element of Union armies throughout the entire war.

Lincoln quickly developed a friendship with Ellsworth and was grateful to him for the good humor that could at the end of a long day at the office override Mary's often sour attitude awaiting him at home. Ellsworth became so close that he spent a good deal of time in the family circle during the last months in Springfield before the Lincolns departed for Washington and the oncoming war, and the love he showed for Willie and Tad endeared him to both the president-elect and the first-lady-to-be. Lincoln finally asked his young protégé to join the family on the inaugural journey to Washington, a request that pleased Lincoln's wife and sons. A less happy note came a few days after the inauguration, when Ellsworth caught the measles from Willie and Tad. All three cases were serious, but more ominous for an adult with measles was that the condition relatively easily degenerated into pneumonia, which it did with Ellsworth, and which made his case more dangerous than the boys' illness.

As a preventive measure against the peril of likely Confederate shelling, soon after Virginia's May 23 secession Lincoln ordered the military occupation of that state's areas lying directly across the Potomac from Washington. Ellsworth and his Zouaves—now formally militarized and styled the "Fire Zouaves," a name honoring the eleven hundred or so of his men from the New York City Fire Department—offered to assist in securing Alexandria, help Lincoln gratefully accepted. Beyond the obvious and urgent objective of keeping the capital from being shelled, the president had a highly symbolic reason for wanting the town brought under federal military control. For more than a month, an enormous Confederate flag had been waving from a building in the center of Alexandria. Although the offending banner was eight miles from the White House, with the aid of a telescope it was annoyingly visible from the president's own home. Lincoln hated seeing it and wanted it gone.

The following evening, after writing a letter to his sweetheart, Kitty, the Zouave commander gathered his men and crossed the river under bright moonlight to undertake his mission to clear Alexandria of its rebels, with the secondary tasks of destroying the railroad track leading to Richmond and dismantling the town's telegraph wires that were keeping it in contact with the rest of the Confederacy. As Ellsworth quickly discovered, rebel troops had already evacuated the town, their commanders aware that holding such an exposed position would be impossible against any concerted federal attack.

While attending to his principal mission, Ellsworth also caught sight of the offending flag fluttering from the roof of the Marshall House hotel. The young officer dashed into the building and up the stairs, where he charged through a door opening onto the roof. With the help of a ladder, he cut the huge Confederate banner off its pole and roughly wadded it in his arms. He then began to run back down the stairs to rejoin his troops. A *New York Tribune* correspondent who was an eyewitness reported, "While on the second floor, a secessionist came out of a door, with a cocked double barreled shot gun . . . took aim at Ellsworth . . . and discharged, lodging a whole load of buckshot in Ellsworth's body, killing him instantly."[10] Ellsworth's fellow Zouaves immediately descended on the shooter, a corporal firing into the Southerner's face. He turned out to be the hotel's owner, James W. Jackson. Predictably, Jackson was soon proclaimed a hero-martyr throughout the South, the Confederacy's first.

Ellsworth's men transported his corpse back across the Potomac to the Washington Navy Yard. An officer who knew of the dead man's relationship with the president sent word of the killing to the White House, adding an account of the skirmish in Alexandria. The news of Ellsworth's death, the first battle casualty of the war, staggered Lincoln so badly that for a time he refused to face visitors in his office; people who saw him that day said that he wept openly over the calamitous events. Mary was immediately driven to the Navy Yard, but because the embalming was in process she wasn't permitted to see the body. That evening both the president and his wife went to arrange for the remains to be brought back to the White House for a funeral. Standing before the body lying on a table, Lincoln looked on the dead face and moaned, "My boy! My boy! Was it necessary this sacrifice should be made?"[11] John Hay noted that Lincoln "mourned [Ellsworth] as a son."[12] While going through the body's uniform pockets, the doctors had found the letter Ellsworth had written a few hours earlier to his fiancée, together with another to his parents.

The president asked the Zouaves to personally bring the remains to the White House, in whose East Room funeral services were held the next day. Colonel Ellsworth's body lay in state, surrounded by soldiers slowly beating muffled drums and bearing the traditional reversed arms. The president and the first lady sat in chairs near the foot of the coffin, while cabinet members stood nearby the candlelit bier. Mary placed a wax laurel wreath on the coffin, laying it so its leaves encircled a photograph of their dead friend. Afterward, the president rode with the members of his cabinet to the train station, where together they bade the coffin farewell on its journey to Ellsworth's parents' home in Mechanicville, New York.

Lincoln himself wrote to his friend's parents that afternoon: "My acquaintance with him began less than two years ago; yet through the latter half of the intervening period, it was as intimate as the disparity of our ages, and my engrossing engagements, would permit. . . . May God give you the consolation which is beyond all earthly power. Sincerely your friend in a common affliction." Lincoln handed the letter to a secretary for mailing, the first of many, many more he would write to wives and mothers and sisters of the fallen.[13] A historian would write that "a vision of Ellsworth's face haunted [the president] for the rest of the war."[14] But he immediately returned to the war. And it was said that after having suffered such sorrow brought into his own home, Lincoln seemed more impatient than ever to begin the fight.

FIXING THE WHITE HOUSE

While the advancing war almost entirely engaged the president, the first lady remained preoccupied with the house she lived in. For all the problems of its current battered state, the White House nonetheless represented a grander home than any lived in by all but a handful of Americans. But Mary Lincoln—or now Madam President, the slightly derisory label the press gave her and one she assumed denoted deference—believed the Executive Mansion's current condition should equal her husband's status as his nation's leader. Mary calculated that the power of the president derived in no small degree from the stateliness surrounding him and his wife, and that any leader understands that his battles are half-won through just such symbolism. Since the first lady judged that the White House was the primary symbol of the president's power, she was going to make sure that it looked the part it was built to play.

During the nineteenth century presidents were expected to live self-effacingly and without undue luxury. Accordingly, Congress provided new chief executives with only a modest sum of money with which to keep the White House habitable. The figure was $20,000, *not* per annum, but to cover each quadrennial term. Even in the mid-nineteenth century, long before galloping twentieth-century inflation shrank the dollar, $20,000 for four years of White House upkeep was unequal to the needs of the hard-used building. Surprisingly though, few of the Lincolns' predecessors used even the little money available to them for any significant White House improvements. Buchanan did, however, spend the bulk of his allotment, in his case to build the glass-roofed conservatory, a move that left his niece Harriet Lane little for renovating the building's infrastructure or refurbishing its decor.

The problem lay most deeply rooted in the reality that the Executive Mansion was not merely a home. At mid-nineteenth century, the public-private building was in large part an essentially unguarded tourist attraction, open to nearly anyone who looked minimally respectable, and the minimally respectable-looking portion of the public believed itself entirely justified in wandering at will through the seat of the presidency, and doing so at almost any hour and on every day of the year. The damage this trampling exacted on the White House was significant and unending. But to make matters worse, tourists often simply took as souvenirs what they wanted if what they wanted wasn't nailed down: Ornaments and bric-a-brac constantly went missing, pieces got snipped from curtains to serve as mementos, and almost anything lying around was liable to end up in some dining room in Duluth or drawing room in Buffalo. Such pilferage wasn't considered "real" criminal mischief nor was it directed at a particular occupant of the building. It was just the way life was for the mansion and its inhabitants, whoever they were. In their case, though, Abraham and Mary Lincoln aroused substantially greater curiosity—not to mention higher sectional passions—than did the average nineteenth-century first family, which meant many more people were eager to snoop around their home, and thus the incidence of mischief rose along with the size of the visiting crowds.

The one part of her overwhelming new home that Mary found entirely to her liking was the Buchanan greenhouse at the west end of the building, standing roughly where the West Wing with its Oval Office is today. In late March of that first year, the first lady happily wrote about it to an old friend: "The conservatory attached to this house is so delightful. We have so many choice bouquets."[15] Mary took up the habit of gathering the conservatory's blooms and making colorful nosegays of them, which she then generously handed out as thank-you gifts for the kindnesses people showed her and the president.

Though happy with her flower house, Mary swiftly began to plan a restoration of the rest of the building to the elegance it knew under Jefferson. In 1861, "elegance" no longer signified the creamy neoclassical look of Jefferson's upper-class colonial America. Instead, it now meant the ultramodern tufted and overstuffed, plush-upholstered mahogany and oak furniture of mid-Victorian middle-class respectability, an interior style both Jefferson and the mansion's architect would surely have found hard to bear. With her $20,000 credit in hand, Mary headed for New York, the capital of American consumerism and in whose shops and department stores she would find what she wanted and where she would be greeted and treated like a queen.

After the war got under way with the Fort Sumter attack, Washington's physical isolation temporarily forced the curbing of the first lady's travel. General Scott not only warned her against a rail journey to New

York through still unsecured Maryland; he even personally and strongly recommended she take the boys and go back to Springfield to remove themselves from the danger of an expected rebel assault on the capital. But after the late-April arrival of the Pennsylvania and Massachusetts regiments into the District of Columbia, Mary was satisfied that train travel northward was safe again. With her husband's blessing, she left home in mid-May to get started on the long list of White House refurbishments she enthusiastically foresaw.

Mary had actually been to New York already when a few weeks after her husband's election she visited Manhattan on a clothes-shopping spree, there replacing her plain Western wardrobe with more up-to-date Eastern fashions. On that occasion, New York merchants eager to gain presidential custom had extended to the first lady the figurative keys to the city. For her part, Mary had learned about the special joy of credit buying and spent far more than she could afford as the wife of a frontier lawyer, justifying her extravagance by maintaining that her wardrobe had to be appropriate for the wife of the new president. The experience also gave her a good idea of where to find the things that would make White House living the pleasant experience the president deserved.

On that trousseau-gathering trip, Mary had been hurt by the criticism she received for seeming to carry on a semi-state-procession of her own—receiving and being received, making little impromptu speeches—and one viewed as making herself appear overly grand. Much of the public perceived the wives of other presidents (and presidents-elect, as well) as having remained staunchly at their husband's side rather than appearing to be independent women. Mary's unfettered behavior brought her the sharpest criticism that could be directed at females of her time and class, namely that of stepping outside the traditional and highly restricted roles of mid-nineteenth-century respectability. The press briskly criticized what it considered her pretensions, behavior magnified by what looked like unsuitable ambition even before her husband had been sworn into office. At the time, though, the country still wasn't at war. That distinction would reverberate harshly against Mary in the wake of this second visit to New York, one she now undertook as the reigning first lady.

William Wood, Washington's new acting commissioner of public buildings, escorted the president's wife on her visit north. As Mr. Wood was the government officer responsible for White House spending and for appointing and paying the doorkeepers and groundsmen, the presence of this officer with the first lady should not have been remarkable. But Mr. Wood's attendance on the first lady became highly significant, principally because of the gossip suggesting that he and Mrs. Lincoln behaved improperly, both in fiscal and in personal terms. It wasn't long after meeting Wood that Mary concluded he was "clever" and thus potentially useful to her. His job paid a comparatively meager $2,000 a year, but the incumbent was in a position to pocket far more on the side by steering the president's wife to merchants eager to gratefully provide him with kickbacks. Little evidence existed that Wood had stooped to any such dodgy behavior, but gossip could damage its target irrespective of the truth of what was being gossiped about. As to any personal impropriety on Wood's part toward Mrs. Lincoln, Mary Lincoln's innocent but incautious familiarity with the acting commissioner did cause tongues to cluck. But their supposed "intimacies" were utterly nonsexual, though they nonetheless stood open to the worst sort of misinterpretation by persons eager to find fault in a first lady married to a controversial and vulnerable man.

Joined by Wood and by her cousin Elizabeth Grimsley, Mary Lincoln processed gaily through the most expensive shops in New York, ordering a rainbow of colorful and usually expensive items for the White House. Mary particularly homed in on the great mercantile emporium of Alexander T. Stewart, a shopping palace many considered the finest department store in the world and a destination where the first lady anticipated every success in having her needs met. One of her biggest purchases at Stewart's was a $2,500 carpet meant to replace the East Room's threadbare predecessor. Sadly for her public image, this was an age when $2,500 exceeded what the majority of Americans earned in a year, a reality ripe for use by Lincoln's opponents in making the administration look to be frittering away public funds. Mary also ordered a seven-hundred-piece set of Bohemian cut glass as well as a number of vases and mantel ornaments for the Green and Blue rooms.[16] Haughwout & Company, whose store wasn't far from Stewart's, provided a large and magnificent set of red-and-gold-trimmed china to complement the Bohemian glasses. The first lady must eagerly have anticipated the effect these glorious goods would make when seen by the ladies of the capital, women who Mary knew considered her and her husband to be hicks.

To cap the trip, Mr. Stewart, the department store proprietor, hosted an elegant dinner in Mrs. Lincoln's honor, undoubtedly looking forward to more presidential custom on the first lady's future shopping expeditions. As it happened, Mary did make two more shopping trips to New York that first year in the White House. Before 1861 ended, the first lady bought everything from wallpapers and draperies to bellpulls and books from the best merchants not only in New York, but in Philadelphia and Boston as well. All her purchases were of the finest quality and most came at high prices.

When Mary returned to Washington, she quickly began the covering of the building's badly damaged walls with her $6,800 worth of French wallpaper, a sum that fortunately included the preparation of the walls and the hanging of the paper. As her purchases were arriving at the White House, she ordered a team of painters, curtain-hangers, and floor waxers to refurbish the state rooms on the first floor and the second floor's private family rooms; during the time the couple's bedrooms were being renovated, husband and wife slept together in what Mary called the "state guest room."[17] The totals spent far exceeded her $20,000 allowance, and anticipation of her husband's wrath began to worry her as the invoices flowed into the White House. This concern led her into "economies," such as trying to have Nicolay and Hay pay the feed bills for the horses they kept housed in the White House stables, costs the president was currently footing. The effects of such spending in Lincoln's presidency would soon require serious damage control, and the bills for Mary's prodigality eventually came to terrify Mary with the fear of political scandal.

THE WAR PRESIDENT

Since the firing on Fort Sumter, the first weeks of the ensuing conflict had engendered little more than a series of armed skirmishes. But the nation's sundered halves were now unmistakably at war with each other, and the president made clear that the Southern states' secession would not stand. For the Lincolns, as indeed for much of Washington's population, the most personal fear throughout the spring had come from the threat of a rebel strike on the city itself. In making certain of its survival, the Northern states' militias rushing to the District's defense had had to hammer their way through highly antagonistic Maryland. In

Baltimore, a mob sympathetic to the South's cause assailed a Massachusetts regiment, leaving thirteen soldiers and civilians dead. The militias
further encountered relatively minor but nonetheless nasty resistance
in the form of belligerent Confederate sympathizers, a threat the Union
forces were luckily strong enough to quickly thwart. But the principal
menace of attacks coming out of Virginia kept everyone in Washington
agitated—everyone, that is, except Southern sympathizers, many of
whom remained in town after the hostilities at Fort Sumter began and
all of whom would gratefully have welcomed a rebel army throwing
the Yankee president and his wife out of the White House and into a
Confederate prison.

The new government of Confederate president Jefferson Davis rejected out of hand every overture that was sent southward offering me-
diation. The men in charge of the insurgency had by now gambled too
decisively to flirt with any Northern proposals for reconciliation, the
rebels truculently insisting that their confederacy represented a fully
sovereign nation, one that the United States would be required to treat
as an equal. Lincoln's policy was to unwaveringly regard the insurgency
as an illegal rebellion pure and simple, denying it and its so-called government any hint of legality. He did not and would never consider the
seceded states "foreign" territory, but rather that they were and would
ever remain states of the United States. Slavery and its extension into
the Western territories was the Confederacy's sole substantive foundation for its self-styled statehood, and continued union and the confinement of slavery within its current borders remained Lincoln's firm
requirements for ending the war. So the two entities found themselves
without a bridge on which to approach one another. Thus for the first
three months of the war, Lincoln's most vital task was to select key combat actions that might defeat the rebels. Over these agonizing weeks of
hesitancy the president became slowly convinced that only a large and
decisive Union victory would represent a feasible way to end the uprising, and by late June the planning for such a war-ending outcome had
finally begun to get up steam.

At the war's outset, many Northerners believed that beating the
South would amount to a quick romp to victory. With its better than
two-to-one advantage in population—some twenty million in the North
against half that many in the seceded Southern states—and its overwhelming superiority in industry, munitions, railroads, and shipping,

the common Northern wisdom in the early weeks of the war had the conflict ending in a few weeks or, at latest, "by Christmas." But saddled with the responsibility of actually devising a winning strategy, Lincoln wasn't nearly as sanguine as common wisdom or the enthusiastic optimism of "most" Northern opinion. He did believe, though, that one hale blow against the secessionists *might* undermine Southern confidence to the point where the still politically shaky Confederacy would cave in. But where to begin, and where would the North's still inchoate superiority be most effectively used in demonstrating to the South the futility in fighting the far stronger Union? And always at the back of Lincoln's mind and in the forefront of his fears was the specter of the border states forsaking the Union and joining their slave-owning brethren against the abolitionist Yankees: Missouri with its command of the Mississippi and Missouri rivers; Maryland, which in league with Southern forces could cut off access to Washington from the north; and Kentucky, the state that controlled the critical southern bank of the Ohio River.

As his first task, Lincoln knew he would have to get a federal army in shape to take to the field. The opening move in achieving that end was to increase the army's size, which in the spring of 1861 was, in a word, minuscule. In the early part of the war, that preceding the introduction of a draft, this translated first into federalizing and calling up the individual state militias. Second, it meant successfully answered appeals to the public for volunteers for both the army and the navy. Both elements did succeed, at least in terms of putting a force in the field adequate to fight what was assumed would be a relatively short war, an assumption fortified by a few small but cheering Union victories over rebel forces in western Virginia. A federal blockade that swiftly closed Southern ports was designed to prevent supplies from reaching Confederate troops and to block the importation of food and medicine sustaining a Southern population that couldn't be adequately fed or kept well without them. On an optimistic note, simply facing a tangible threat—one the president believed could successfully be dealt with—finally began to vitalize and strengthen Lincoln after his early weeks of indecision. Secretary of State Seward, who had until now held that he himself would have made a far more successful president than the man who actually occupied the White House, wrote to his wife with rare words of praise for his chief, albeit words mixed with a shadow of concern: "Executive skill and vigor are rare qualities. The President is the best of us; but he needs constant and assiduous coöperation."[18] By mid-June, Lincoln had decided where the North's forces would strike, and preparations began in earnest for a much anticipated first real showdown between North and South.

When a few weeks earlier the Confederates had moved their seat of government from Montgomery, Alabama, to Richmond, Virginia, the capital of the Confederacy ended up a mere one hundred miles south of the federal capital. The new Confederate congress planned to convene there in July, fueling a response of "Forward to Richmond!" from countless Northerners egging on a Northern attack against the cockpit of the rebellion. Under the overall command of General Joseph Johnston, the rebels further chose northern Virginia in which to locate their largest army. There it would both protect Richmond against any Union advance on the city *and* be within striking distance of nearby Washington. The epicenter of Johnston's forces was at Manassas Junction, an undistinguished crossroads town just south of the sluggish Bull Run, a stream not far south of the Potomac. The village didn't amount to much, its importance lying only in the "junction" part of its name: There the main rail line south and west from Washington into the heart of Virginia joined with another line heading due west into the Shenandoah Valley. The convergence meant that the Confederates could rush trains full of additional troops to the area to help thwart any threat to their army already there.

Regardless of the site's advantages to his opponents, Lincoln was still convinced that Manassas was the best place to face off against the Confederate force, troops serving under General Beauregard, the same confident little Creole who had commanded the attack on Fort Sumter. Unfortunately, Lincoln possessed no obviously qualified counterpart for Beauregard: Unavailable were the admired but elderly and infirm Winfield Scott and the esteemed West Pointer but now-gone-South Robert E. Lee. To lead the attack in the field against Beauregard, the president settled on the relatively obscure General Irvin McDowell, another West Pointer with a history of having served with distinction in the Mexican War.

To reach Manassas before the Confederates were able to reinforce it with reserves from the Shenandoah Valley, Lincoln wanted to attack in early July. But McDowell well understood that his army wasn't yet ready to fight a major battle. Consequently, on July 9 the general began a week of intensive training meant to whip his force of thirty-seven thousand volunteers into the closest possible state of readiness before marching them across the Potomac and into Virginia. A mere twenty miles separated the federal capital from Beauregard's thirty-two thousand men at Manassas.

Sadly, McDowell's week of training was a week too long. Confederate spies and sympathizers in Washington—the most damaging was the widow Mrs. Rose O'Neal Greenhow, whose stylish parties were routinely filled with politicians and officers eager to boast of, and give away, their knowledge of Union plans—had informed President Davis and important Confederate officials about the gathering federal attack aimed at Manassas. The intelligence proved crucial, leading the Confederates to strengthen Beauregard's force by bringing troops by train from the Shenandoah Valley. The rebels were fully as inexperienced at warfare as were the federals, but they possessed the unmeasurable but critical advantage of defending their home ground, not to mention the zeal of being the presumed underdog in facing whatever Lincoln would throw at them.

The battle of Manassas—usually called Bull Run by Northerners—turned out to be a near miss for the North. If the federals had gained knowledge of the rebels' true strength, victory would likely have gone to McDowell, whose swollen estimate of the enemy's forces led him to give up the field though victory for him had probably been attainable. Conversely, without the espionage intelligence received from Washington's spies, the South would probably have lost. As for the president, Lincoln seemed to have earnestly believed at the outset of the fight that his men would carry the day. He also believed, wrongly, that the shock of its heavy losses on the field would bring down the Confederacy's shaky structure, at least to the point of forcing Davis and his government into a negotiated settlement.

Lincoln wasn't alone in his miscalculation. A large part of Washington had also been confident that the overwhelming Northern superiority in men and equipment would carry the day. Washingtonians' spirits had been high as the city watched long columns of troops and wagons cross the Potomac to head toward Beauregard's army. Accompanying the units were military bands optimistically blasting out popular march tunes of the day, including "John Brown's Body" and "Ach, du lieber Augustin." The city's newspapers breathlessly reported the spectacle for all to enjoy, ensuring that everyone knew the fighting was about to get under way. After the shooting began on Thursday, July 18, the news that seeped back to the capital brought about wild excitement alongside hopes of victory. By Saturday, countless Washingtonians—members of Congress, the town's social lions both male and female, the simply curious—drove or walked across the Long Bridge toward the sound of the distant cannon fire that could clearly be heard throughout the capital area. Many of the spectators had packed portable feasts to lend them sustenance while watching the fighting, allowing knots of civilians to enjoy their picnics from the heights surrounding the battlefield; Washington caterers had been kept busy packing hampers for the capital's better-off citizens all that Saturday morning, some trebling their ordinary prices to take advantage of the ripe pickings occasioned by the drama of the day. The main clash, though, would actually wait one more day—until Sunday, July 21.

The critical part of that day's climactic fighting began while Lincoln was in attendance at weekly church services near the White House. It was a tense Sunday in the capital, with the population anxious about what the day would bring on the banks of Bull Run. Following the church service, General Scott approached the president and solemnly reassured him of federal success. Later that afternoon, strollers in the White House area saw Lincoln wearing a soft felt hat and scurrying across from the mansion to the telegraph office in the War Department. Like most everyone else in the city, the president could hear the steady thump of cannon fire wafting northward across the Potomac. Eager to get closer to the source of the noise, Lincoln himself then saddled up and rode across the river to Scott's headquarters in Robert E. Lee's vacated mansion at the top of Arlington Heights. Then the ax fell. On his 6:00 P.M. return to the White House, the president found the secretary of state awaiting him, the somber Seward having just gotten news directly from the front. Seward's message was devastating. "The battle is lost," he told the president. "McDowell is in full retreat and calls on General Scott to save the capital."[19] Seward produced a telegram from a captain at the front informing his superiors that "the routed [federal] troops will not re-form."[20]

Along Bull Run, the scene was one of pure horror. What had looked to be a seemingly sure Union triumph had changed direction late that day into a victory for the rebellion, Beauregard's and Johnston's armies routing the superior Union forces and sending them fleeing in panic back toward the Potomac and the relative safety of the capital. As the day was described by a South Carolinian who witnessed the devastation: "For ten long hours it literally rained balls, shells, and other missiles of destruction. . . . It is heartrending. I cannot go any further. Mine eyes are damp with tears."[21]

His expectations in ruins, Lincoln was staggered. For that entire night and into Monday morning, he remained on his feet in his White House office, receiving visitors from the site of the battle. Each etched a scene of the fighting, one worse than the last, but all telling of the thousands of deaths, by any measure the deadliest horror the American people had ever experienced. The truth finally sank into the president's consciousness that this war was not going to be over in a few weeks, or even a few months—and, furthermore, that no one could begin to see when an end would come to the struggle that would conclude with either the Union saved or the Southern states permanently severing their bonds with the rest of the nation.

For that night and for many days and nights following, Washingtonians beheld bloodied shards of McDowell's routed army flowing back into the city, thousands of military wagons and buggies filled with the dead and injured, and all whipping up banks of mud on the city's rainsoaked dirt streets. Among the battle's losses were a handful of the politicians who had gone out to see firsthand the rebellion crushed: The Confederates had captured senators and representatives, a few of whom were now on their way to Confederate prisoner-of-war camps. Standing and smirking on many a house's stoop, the city's Southern sympathizers gloated over the miserable parade of soldiers in the streets, these Southern fellow travelers triumphantly certain that the capital would soon be in Confederate hands. One braying secessionist so maddened a young blue-clad army officer that he chased the man down the street until the offender ran into a building, from which the disdainful women of the house slammed the door in the officer's face.[22]

Though the defeat was not catastrophic in terms of damage done to the North's military force—the federals had inflicted a nearly proportionate toll of death and mayhem on the rebel army—what quickly became clear was the Union's startling lack of the military preparedness needed to take on the Confederacy. Unquestionably though, the defeat had represented a grievous injury, a message that no light of victory shone at the end of any tunnel, *and* that Washington and its hinterland stood in direct and immediate danger of invasion from Jefferson Davis's soldiery. Federal officials now had to believe those forces were being regrouped even while Bull Run's blue-uniformed survivors were flooding the Union capital. But in truth, the rebels were also exhausted, in such injured condition that Johnston and Beauregard gave up their chance to attempt a march on Washington. For the present, the city would remain free. A stunned Lincoln now had to hastily reconsider how to save the Union.

THE FIRST FAMILY AT HOME

With the disillusionment of Bull Run and the threat of Confederate attack, a frightened Washington drew in on itself. In his White House councils, Lincoln and the men planning the war with him understood that their most urgent priority was to turn the army that had fled the field at Manassas into a force capable of confronting and defeating the enemy. To that end, for the remainder of the summer and into the fall Washingtonians saw their city transformed from a small and languid town whose only real business was politics into a large and booming military nerve center whose new business was war. Indeed, the capital was becoming an urban encampment of soldiers on a scale the nation had never before dreamed of.

Unlike their immediate predecessors in the White House, the Lincoln family decided to remain in residence in the Executive Mansion during the summer of 1861, even though in the pre-air-conditioning age those months were a purgatory for the people of the city. Earlier presidents and their families had escaped—the term isn't inappropriate—to a wooden cottage at the Soldiers' Home, a few miles north of the White House but because of its greater altitude and lesser humidity a world away in terms of tolerability. But Lincoln decided that he and his family should stay put, probably both because of what he saw as a vital need for security and to remain close to the city center and its communication facilities (the telegraph machine in the nearby War Office quickly became critical to overseeing the war's progress, but for unknown reasons no telegraph capability would be installed in the White House during Lincoln's years; had there been, it would have represented a great convenience to the overworked chief executive). The price Lincoln and his family paid for remaining in the Executive Mansion was nearly unrelieved misery during the worst weeks of that summer.

In truth, daily life for every family member was rarely without its torments at any season, not least for the hardworking president. Lincoln's working conditions were primitive compared to the comforts enjoyed by modern presidents. Almost nothing in the White House was truly splendid, certainly not the room where the nation's most important political decisions were taken. The president's White House office resembled that of the head of any middling business enterprise, little different from those filling countless office buildings all across mid-Victorian America. Serving as Lincoln's personal workroom as well as the chamber in which the cabinet met each week, the space measured a comparatively modest twenty-five by forty feet. The window on the east wall faced the Treasury building, a looming structure then still uncompleted. The south windows overlooked the president's small private park and farther to the perpetually rank-smelling Tiber Canal with its steady flow of garbage, offal, human waste, and bugs. In winter, a white marble fireplace struggled to warm the room's occupants, and in summer open windows tended to let in little more than hot air and the winged vermin reconnoitering from the canal. John Hay wrote about these insects that tormented every White House occupant: "The air is swarming with them, they are on the ceilings, the walls and the furniture in countless numbers, they are buzzing about the room, and butting their heads against the window panes, they are on my clothes, in my hair, and on the sheet I am writing on. They are all here . . . they hold a high carnival, rather a perfect saturnalia."[23] And whenever the window was left open for the president to catch the occasional breeze, they ceaselessly tormented him as well.

Light other than daylight came either from the kerosene lamps placed around the room or from overhead gas jets shaded by cut-glass globes. The sparse furnishings consisted of a desk for the president, a tall cabinet fitted with pigeonholes, a pair of horsehair-stuffed sofas, and a table with several side chairs around it used for cabinet meetings. Maps covered a good part of the white walls. One useful device, a bell cord, hung near the president's desk and was pulled to summon either of the presidential secretaries from their adjoining offices.[24]

Consider other aspects of life for the Lincolns in that summer of 1861. Start with clothing, the most ordinary reality of existence. There were then no such things as "summer" clothes. Garments worn in the summer might be somewhat lighter than those used for the colder months, but not by much. Both convention and technology prevented any great diversity in the pursuit of comfort. Mary would be dressed with an initial layer of linen or cotton underwear. The individual items would include drawers and a chemise and relatively heavy, nonsheer stockings, likely black; all of the above were partially or entirely encased by a whalebone-stiffened corset whose uncomfortable stays were sewn into channels all around and whose back was laced up by threading cords through metal eyelets. Mary would need her maid to pull this contraption's lacings tight so as to compress the intestines and elevate the wearer's innards as high as possible, the idea being to form a fashionably rounded bosom under either the bodice of a day dress or an evening gown's more deeply cut décolletage. Hanging from the top of the lower part of this rig, which is to say from around the waist, was a great cage-like, bell-shaped contraption, its straps held together with smaller so-called tapes, at the bottom of which hung a steel hoop in suspension and which spread out nearly a yard from the fulcrum of the legs. This cage was usually covered with a light fabric, the whole forming a sort of stiffened gown-under-a-gown.

Over all this would be, of course, *the* gown. In a summer's daytime, it could be made of comparatively cool cotton or linen, but rarely did it come without a battery of ribbons, frogs, blossoms, stripes, hangings, gewgaws, and furbelows attached to it by the needle and thread of Lizzy Keckly. No matter how fluffy or "light," it would never by any modern definition be what could be called an airy body covering. Mary's shoes—in any season—would be in modern terms simply high-heeled boots, usually made of leather, laced up the front, their tops rising to perhaps three or four inches above the wearer's ankle. The first lady could not have her hair cut coolly short or arranged in a comfortably loose cascade.

Instead, it was oiled, parted in the center, and pulled down tight (again by a maid), the whole formed into a bun and pinned to the back of the skull like a small cushion. Some kind of lace caplet almost always was bound up in the arrangement. Finally, stepping outside one's front door required the putting on of gloves, probably kid—summer, winter, it made no difference.

Her husband could, blessedly, expect to be somewhat cooler in the capital's summer. Lincoln's suit would be, rather than the heavy worsted wool of winter, comparatively thin *light* worsted wool. Underwear was cotton or linen and came in two pieces: a short-sleeved shirt that buttoned up from midchest and a pair of drawers extending to the ankle and equipped with a button fly. (One-piece union suits were still a few decades in the future.) The president's shirts were also cotton or linen. His neck was wrapped with the unavoidable tie, then wider than those worn today. Shoes resembled a modern desert boot, or high-top oxford. Going out-of-doors required a hat, which for Lincoln generally meant the famous stovepipe beaver, a heavy and expensive model that served the president double duty as a portable filing cabinet, a kind of briefcase-on-the-head in which he tucked everything from memorandums to state papers. Only Willie and Tad were afforded anything like *genuinely* light summer wear, and that only because they were young enough to get away with short pants. The fabrics they wore were the same as those worn by their parents, though generally cut a little fuller and therefore, one hoped, a bit cooler.

Living conditions were extraordinarily wearing in the White House on summer days, few of which are not hot and, particularly unpleasant, humid. Washington's withering heat and dampness rapidly putrefied the human and animal slop that was sluiced into the town's waterways, with the principal canal flowing just a few hundred yards from the south front of the Executive Mansion. The slightest breeze wafted the stench into the building's open windows. Along with the nauseating smell came squadrons of flies and mosquitoes, each one a potential carrier of some deadly or at least debilitating disease, malaria being a particular danger to the White House's occupants in the summer; that illness—pervasive enough to be considered almost run-of-the-mill—was carried to humans by way of the mosquito's mouth. Since screens hadn't yet been invented, all of the building's windows and doors served as entrances for these airborne terrors.

It was not only odors and insects that unvaryingly gained easy entrance to the building. The public character and physical openness of the president's house meant that legions of people—clemency seekers, tourists, the curious, those looking for a toilet—clambered through the place every daylight hour. But it was the never-ending office seekers lined up outside the president's office who could be the most troublesome. Having journeyed from almost everywhere in the country to present their pleas to Lincoln, these importuners were strongly indisposed to ever being told to come back another day. Almost all of them could be expected to stink in the summer, since nothing like deodorants or antiperspirants yet existed. Few people bathed daily, or even weekly, and the woolen clothes of the time reeked because dry cleaning didn't exist and any effective purging of outerwear was difficult and time-consuming.

Tobacco stood high on the list of dreadfulnesses that made White House life—especially summer life—so miserable. In Lincoln's time, most of the stuff was smoked as cigars or chewed in wads jammed in the cheeks or behind the gums. The latter meant that the chewer was constantly ejecting juice. When this was done nicely, it went into the cuspidors, reeking spittoons that were then standard equipment in every room. When not done nicely, it ended up all over the floor. As for cigars, summer at least meant open windows and therefore some relief from the miasma of eye-burning and throat-choking smoke they created.

In addition to all the unpleasantness *inside* the White House, in those summer weeks of 1861 tumult reigned in the streets immediately adjacent to the building. As we've seen, the city had become a vast military depot, a teeming swirl of soldiers together with all their accoutrements and hangers-on: the sutlers who served as the traveling post exchanges of the time, the thousands of wagons that carried soldiers' supplies, the horses that hauled or carried everyone and everything, and the massive deposits of animal feces (a much greater problem since the war started) that covered the city's roadways. The army quartered its soldiers just about anywhere a spare patch of ground or unused space existed on which to pitch tents and build cooking fires; even the Capitol's basement becoming a gigantic military bakery. Soldiers surrounded the White House itself, some acting as a guard for the first family, and some there simply because no place else existed for them. No one prevented the mansion's grounds from being turned into a habitat for soldiers during the time they awaited their orders to go off and fight the rebels. Some of the more sociable men even pitched in as playmates for Willie and Tad.

It is understandable that Mary Lincoln wished to turn this unlovely disarray into as pleasing a home as possible for her family, chiefly for her beleaguered husband. Having left an orderly and comfortable residence in Springfield for the disorderly and largely uncomfortable house at 1600 Pennsylvania Avenue, Mary decided that the least she could do for the president was to make things as agreeable as she could for him. She did often forsake good sense with her spending and overspending, and she was overly acquisitive, but perhaps only to compensate for having left behind a genteel childhood for a just-barely-middle-class adulthood. Finally, her delusions of grandeur could be genuinely maddening but also forgiven when seen in the light of the unkind treatment she suffered from so much of Washington's established society. But through it all, the first lady considered as her chief responsibility the comfort and happiness of her husband and her children. The approaching tragedy of her life in Washington was rooted to a large degree in that everyone saw her flaws, while few stopped to consider the reasons for those flaws.

ROBERT

One great joy came to Abraham and Mary Lincoln in a summer dominated by war and the phenomenon of the constant death of loved ones. Their firstborn son, who by this first year of war had become almost a stranger to his family, visited the White House. On July 17 he wired his father, "I have the mumps. Home in a few days. Not sick at all."[25] It was, coincidentally, Robert's vacation period from Harvard. Even though the prospect of her eldest son threatened by a dangerous disease was one more and much unneeded upset for the first lady, the whole family nevertheless looked forward to being reunited with the son and brother who so clearly looked to be steering a handsome course for himself in life.

From soon after his entry into the family eighteen years earlier, Robert had seemed to stand slightly off the centerline of his parents. As we've seen, the historical cliché has it that he inherited more

"Todd" from his parents than he did "Lincoln." But perhaps to state it with greater precision, he grew less in either Abraham or Mary Lincoln's mold than he did in that of his namesake, his proper and businesslike maternal grandfather, Robert Todd of Lexington. And as he grew, his personality seemed to take wing in a different direction from those of his parents, and especially so from those of his brothers Willie and Tad. The youngest two boys developed as one unit, Robert as another. Had death not taken Eddie—the second son, and three years his older brother's junior—he and Robert might have become a kind of unit to themselves within the family, much as Willie and Tad did later. But with the loss of Eddie a month short of his fourth birthday, that scenario never happened.

In the early formative years of Robert's life, his father possessed little notion of the hows and whys of children. Abraham Lincoln's relationship with his own father had been problematic, the cause likely the chasm of difference in their personalities: Thomas Lincoln cared not at all for intellectual self-improvement, while his son lived to learn about a universe that lay beyond his immediate surrounds and daily needs. The difference between Abraham and Robert wasn't that stark, but it was enough to keep them from achieving anything like the astonishing closeness that ripened between Abraham Lincoln and his third and fourth sons. A famous and telling remark made about Robert by his father—"I sometimes fear he is one of the little rare-ripe sort, that are smarter at about five than ever after"—suggests to many the onset of a father's disappointment in his son's developing personality.

Robert's earliest years appeared normal and contented. His father described him as a boy with "a great deal of that sort of mischief that is the offspring of much animal spirits." The family's neighbors grew used to the customary mischievousness of a noisy little boy whose parents believed in the then unusual course of letting their children have pretty much their own way as far as manners and comportment were concerned. And in turn, Mary became accustomed to Springfielders' complaints of the rambunctiousness of all her children, very much including the eldest of the lot. But with his next brother Eddie's passing, Robert lost a mate in youthful play and started to grow apart, his personality shifting from boisterous to contemplative. In his early schooling years he saw that his father often favored Willie and Tad, the father perhaps making up for not having gotten closer to Robert and the sad reality that Eddie hadn't lived long enough to become close to him.

Physically, Robert certainly seemed to enter manhood with a greater proportion of Todd characteristics than those of his Lincoln heritage. In height he was about a head taller than his mother, which still left him considerably shorter than his father's six feet four inches. His eyes were noticeably saturnine and his face round, making him look like old drawings of his grandfather Todd. From youth, he was inclined to stoutness, just avoiding fatness until his later adult years. From about eighteen onward, the young Robert was handsome in a way that looks contemporary today, wearing none of the facial hair of his father and keeping the hair on the top of his head combed in a neat and short style, contrasting peculiarly with his father's bushy-topped appearance. He was born with a cast in one eye that left him slightly cross-eyed, but Robert's mother had the condition surgically corrected while he was still in his teens; given the knowledge of eye surgery in the 1850s, he was lucky not to have come out of the treatment worse off than when he went into it.

Both parents harbored lofty expectations for Robert's future, and his lawyer father was earning enough to pay to see that those expectations were fulfilled. So in the summer of 1859 the Lincolns sent the sixteen-year-old to Cambridge, Massachusetts, to take entrance examinations for Harvard College. Lincoln, though, was wary of his son's picking up the snobbish ways of Eastern society, notions that might throw him into direct contrast with Lincoln's own astonishingly liberal values. As it happened, Robert passed only one of the sixteen entrance tests, his Springfield schooling evidently having come up far short of the mark. Nevertheless, the boy single-mindedly fought to get into what was already then the finest college in America. His parents enrolled him at Phillips Exeter Academy to complete a year of hard cramming designed to enable him to broach Harvard's rigors, especially the required curriculum of Greek, Latin, mathematics, chemistry, religion, elocution, rhetoric, composition, history, and botany.[26]

While Robert did greatly differ from his father in many aspects, that is not to imply that he was by any means unintelligent. He did lack the older man's genius, but so did almost everyone else in the country.

Robert was a quick study, and he possessed a gift for words, though in college he often wrote in an oddly elevated and affected manner. He mastered what he had to at Phillips Exeter and earned himself a place at Harvard for the following summer, becoming a freshman in the class of 1864. That was the summer his father won the Republican nomination for president of the United States, and from that turning point Robert would be largely separated—and in many ways alienated—from his family for the rest of his father's life.

Robert Lincoln and Harvard agreed with one another. By demonstrating to his fellow students—every one then a male, of course—that his father's political prominence was more of an embarrassment to him than a source of satisfaction, the newly socially smooth young man immediately began to fit in. The year at Phillips Exeter had seemingly washed out Robert's prairie naïveté, and he found the transition to the more prominent institution to his liking. When a group of upperclassmen intent on humiliating the freshman asked him what kind of man his father was, Robert coolly answered that the president-elect was "the queerest old cuss you ever saw,"[27] a reply that firmly linked him to his new environment. Then as now, the Harvard student body was disproportionately composed of the sons of America's social and economic elite, and the mores he learned and the friends he made benefited the young Illinoisan socially and economically for the rest of his life.

As for relations with his father, the new Harvard-molded first son quickly became comparatively remote from the president. Robert was at the White House for only short periods during the war, he and his father growing politely but unmistakably distant in those years. Instead, the president's two secretaries provided Lincoln with the relationship that the adult Robert might have had with his father; in fact, Lincoln came to regard John Nicolay and John Hay with tremendous affection, indeed almost as sons. Pointedly, the secretaries were the men the family's two youngest sons looked up to as stand-in elder brothers. Little evidence indicates this drift away from his president-father greatly bothered Robert. While there was no sharp or clear split between the two in the White House years (for example, the president was volubly proud of Robert's academic achievements and had even visited him at Harvard on his campaign travels), neither was any particular attempt made by either to restore the comparatively greater warmth that had characterized their earlier relationship in Springfield. Only scant correspondence passed between father and son in the Harvard years, largely, of course, because of the president's preoccupation with the war, though Lincoln did routinely mail checks to Robert to cover his student expenses.

However one looks at the father-son bond, during these years President Lincoln was overwhelmed by his job, by his responsibility, by the war, and by his own complex emotions regarding people. Some observers of Lincoln believe that he kept the deepest part of himself to himself, as viewed by the near certainty that he had only one truly intimate friend in his entire life. As president, he allowed his spirits to fly entirely free only with his two youngest sons, children who sought nothing from him but the physical adoration he heaped so freely on them.

Robert's relationship with his mother was significantly closer than that with his father. On their mother-son visits he talked to her, if only because, unlike his father, she had the time to do so and probably because he didn't doubt that she loved him as much as she loved her other children. Maybe the two understood that their self-righteousness and quick tempers matched one another's, traits that made them companionable, but sometimes alienated them as well. In any case, Mary Lincoln unabashedly adored her eldest son and during her initial months as first lady sought him out as much as possible, including him in her social life as a substitute for her occupied husband. Because "proper" ladies of the time rarely traveled without a male escort, Mary considered Robert the perfect companion for the routine rail journeys to which she became passionately addicted as an escape from the social and climatic trials of Washington.

Soon after Lincoln's election, Robert had joined his mother's pre-inaugural shopping expedition party in New York and later came down to Washington to stay with his parents for the swearing-in ceremony. By this time the press had begun referring to Robert by what it considered the humorous nickname of Prince of Rails, in joint reference to his father's rail-splitting reputation and to the Prince of Wales, the heir to the British throne, who had famously visited President Buchanan's White House in 1860. Characteristically, Robert found the term embarrassing, especially among his classmates in Cambridge.

With her eldest son home in early August on his summer vacation, Mary wanted to show off the Harvard undergraduate to official Washington. She likely knew much of the capital's society judged the first family's parenting abilities by Willie's and Tad's wild behavior, already much discussed around town. Mary reasoned that Robert would look a becomingly proper presidential son at her first reception for real European royalty.

The first lady firmly believed that, irrespective of the war, the White House should remain a place of social activities, despite that many Americans, even prominent Washingtonians, believed social display in the Executive Mansion had become inappropriate in the tragic circumstances of the nation's conflict. But Prince Napoleon of France, the cousin of the emperor of the French, Napoleon III, was honoring the capital with a visit, and Mary delighted in arranging a sumptuous reception for the prince. She justified her lavishness in the cause of paying homage to France, whose friendship, or at least continued denial of diplomatic recognition to the Southern rebels, was a state-to-state courtesy for which her husband's administration was deeply appreciative.

Unhappily, Prince Napoleon's wife, Clothilde, chose to remain on the couple's yacht, moored in New York harbor, rather than journey to a city considered too hot and unhealthy. Lincoln's two secretaries chalked up the princess's absence to a desire to avoid the "profanation of vulgar eyes," possibly meaning the first lady's eyes.[28] In any case, the Lincolns' earlier regular levees had proven successful, and it couldn't be imagined that the honoring of a royal visitor would be criticized.

On the afternoon of August 3, 1861, Prince Napoleon Joseph Charles Paul Bonaparte arrived at the White House to meet the president. Embarrassingly, only Willie was at the front door to show him in, obviously a very different situation from what Napoleon would have found in the palace of any European head of state. (The imperial visitor wrote in his diary that "one goes right in [the White House] as if entering a café.")[29] Whether it was truly because his guest had been greeted so informally, Lincoln's initial talks with the intensely status-conscious prince got off to a shaky start; according to witnesses, in retaliation the prince appeared to take a "cruel pleasure in remaining silent."[30] The snide Napoleon later wrote that the president looked like a "bootmaker."[31]

Luckily, at their party the Lincolns had a chance to make things up with his French majesty's cousin. Though Mary was the official hostess, she herself had not planned the affair, her husband having assigned responsibility for the details to John Nicolay. Mary smarted at the undisguisable insult, but Lincoln knew his wife didn't possess the necessary political acumen to oversee such important state affairs and that any errors she might make would reflect poorly on the administration. Unfortunately, Nicolay was forced to turn down some of Mary's choices regarding the guest list. The situation augured poorly for the future in that Mary's antipathy to the young secretary, a man critical to Lincoln's ability to run his office, would eventually grow to a truly disturbing level.

The state dinner for Prince Napoleon, one of the grandest festivities in the Lincolns' first year in the White House, turned out to be almost entirely a stag affair: Only the first lady, magnificently gowned in a long-trained creation of white silk swagged with white grenadine, and her houseguest cousin, Elizabeth Grimsley, joined the thirty-eight men deemed most essential for a meeting with so important a guest. Glowing, Mary entered the dining room on the arm of the prince, a regal honor that must have deeply gratified the royalty-intoxicated first lady. At the table, Cousin Elizabeth sat on the president's right, while Mary assumed the female seat of honor as the prince's partner. The chief guest arrived in full imperial kit, his breast described as "a flame of decoration" with its banks of medals and orders lined up in heavy rows. Mary chatted away with him in the prince's native language, her boarding-school French lessons from Madame Mentelle put to their best possible use, a development that could hardly have been foreseen in those long-ago Lexington days of her youth. At the climax of the evening, the Marine Band played the "Marseillaise" in the prince's honor, mistakenly concluding that the republican anthem was the proper one for the prince rather than the correct imperial air, "Partant pour la Syrie." Asked later about the musical faux pas, Prince Napoleon murmured diplomatically, *"Mais oui, ici je suis républicain—en Amérique."*[32]

But an electorate already finding itself disenchanted with the war had begun to regard this kind of luxurious behavior as inappropriate, irrespective of the strategic diplomatic justification behind it. Grumbling about the president's—and, ominously, the first lady's—lack of judgment was rapidly growing more vigorous in Northern editorial columns, a dangerous situation for an administration already widely viewed as unsteady, even flailing, in its conduct of the war.

THREE

———

CALAMITY IN WAR,
CALAMITY AT HOME

THE BOYS

It is hardly possible that any presidential children ever had more fun in the White House than did Willie and Tad that first year. From the day their parents took possession of the mansion, the president's sons—the Little Codgers, as Lincoln affectionately referred to them—made it their business to have a good time. For eleven months, the boys possessed their own magic fort.

Abraham and Mary Lincoln were very much in the minority of their countrymen where it came to the rearing of children, especially their last two. As a young boy, even Robert had been allowed wide latitude by his parents in a way mid-nineteenth-century American children were generally not. Admittedly, Mary Lincoln had never been averse to corporal punishment when she thought the oldest of her four sons needed it. Lincoln is never known to have struck his oldest son, but neither did he allow Robert to become an irrepressible whirlwind like Willie and Tad.

Why Lincoln departed so far from the norm in the latitude he allowed his sons isn't readily answerable. Mere preoccupation with his other business affairs—especially a time-consuming law practice and an ever-deepening involvement with politics—doesn't come close to explaining why he became the kind of father he was. Many nineteenth-century fathers were busy, yet those of the class to which Lincoln aspired hardly ever gave their children such leeway. Long before their father's election to the presidency, Willie and Tad had made themselves well-known in Springfield. Their behavior was far from shameful or cruel and certainly did not rise to what normal society regarded as juvenile delinquency. But the boys could be terrors, especially when acting in unison. They routinely ignored their mother's attempts at discipline, though in truth Mary wasn't overly demanding of her two youngest sons. Lincoln himself seems to have regarded their antics as cute, or endearing, overlooking others' opinions when the two would burst into his meetings with clients or trash his paperwork or anger neighbors with their cyclonic sprees around town.

William Herndon, Lincoln's last law partner, remembered Willie and Tad with a surprising repugnance, especially so considering his lifelong veneration of their father's memory. The man whose daily life was long entwined with Lincoln's could find scant sympathy for the brats who often visited the partners' office in downtown Springfield. He wrote of the boys as "little devils." "These children would take down the books," he noted, "empty ash buckets, coal ashes, inkstand, papers, gold pens, letters, etc. etc. in a pile then dance on the pile." What astounded Herndon was that Lincoln would "say nothing, so abstracted was he and so blinded by his children's faults. Had they s__t in Lincoln's hat and rubbed it on his boots, he would have laughed and thought it smart." Herndon more calmly concluded, though, that his partner "worshiped his children and *what* they worshiped; he loved what they loved and hated what they hated—rather, disliked what they hated which was everything that did not bend to their freaks, whims, follies and the like."[1] Having loathed Herndon from the day she met him (on that occasion he supposedly offended her while they danced together), Mary later disagreed with his picture of her sons, saying she and her husband refused to strongly discipline the boys in order that they would become "free-happy and unrestrained by parental tyranny." But as she also admitted, "We never controlled our children much."[2]

The inconsistency in Willie's and Tad's often unruly behavior was that both boys were habitually kind and lovable. In this regard they seemed to have inherited the best of their father's characteristics, unlike Robert, whose more brittle disposition mirrored his unpredictable mother. Historically, modern observers tend to weigh Robert by his somber postadolescent character, which he carefully controlled probably in an effort to distinguish himself from what he held to be unsophisticated frontier folksiness on his father's part. We of course cannot know how either Willie's or Tad's personality would have matured. But from the numerous accounts left by friends, relatives, and observers, Willie would likely have retained throughout life the sweet-tempered disposition remarked upon by so many. By the time Lincoln was in the White House, he viewed the boy as indispensable to his own peace of mind, as well as a joy to share his life with. It seems certain that Willie was the son whose character the father most admired.

In the first White House year, Tad grew more into the pet of the family, especially of his father. Possibly because of the boy's physical difficulties, Tad's fiery temper often flared whenever he was thwarted. His speech impediment meant that strangers sometimes could not understand what he was saying. Fortunately, his parents were able to make out Tad's indistinct words, and with their special understanding gave him the sympathy he needed when others could not. He was indulged in the family circle, a haven in which his parents overlooked his shortcomings—and saw to it that others did the same. Along with Willie, Tad received his lessons from a tutor (this wasn't only because of security concerns; Washington schools were closed in the early part of the war) in the second-floor Oval Room, a chamber that also acted as the family's living room. But the reality remained that while in Washington the youngest Lincoln son was handicapped to a degree, and his parents never, for example, forced him to dress himself during those years.

As for Abraham and Mary Lincoln—called Pa and Ma by Willie and Tad—their chief family principle in the White House was simply to "let the children have a good time."[3] The first couple followed this dictum from the beginning of their life in Washington, the president especially rigidly adhering to it. Given the president's wartime role as commander in chief, from the beginning of the Lincolns' life in Washington their existence was saturated by the trappings of the military. It could hardly have been otherwise. A large proportion of visitors to the White House arrived in uniform, and the bulk of the presidency's business revolved around the war. Army units were routinely bivouacked on the mansion's grounds, and round-the-clock formations of marching men and horse-drawn supply wagons rumbled along the surrounding streets. From the outset, Willie and Tad lived a make-believe military life in their new home. They used its roof as grounds for a private fort built of foraged logs, and they gravely saluted the soldiers guarding the family. The pair conducted court-martials on uniformed dolls, sat in judgment on little rag soldiers who "fell asleep" on duty and when found guilty were sentenced to executions that the boys performed with tiny lengths of rope. And they begged their father for uniforms and muskets, which Lincoln cheerfully obtained for the boys, though the president carefully saw to it that the guns were neutered of their firing capacity.

Within days of the inauguration, two young brothers came to the White House to join the Lincoln boys, the Taft boys sharing for the better part of a year this magical world with Willie and Tad. Bud and Holly Taft were the sons of Judge Horatio Taft, whom President Buchanan had appointed to head the Patent Office. That relatively high post meant that Taft and his wife became part of the upper level of the city's officialdom and thus were among those who visited and welcomed President-elect and Mrs. Lincoln on their arrival in Washington. After learning that the Tafts' sons were the same ages as her own boys, Mary requested that they be brought to the White House to meet Willie and Tad. On their first visit, their sixteen-year-old sister, Julia Taft, joined the pair. Within days, Bud, Holly, Willie, and Tad were inseparable, and Julia quickly came to be looked upon by the president and the first lady—who always felt that one of their greatest misfortunes was not having had a daughter—almost as their own child. Mary called Julia by her correct name, but the president and his sons always knew her as Jewly. The Lincoln sons and the virtually omnipresent Taft children enjoyed each other's company immensely. The group was even able to lighten the burden of war that constantly weighed on the president.

The Lincoln boys and the Taft boys nearly melded into a single unit during these days and sometimes nights together. When Mary left on one of her shopping trips to New York or to visit Robert in Boston, she knew that her young sons remained in safe hands with Julia at the White House, or on sleepovers at the Taft home a few blocks from the Executive Mansion. Tad and Willie came to regard the Taft home as an adjunct of their own, while on the other hand all three Taft siblings spent nearly as much time with the Lincolns as they did with their own parents. While the four boys raced around the Executive Mansion's grounds in search of adventure, Julia spent decorous afternoons with the first lady, the two sitting together on a sofa, sipping tea, the girl learning womanly secrets, the woman listening to Julia's thoughts and likely being transported in her mind back to her own youth in the remembered softness of antebellum Lexington.

The four boys spent many hours together in activities more serious than play. In the fall of 1861 the president hired a tutor for Tad and Willie to come to the White House, and he generously invited Judge Taft to allow Holly and Bud to share the classroom. Mary had a blackboard and desk installed at the end of the State Dining Room, and in the unfrontier-like grandeur of that chamber Abraham Lincoln's boys studied the basic building blocks of knowledge in a setting a world's difference from the prairie cabin in which their father had taught himself. Sadly, the perpetually fidgety Tad absorbed little of his tutor's lessons, though the president understood his son's limits and asked that the boy not be pushed overly hard. Willie did study hard though, judging from the growing writing ability he demonstrated that first presidential year. His composition in letters to old family friends in Springfield showed remarkable ability for a ten-year-old.

Willie sometimes tried to put a brake on his younger and as yet lesstamed brother. In her written recollections of those memorable days, Julia told the story of the Lincoln boys playing with a ball in the White House's grand vestibule. Oblivious to his surroundings, Tad kicked the ball against walls and delicate furnishings alike. Finally, one smash sent it into a large mirror, splintering the glittering object into giant shards. Swaggeringly, Tad then kicked the pieces into smaller bits. While an alarmed Willie looked on, the younger brother calmly chirped, "Well, it's broken. I don't believe Pa'll care." Willie shot back, "It's not Pa's looking glass. It belongs to the United States government."[4] "Pa" likely *wouldn't* have done much other than just direct a solemn remonstrance to his son to play ball somewhere else—but hardly anything that would have been apt to seriously hurt his beloved child's feelings.

Occasionally, though, the childish fun went unforgivably overboard, which meant the indulgent president found himself forced to halt the boys' misbehavior. Once when reviewing troops passing in front of the

White House, Lincoln turned to find his youngest son crouched behind his back, gaily waving a Confederate flag. It was the Alexandria banner Elmer Ellsworth had died removing, and which had been presented to the first lady at his funeral. Tad had found it in his mother's bureau and was overcome by the urge to wave it in his father's presence, clearly innocent of the symbolic meaning of the rebel symbol. Lincoln quickly turned his son over to an orderly and asked him to remove the boy from public view.[5] Tad's inclinations even came between Lincoln and Robert, sometimes representing a serious source of friction between the two men. One of these disputes arose when the secretary of war acceded to Lincoln's wish to please Tad by commissioning him a "lieutenant." After the boy received his new blue uniform, Tad decided to treat the White House servants as his own little army, going so far as to give them weapons with which to be drilled. When Robert saw this charade on a family visit home from college, his Harvard instincts judged the behavior inappropriate and he told his father. The president considered the matter trivial and so told Robert, but the incident hammered another small wedge between the lives of the two.[6]

McCLELLAN

After Bull Run, Lincoln's government directed itself to the critical job of turning the federal army into a machine capable of defeating a newly understood and obviously determined adversary. Seen in the light of Bull Run, the rebel army would clearly not be a walkover, and Lincoln knew that the federal army had better rapidly reinvent itself as a first-class fighting force or, short of divine intervention, the Union of North *and* South was finished. More than anything else, high-quality leadership was what the president needed in the field. General Winfield Scott, the long-past-prime commanding general, was too old to direct the federal force with the vigor the job demanded, and General Irvin McDowell—the Potomac forces commander at Bull Run who had failed to stop, let alone crush, the rebels—had not shown the command ability needed to defeat the enemy.

Perhaps a deeper analysis of the reasons for the Manassas disaster should have been Lincoln's first task. But instead, the hard-pressed president decided he had to quickly do whatever was necessary to stop a

Confederate advance into the North, and above all else that meant finding an able commander. The officer the president finally settled on was
a thirty-four-year-old West Pointer, a trained engineer who until that
summer had been all but unknown to the general public. His name was
George B. McClellan.

For the first half of the war, the Northern public would see this astonishingly young general as the brightest field commander Lincoln
possessed. That standing appealed enormously to the man himself,
who believed it was wholly deserved. Besides possessing a quick
mind, Major General George McClellan also bore matinee-idol looks,
which compensated for his lack of physical stature. When fully
stretched, McClellan stood five and a half feet tall, his disproportionately large head bearing small but penetrating eyes and topped by
thick black hair. The whole of his handsome appearance caused many
Northern ladies to regard him as a demigod, though many others routinely described him as "banty," a term that conveys as much of his
egocentric personality as it does of his cock-of-the-walk physique. But
more important, McClellan's prewar accomplishments had genuinely
been worthy of respect: He graduated second in his class at the military academy, gained distinction in the Mexican War, and served well
in the elite Corps of Engineers. In his recent civilian life he had
achieved notable success as a business executive in the running of two
railroads.

McClellan began the war as a relatively anonymous military leader,
but by the summer of 1861 he had managed a few minor victories in
western Virginia (the rebels enjoyed comparatively little support in the
area, which would soon break away from Virginia so it could remain in
the Union), for which Lincoln's attention fell on him. Mainly for lack of
anyone with greater obvious potential, in a large gamble the president
appointed the meticulous and disciplined officer commander of the Military Division of the Potomac, which meant McClellan was going to control what was, in effect, the eye of the war's hurricane, the area that
represented the conflict's most critical theater of operations. What the
president needed most was a general who would not allow another Bull
Run, and he believed he saw that commitment in the new commander.
The irony was that McClellan would indeed see to it that his army did
not suffer any more such distressing losses, but he achieved that goal in
large part because he avoided substantive confrontations.

McClellan spent the war's first winter training his army, an appropriate enough undertaking: The Northern forces admittedly possessed the North's economic power behind them, but they were grievously unprepared to take the field against so committed an enemy as the Southern rebels. In addition to teaching inexperienced recruits the fundamental elements of soldiering, McClellan also planned and constructed a ring of forty-eight forts around Washington, defenses backed up with a barrier of felled trees fifteen miles long and over a mile wide. The scheme made the city one of the most securely protected places in the world and shielded it from the unthinkable catastrophe its loss would have represented to the Union cause.

But while Lincoln's new commander oversaw the creation of a capable fighting army, the president grew increasingly frustrated as McClellan withheld that force from actual battle. For example, even as the general meticulously planned a drive on the Confederate capital of Richmond, he seriously overestimated the size of the Southern army. The error came largely from poor military intelligence, but Lincoln read the general's caution as missing the opportunity to defeat the rebels and perhaps even produce an early end to the war. During the Civil War, intelligence remained a shaky science, and many observers credit McClellan's actions to his determination not to throw his men to wasteful deaths by failing to carefully prepare the ground. For this reluctance, he was, unsurprisingly, idolized by his troops, men who affectionately called him Little Mac. But the public—and Lincoln—grew increasingly frustrated at the lack of a real assault against the enemy. As McClellan painstakingly trained his own forces, the opposing Confederate army gainfully spent this same period developing its own competence. The upshot was that McClellan's ostensible inertia was starting to politically damage the commander in chief, making Lincoln the growing target of scorn in Northern newspapers for not more forcefully pressing the war home.

Paradoxically, one beneficial consequence of the reluctance of Mac the Unready (the press delighted in coining names aimed at deriding the general) to take the field was Lincoln's own heightened involvement in the details of the actual war on the battlefield. Because Lincoln had understood that his own military experience was essentially nonexistent, at the outset of the conflict he gave his commanders almost unrestricted lead, reining them in only when their generalship crossed over into the political realm, territory the president jealously guarded against intervention by serving officers. But McClellan's slowness so disappointed Lincoln that he took it upon himself to gain an intellectual and technical command of how to win the fighting war. And, gradually, he became good at it. McClellan's slowness in pressing the fight, as well as the growing disrespect he openly directed at the president himself, would have an enormous effect on the war, one that probably contributed to the conflict's lasting far beyond a time anybody could have foreseen when it started.

These latter developments still lay in the future in the late summer and early fall of 1861, when McClellan's energy seemed unquenchable and he continued to enjoy Lincoln's confidence. Many even took to referring to the commander as Young Napoleon, comparing him not with the posturing hack mismanaging the French state at that time but rather with the first Bonaparte. Aware, though, of increasing press disapproval for his deliberateness, McClellan said of his accomplishments, "Let those who criticize me for delay in creating an army point out an instance when so much has been done with the same means in so short a time."[7] And in the near term and so long as he had the president on his side, Little Mac could stick to his own careful timetable.

DEATH COMES HOME

The war's tragedies continued to hammer the White House family hard, just as they did so many thousands of ordinary families in both the North and the South. Not widely noted but affecting the close circle in the Executive Mansion was the loss that August of George Keckly, Lizzy's only child (he was the son of the dressmaker's white former employer, but the child's illegitimate birth meant that he had had to take his mother's last name). The army barred George from openly joining the service as a Negro (the few blacks then serving in the Union army did so almost exclusively as cooks and as servants to officers), but his light complexion had allowed him to pass as white. After leaving Wilberforce College, he enlisted in the First Missouri Volunteers, and on August 10 died in his first experience of battle, at Wilson's Creek, in southwest Missouri. While in New York City, Mary Lincoln found out about the death and immediately sent Lizzy, who had by now become a close friend, a "kind, womanly" letter, a gesture that its beneficiary deeply appreciated.[8]

Edward Baker, a friend from the Lincolns' prairie years and for whom the couple had named their second son, was killed in the fighting at Ball's Bluff that October. The young and highly intelligent lawyer had worked with the nearly equally young Lincoln in Springfield and eventually became a much praised orator and politician. William Herndon described him as "hot-headed and impulsive, but brave as a lion." As the Republican senator from the new state of Oregon, Baker had been assigned the honor of formally introducing the president at Lincoln's inauguration. Just before his death, he visited his old friends in the White House, joining the first family at the mansion on a bright October afternoon. The senator and the president sat on the lawn under an old tree, and while Willie played at their feet, leaves fell all around. As Baker went to leave after this pleasant interlude, he picked up Willie and kissed him fondly, then rode away from his friends, this time forever. The next afternoon, near Leesburg, Virginia—Ball's Bluff lay just outside the town, about thirty miles upstream from Washington on the Potomac—Edward Baker died, his unit overpowered by rebels in a botched confrontation that was meant only as a reconnaissance but, with the troops under Baker's inexperienced leadership, ended with nearly a thousand Union casualties. For days afterward, the bodies of men killed at Ball's Bluff washed ashore as far downriver as the capital.

News of his friend's death hit Lincoln with tremendous force, leading him to the rare act of canceling his White House schedule on the next day. As for Willie, his joy of playing at war must have died a little with Colonel Baker's death. And Mary's sadness was worsened by yet more criticism of her actions in the wake of the tragedy, when Washington ladies took her to task her for an inappropriate "lapse"—wearing half-mourning lilac instead of full-mourning black at Baker's funeral. Grieved at Baker's loss, Mary was badly stung by the criticism, lashing out in response with the plea that she couldn't "muffle herself in mourning for every soldier killed."[9]

The day his parents told him about Baker's death, Willie sat in his room and wrote a poem about his family's old friend, the verses later being published to widespread admiration in the *Washington National*

Republican. Though the refined grammar of the lines suggests a parent's helping hand—Willie was only ten years old at the time—the depth of this exceptional boy's feelings clearly comes through.

> There was no patriot like Baker,
> So noble and so true:
> He fell as a soldier on the field.
> His face to the sky of blue. . . .

> No squeamish notions filled his breast,
> The Union was his theme,
> "No surrender and no compromise,"
> His day thought and night's dream.

> His country has her part to play,
> To'rds those he left behind,
> His widow and his children all—
> She must always keep in mind.

THE FIRST LADY

Sadly for Mary, the national sentiments against her were far more complex and intense than mere criticism of the color of the dresses she wore to funerals. By the fall of 1861, the first lady had become widely disliked in both halves of the divided nation. This wasn't especially surprising in the South. There the president's wife embodied Yankee treachery, a Southern-born gentlewoman having gone over to her own people's deadly adversary, living in a home that stood as the very symbol of the North's effort to destroy the South, and married to the enemy's commander in chief. It is difficult to see how any woman from her background and in her position could have been characterized in the Confederacy as anything *other* than a living devil. But the low esteem in which Mary Lincoln was held had also spread widely throughout the North.

No first lady before or since has seen her reputation so deeply sullied as did Mary Lincoln in those days of national fratricide. Prior to her husband's incumbency, presidential wives were regarded somewhat like children, which is to say little seen and heard even less. A few first ladies—women like Dolley Madison and Rachel Jackson—had been viewed as genuine personalities, women who uttered serious thoughts and weren't afraid of the consequences. Most of the others, though, had remained largely silent on matters that even remotely touched on politics or "men's business." Pre-Lincoln presidential wives did not rock boats, did not change protocol, did not traipse through the nation's cities in search of White House furnishings, and—most decidedly—did not raise their voices, show that they possessed a temperament, much less a temper, or interrupt their menfolk. From the outset of her husband's entry into national presidential politics, Mary Lincoln broke all of these "rules."

That was just for starters. In the same way Southerners despised her for being one of them who had transferred her allegiance to the North, Northerners equally despised her for being a Southerner who they surmised *had* in fact retained her allegiance to the South. In other words, people in both sections of the country assumed she was a traitor. What the people of the North knew of her that concerned the war was that Mary Lincoln's own brothers (that most were only half brothers didn't matter) were fighting for the *South,* and doing so in responsible command positions. The reality was, of course, that the war had divided thousands of American families, with siblings and all sorts of other relations fighting on opposite sides. The Lincoln family was not by any means unique in this regard.

Beyond these issues stood the belief that Mary Lincoln's personality was larger-than-life—at least, larger than *previous* first ladies' lives. Sadly typical of a large part of the national press's attitude toward Mrs. Lincoln was Murat Halstead's observation from the *Cincinnati Commercial Gazette.* The writer concluded that Mary was "a fool—the laughing stock of the town [Washington], her vulgarity only the more conspicuous in consequence of her fine carriage and horses and servants in livery and fine dresses, and her damnable airs."[10] This astonishingly unrestrained criticism was so painful because such sentiments were often brought down on Mary's head as a result of her own unwise actions.

Mrs. Lincoln was not a virago. Most of her efforts at being a successful first lady were based on kindly motives, but her intentions often backfired because of her brisk and fidgety personality that had been heavily shaped by an education far superior to that received by all but a tiny minority of mid-nineteenth-century females. Her efforts were thwarted from many quarters besides public disapproval. As to managing the White House and its social activities, both the State Department under Seward—a man she loathed—and her husband's office under Nicolay and Hay stood squarely in her way. Official precedence gave State final approval in how foreign visitors were to be entertained, and Lincoln himself gave oversight authority to his two secretaries affecting nearly all other *official* social activities in the mansion. Mary often asserted herself and frequently got her way, but in any real contest of wills her preferences as mistress of the house could be countermanded. She came to Washington undoubtedly determined to run the White House as she had her Springfield home, to be *Mrs. President* in the full sense of the job. When she found out how things were really going to work, it surely was a heavy blow to her fragile emotions.

A word about her relationship with John Nicolay and John Hay helps explain the domestic battlefield Mary faced. These two highly intelligent men were devoted unto death to the president, at least in respect to his and their official duties. But where his private life was concerned, the secretaries did not serve Lincoln as wisely as they might have. Both were conscious of Mary's emotional unsteadiness and should have comprehended that her often prickly, even rude, behavior was partly rooted in insecurities about how she would be publicly viewed and how she could help her husband with his formidable responsibilities. With the superciliousness of youthful brilliance, Nicolay and Hay instead saw her as an adversary, someone from whom their boss frequently needed to be protected. It wasn't long after they had settled into the White House that they started referring to the first lady as "the hellcat," a "witticism" that likely lost little time in getting to Mary's ear. The more she asserted her authority in the White House, the more Nicolay and Hay ridiculed her; the more she apprehended their disdain, the more she disliked the two men and, unquestionably, the more dejection she suffered.

Shopping and traveling became near addictions for Mary in the first White House year, an inclination that had started when as a congressman's often lonely wife she'd learned that she could find contentment in the treasure-laden shops of Washington. And now, because of her high profile as first lady, she could easily find new friends and allies. But Mary's personality was especially susceptible to male flattery, and some of the new friends and some of the allies proved to be less than desirable. One, in fact, was disastrous. Washington's insiders may have regarded Henry Wikoff, widely sneered at as a "professional gossip," as little more than a mountebank. But he smoothly sucked a first lady unable to distinguish between real friends and false into the shiny residue of his oily sophistication.

Wikoff's legion of supporters included many names of the good and the great of Europe, royalty like Queen Isabella of Spain, faux-royalty like France's Napoleon III and Eugénie, and innumerable personages of title and fortune. Wikoff's chest was paved with European decorations, and for himself he used the ill-defined honorific of "chevalier," a title that sounded impressive to American ears. After establishing a friendship with Mary, he promptly took to referring to himself as the first lady's "social adviser." Journalist Henry Villard said that the president's wife "accepted Wikoff as a majordomo in general and in special, as guide in matters of social etiquette, domestic arrangements, and personal requirements, including her toilette, and as always welcome company for visitors in her salon and on her drives."[11] Wikoff became even more visible by accompanying Mary on her White House buying trips to the Northeast, where his advice on any given article signified thumbs up or down to many a merchant. The "chevalier" was, unknown to all but a few, in the hire of the *New York Herald*, the paper then running an ongoing column called "Movements of Mrs. Lincoln." Wikoff's dishonorably obtained information on the first lady's lavish shopping led to a number of *Herald* headlines. Those stories lent untold damage to Mary's name and, by extension, to the repute of her husband's presidency. When Wikoff's *Herald* connection was disclosed, Lincoln ordered that he never again be allowed to set foot in the White House, but it was too late to repair the public relations damage.

Another scandal muddying the waters involved two more characters in circumstances that can be viewed as reflecting Mary's growing disengagement from common sense. As we've seen, the redecoration of the building's interior brought about a clean and livable White House the likes of which hadn't been seen in many years. A fresh coat of white paint was even applied to the exterior. Potomac River water was newly piped into the house, as was gas to fuel the gasoliers replacing the building's candles, and workers installed a furnace so that fireplaces would no longer serve as the sole source of heat. With everything finished and in place, the Executive Mansion did present an astonishing transformation, going from the decrepit mess the Lincolns had confronted on inauguration day to a magnificent home and office appropriate for the nation's chief executive. And it couldn't have been lost on the president that the building had become a powerful symbol that the administration remained confident. One thing was troubling though, and that was the cost of this symbolic splendor to a nation now mired in a ruinously expensive war, a conflict that looked as if it would go on for a long time.

The first lady's desperate attempt to hide her spending was the scandal's principal cause. Today we wonder why Mary hadn't been running a flying total of her purchases, and why she evidently ignored the probability that her recklessness would generate serious trouble. The storm broke in the latter part of 1861 when the bills from the merchants of New York, Philadelphia, and Boston started arriving at the White House. The totals far exceeded Congress's $20,000 appropriation, the overage amounting to $6,700, a sum whose magnitude she realized could damage the president's reputation for probity. Trying to disguise this information, the first lady turned to her head groundskeeper, John Watt, who, evidently flattered that the president's wife would take him into her confidence, offered advice on how the accounts might be rearranged, "cooked" in modern terms, thus keeping the overdraft from her husband. One of Watt's suggestions was for the first lady to discharge the White House steward and have *Mrs.* Watt formally assume the position, though Mary Lincoln would be doing the actual work of the steward *and* retain the salary for herself.[12]

Facing a confrontation with her husband, Mary then begged the commissioner of public buildings, Benjamin French, to intercede for her, pleading for him to tell the president that "it is common to overrun appropriations—tell him how *much* it *costs* to refurnish." Lincoln's unsympathetic reaction is famous for its sharp repudiation of Mary's behavior. "I'll pay it out of my pocket first," Lincoln exploded. "It would stink in the nostrils of the American people to have it said the President of the United States had approved a bill over-running an appropriation of $20,000 for flub-dubs for this damned old house, when the soldiers cannot have blankets."[13]

In reflecting on the brouhaha, historians have questioned why the president was so needlessly unaware that serious trouble might be brewing, he surely having taken in the dramatic makeover going on in the White House. In Lincoln's defense, observers note the president's almost total indifference to his surroundings, even to the extent of the food that was put in front of him or to the condition of his clothing. He was, furthermore, enormously, almost superhumanly, involved in running a war. And since Mary had overseen the family's household finances in Springfield, Lincoln likely assumed that pattern would be the case in the White House. Yet the latter didn't stop him from taking good care of his own $25,000 annual salary as president, the vast majority of which he saved in an account at Riggs & Company Bank in Washington; in fact, over his presidency Lincoln's estate grew from the $15,000 he had when he was inaugurated to more than $85,000 at his death. (As to interest on his salary, his savings would have grown even faster had he promptly cashed his government checks, then defined as "warrants": He forfeited some $2,000 in interest by keeping the warrants in his desk, at one time having eleven of them tucked away, undeposited, in a cubbyhole.[14])

Lincoln was not stupid about anything, and he was never truly unaware of the real world around him. His secretaries, Nicolay and Hay, knew that the first lady's spending was getting into dangerous waters, and that a flood might just overwhelm the office of the presidency. According to historians Justin and Linda Turner, they also knew about the Watt shenanigans.[15] It is hard to accept that they didn't bring something of these ominous realities to their boss's attention. In a cautious frame of mind, Lincoln might have ordered his wife's redecorating efforts more closely monitored, particularly given his belief that the White House as it was when he'd moved in was acceptable and was, he pointedly added, the most luxurious home his family had ever known (ironically, Mary ignored his own office in her redecorating efforts). The "flub-dubs & blankets" bromide is probably a historical approximation, repeated so often that it is accepted as literally true. If he did say those words or something close to them, they were probably hyperbole uttered in anger: The Union army could certainly afford to provide blankets for the troops, although *getting* them to soldiers was sometimes mismanaged because of the poor transport facilities of the time and the unavoidable difficulties inherent in wartime conditions.

In any case, Commissioner French did resolve the problem without the president having to pay the overdraft from his own pocket. To save the president and the administration embarrassment over the episode, Congress passed two appropriation bills to cover most of the amount (funds were shifted from other government projects) the first lady had spent to turn the chief executive's home into something recognizably like the White House we see today.

Sadly, Mrs. Lincoln's integrity issues didn't end with Congress's benevolent rescue. Watt got himself into even hotter water over a contretemps involving the leaking of Lincoln's first State of the Union address. What was more, he also appeared to attempt to blackmail the president, the $20,000 he supposedly demanded meant to keep three of Mary Lincoln's indelicate letters he possessed from being publicly released. In the end, the threat of prosecution kept this matter from flowering into a nationwide scandal.

Probably the most potentially harmful threat to Lincoln and his administration concerning Mary was the matter of his wife's fundamental loyalty to the Union. The underlying cause of such questions was founded on Mary's Southern, slave-state roots and that her brothers and brothers-in-law were serving in positions of high rank on the Confederate side, something that Mary could not alter and which was, as we've seen, shared by many families on both sides of the war. But in an effort to raise doubts about her allegiance, opponents to Lincoln's policies—including even Republicans—spread distortions and lies through Northern newspapers' editorial columns. Anything that belittled or questioned the first lady's loyalty furthered their malicious denigration of the president's efforts to keep the border states from seceding, such secessions remaining a frightening possibility if Lincoln were to be seen by those states as adopting too radical a policy regarding abolition. One of the falsehoods against Mary portrayed her as sending military intelligence to one or more of her Confederate brothers. The first lady herself shredded any substance in such an allegation with her pointed observation that the Confederates would gladly have hanged her husband had they gotten the opportunity—and that they would probably have done the same with her. It is, in the end, unimaginable that the wife of Abraham Lincoln would have sympathized with a government or a cause so opposed to her husband's policies and such a threat to his very existence.

It has been said that the belief in Mary Lincoln's disloyalty to the Union was so pervasive that Congress investigated the charge. There is no hard evidence that such a probe ever took place. But legend has it that when Congress's Committee on the Conduct of the War undertook to look into the first lady's activities for evidence of disloyalty or aid lent the Confederate cause, Lincoln himself appeared unannounced before the members and said that to his certain knowledge the aspersions bore not the slightest truth, and that no one in his family had ever held "treasonable communication with the enemy." The legislators supposedly dropped any further consideration of the matter.[16] But the committee certainly existed, and the mischief it may have caused is only today coming under serious investigation.

The Joint Committee on the Conduct of the War was established (first by the House and soon thereafter turned into a joint House-Senate effort) to root out corruption and the scandalous profiteering that went hand in hand with the unprecedented wartime militarization of the North and its economy. Allegations of shoddy equipment that fell apart in the rain and of ordnance more dangerous to the men firing it than to those it was fired upon—both under Secretary of War Cameron's aegis—demanded that Congress attempt to find the truth of such charges. Congress granted its committee subpoena power, which was liberally used. Probably the body's greatest weakness was its partisanship, which predictably favored the Republicans in a Republican-dominated Congress. And dominating the committee were the archabolitionists who spent much of their time castigating the president for his cautious policies on abolition. Throughout the war, the committee tried to micromanage the conflict, but in doing so it erected obstacles and created difficulties for Lincoln that were often counterproductive.

By the fall of 1861, events had disabused both the president and the first lady of all illusion of unbounded glory in their high positions. The president knew by this time that the war was going to be horrible and long, and that nothing less than an ocean of blood was going to be spilled in bringing it to an end and the two halves of the nation back together. No great faction of the Northern population unreservedly supported him. The abolitionist Republicans wanted him to at least symbolically free the slaves, which he knew would set the stage for disastrous consequences. The Democrats still in the Union were split between the Copperheads (those who sympathized with the South and supported Southern views on slavery and who for obvious reasons hated Lincoln) and the War Faction, whose support for the White House often seemed shallow. Much of the press editorialized against his administration's initiatives and policies, this at a time when daily newspapers represented the overwhelming bulk of what we today call the media. Even the president's cabinet made its disdain for its chief abidingly clear: Virtually every member of that body *knew* he could do a better job as president than Lincoln, and cabinet rivalries were so bitter that it often made Lincoln's "war council" unable to work in a concerted and purposeful manner.

Mary in late 1861 remained to some extent oblivious to the growing animosity directed against her (although it was usually her husband who was the true target). That fall she was even enjoying a small window of happiness. She would survive the overspending crisis when French managed to get the pressure lifted from her shoulders. And she *had* made the White House look marvelous, an accomplishment she genuinely believed reflected well on her husband's presidency. Just as the continuing construction on the Capitol dome gave notice that the Union and its Congress would endure, so, too, the newly brightened White House signaled that the nation's chief executive and his administration would overcome their adversities.

Most important, Mary's family was healthy in an unhealthy age: After recovering from the first illnesses her husband and two youngest sons had contracted in the White House, all were now thriving. And Robert was safe from military duty in his studies at Harvard. To the first lady, the drawbacks of life in her great house had become clear. But still, she hoped the trials could be survived, and that her husband could achieve the blessings of a reunited nation. It seemed possible that all would yet turn out well.

THE CONFEDERATE LEADER

On the first day of August 1861, a gathering of great moment was taking place in western Virginia. General Robert E. Lee arrived that day to inspect the Confederate forces in the western part of the rebellion's strongest state. The most important adviser to President Jefferson Davis, Lee would shortly take command of Virginia's armies and begin putting together long-term plans to fight and destroy whatever military might the federals could throw at the South.

A mere hundred miles south of Lincoln and the White House, Davis himself was at the same time busy setting up a simulacrum capital in Richmond to match in every possible respect the one in Washington that had served the now disunited nation for the last sixty years. Lincoln and Davis shared few similarities in either character or political philosophy. But a much noted coincidence did bind the two American presidents: Both had been born in Kentucky, within a year and a hundred miles of each other. Beyond that, their lives diverged dramatically, one making his career in Illinois, the other settling in Mississippi, though both would eventually find themselves entering politics. With the onset of the war between their two ways of life, they again ended up a hundred miles apart, each leading his section of the country and each the other's enemy. And, in time, the two men would each experience a father's nightmare, two tragedies that would be heartbreaking and entirely personal.

In most important respects, the Mississippian's personality stood at the opposite end of the spectrum from that of the Illinois lawyer. Formal and doctrinaire in his deportment and thinking, Davis was nonetheless a superior administrator—though one far less able than Lincoln to make the compromises mandatory to successfully running a national government and a war. The Mississippian's perfectionism got him stuck in failed policies, and his inability to suffer any degree of fool often made it nearly impossible for Davis to work with a legislature full of men whose first, and sometimes only, loyalty was to their state. Davis's greatest challenge—and eventual failure—was to turn a group of fractious states into a real nation, one that would function as an undivided whole and that stood for a validation beyond a simple states' rights rationale that upheld little more than the increasingly morally untenable endorsement of slavery. Where the North could effectively, though often imperfectly, act as a nation, the Confederacy could never amount to anything but independent parts united only in their defense of an image of a common "culture" and independence whose purpose was to ensure the region would retain its slave system. And in the end, Davis's personality and temperament were such that he possessed neither the drive nor the charisma to unite its disparate elements.

Throughout much of his adult life, Davis had been handicapped by poor health; his wife once described him as a "man of throbbing nerves."[17] The shock from the early loss of his first spouse, the daughter of future president Zachary Taylor, soon turned what had theretofore been a reasonably normal young man into a depressed middle-aged widower. But in late life he found a new mate, Varina Howell, a wealthy and educated woman of exceptional intelligence and beauty, and as such a rare spouse for any antebellum Southern gentleman. What was likely viral herpes (which had been contracted before his second marriage) further permanently and significantly damaged the robust health of his younger years.[18] This illness led to periodic inflammations of the eyelids and corneas, covering the latter with a film and causing intermittent blindness as well as the weakening of his muscular system, the entirety of which flared anew under any stress or fever. The disease brought with it horrendous headaches, a debility that weighed disastrously on Davis's performance as the Confederacy's commander in chief.

In the run-up to Fort Sumter, Davis had not been one of the South's "fire-eaters," the secession-obsessed men who gained the upper hand over Southern politics and who forced the armed confrontation that ignited a civil war. He had become a politician and gentleman farmer after his early military career had ended. As a planter, he owned slaves and he earnestly believed that African-Americans were better off under a forthright slave system than they would be as landless, disfranchised, segregated serfs, as were found in Russia and which example he saw as the inevitable black condition in a slave-free America, particularly in the South. Indeed, he provided his own slaves with good living conditions, he never physically punished them, and he allowed them to be educated to a moderate degree, the latter actually an illegal act in some slave states. The lives of Davis's slaves obviously colored his overall view of the institution itself, and he ignored the reality that many blacks held as chattels in the South did not live under such relatively humane conditions. As for any desire on the part of African-Americans to become full-fledged citizens of the United States, let alone to achieve social parity with white Americans, the thought probably never entered his mind any more than it did the consciousness of the vast majority of Americans, North and South.

Until war came, Davis energetically worked for the continued unity of his country, at least in restraining his colleagues' overcharged emotions on the issues of slavery and states' rights that upheld the Southern system. He served as a senator from Mississippi and was a capable secretary of war in President Pierce's cabinet. His last position in prewar Washington was again as a senator, acting as such throughout the entirety of the Buchanan administration. For his resistance to the onrushing breakup of the Union, Davis achieved a reputation as a statesman, arguing, frequently powerfully, for preserving the Union—though demanding the South be allowed to retain slavery. The election of Abraham Lincoln convinced him that no realistic solution to this titanic sectional impasse existed other than disunion, but to the very end he continued to raise his voice in the Senate against actual war between the states.

BLESSED SPEED

When the cooler days of autumn settled on Washington, living in the White House became pleasanter for the first family. Despite her husband's wrath over her spending, Mary's restoration of the presidential residence did bring her a measure of praise from many quarters, and she loved the building when it was full of people who could share her pride—and be awed at her achievement. Dinners in the spruced-up Family Dining Room on the State Floor stood particularly high in Mary's esteem. In the last week of November, the president himself was overjoyed with having the greatest friend of his life join the family for dinner on Thanksgiving (then still an unofficial holiday). That afternoon a large party of guests close to the presidential family surrounded the dining room table, but Joshua Speed's presence especially gratified the host.

Abraham Lincoln and Joshua Speed chanced into each other's lives on April 15, 1837, a day both men remembered forever. Early that morning, Lincoln had left his home in New Salem, Illinois, and ridden horseback to Springfield, where he was to join attorney John T. Stuart in a law practice as a junior—a *very* junior—partner. The older man had been lending law books to the aspiring lawyer from New Salem and apparently judged him a likely successful aspirant for the bar. At this same time, Lincoln was also an elected representative to the Illinois legislature, that body then seated in Vandalia; the three towns—Springfield, New Salem, and Vandalia—all were located within a day's ride of each other.

When Lincoln arrived in Springfield that afternoon, he first stopped at a carpenter's shop, where he ordered a single bedstead, one specially lengthened to accommodate his six-foot-four-inch frame. Leaving the woodworker, he made a second stop, this time at the little general store of A. Y. Ellis and Company, named for one of its co-owners. Standing behind the counter was Ellis's partner, twenty-four-year-old Joshua Speed. The young clerk was slender and black-haired, his blue eyes set in a graceful face, and the inelegant-looking Lincoln surely noted, as did most everyone in Springfield, that the man facing him from across the counter had the self-possession of a born gentleman. Their first recognition of each other took only a moment, an instant Carl Sandburg described: "As Speed looked into Lincoln's face, [he] caught in the eyes a sad look that melted him."[19] Lincoln said what he needed to buy: a mattress, a blanket, some sheets, a pillow. Speed said those items would come to $17. Lincoln said he couldn't afford $17, fair though the price was, and couldn't even be sure how long it would take him to accumulate that much money.

Speed spontaneously made the exhausted Lincoln an offer. As he told the story years after Lincoln's death, he had felt sorry for the forlorn-looking traveler. He thus offered his own modest quarters, with its one bed (a "double," he explained), saying to Lincoln that he was free to share as long as he needed to. Speed then pointed to the stairs leading to the crude store's upper room. Lincoln turned and looked at the staircase, bent down, and picked up his saddlebags—his only luggage, which held the entirety of his possessions—and almost ran up the short flight. A moment later he was back, without the bags, and happily announced to his new roommate, "I'm moved!"—this in spite of the fact that Lincoln's friend William Butler, clerk of the county court, had offered him a bed in his own home (though the lawyer-to-be did accept Butler's wife's offer to wash his laundry). But it was Speed to whom Lincoln inclined, and on that day four years of physical closeness between the two men began, as did a lifetime of friendship that would help guide them both through some of the most difficult personal straits either ever encountered. Speed wrote years later that "no two men were ever more intimate."[20]

Joshua Speed's presence in then forlorn Springfield was unusual for a man of his class and family's status. He was born outside Louisville, Kentucky, four years after Lincoln's birth in the same state. But sharing a Kentucky birth is about all the two had in common. Where Lincoln was the product of humble and uneducated parents who rarely lived more than a few dollars above destitution, Speed was the son of America's frontier gentry, his parents anything but humble about their proud provenance. His father, Judge John Speed, owned some seventy slaves, who tended his beautiful estate called Farmington, its manor house a wonderfully luxurious home distantly removed from Thomas and Nancy Lincoln's ramshackle cabins. Joshua gave up the luxuries of Kentucky to follow the same path taken by countless other adventurers in early-nineteenth-century America, chasing the arc of the setting sun to help build up the vast and little-populated plains that ran up against North America's then all-but-unbridgeable dividing range. The wonder, though, is where he broke his journey. Rather than homing in on St. Louis, or on New Orleans, Speed stopped at the settlement of Springfield, whose fifteen hundred people in the spring of 1835 couldn't have foreseen its future as a real prairie city, much less as its state's capital. There Speed bought a half-interest in the general store, whence two years later Abraham Lincoln stepped through the front door.

No certain knowledge exists today of the entire emotional range of the new friends' relationship. But with the question of Lincoln and homosexuality increasingly raised today, this famous relationship has generated public interest. For the four years after their meeting, Lincoln shared Speed's double bed in their upper room. They were not always alone: William Herndon, Lincoln's last law partner, writes of having occasionally bunked with them, describing the arrangement as having been a matter of convenience. Lincoln even when president spoke publicly about this part of his life, obviously proud of the deep friendship that had sprung from it. Assessing a possible sexual element is complicated in that "homosexuality"—meaning the word itself—didn't yet exist in 1837 and wouldn't for many more years. And today's understanding of a "gay" relationship remained so far in the future as to be without any substantive meaning at all in Lincoln's time. Indeed, relevant to the sixteenth president and his experiences in frontier Springfield, Abraham Lincoln would not likely have seen homosexual men (assuming he had knowledge of the idea the word describes) as persons of a sexual orientation, but simply as men who loved each other and whose love extended to the physical. That he himself would have viewed such men or such acts as immoral isn't likely, given his lack of dogmatic religious beliefs and his own deep friendship, physically expressed or not, with Joshua Speed.

It cannot, of course, be thought that same-sex erotic relationships during Lincoln's young manhood didn't exist merely because it was an age when language and latter-day concepts encompassing them had not yet been formulated. The specifics of Lincoln and Speed's mutual love—which emotion the men expressed for each other in their correspondence and which was unquestionably genuine—leads an open-minded observer of America's sixteenth president to believe erotic and physical ties between him and Speed were possible, and perhaps even probable. Neither man would have thought of these bonds—had they existed—as leading to a life together, complete with home and hearth. But given the all-but-unarguable certainty that same-sex sexual attraction has existed since the beginning of humankind, the form of the love Lincoln and Speed shared, and the physical setting which they freely chose over a long period and where they clearly wished to be together, points toward the possibility of physical desire for each other.

The stance taken by historians that any same-sex relations on Lincoln's part were unlikely, or even "impossible," is based on certain assumptions. The first is that men living on the nineteenth-century Western frontier routinely shared quarters with each other only because quarters were scarce. Second, in an effort to abjure the possibility of same-sex involvement between Abraham Lincoln and *anyone* else, historians posit that the loving endearments in the letters Lincoln sent to Speed were merely the ordinary flowery nineteenth-century writing that routinely passed between many men. Third, some writers assume that because Lincoln became *president*, an office they say he could never have achieved had his sexuality been anything but "normal," the case against any same-sex history on his part becomes foreclosed. Fourth, stories from Lincoln's friends testify to his attempt to buy the services of a female prostitute. And, finally, the fact cannot be ignored that both men married, which supposedly implies that their marriages alone mean that neither Lincoln nor Speed could have experienced same-sex longings, much less acted on them.

But these assumptions don't add up to the certainty of a heterosexual Lincoln, at least not an exclusively heterosexual Lincoln. Most men on the nineteenth-century frontier did not sleep together, in the same bed, and for four years. Accommodations in that environment were indeed scarce, especially any that served as an inn or some kind of public or quasi-public keep. Lincoln resorted to the latter on countless occasions while on his circuit journeys practicing frontier law; many references are made in the Lincoln canon about his sharing of beds with sundry lawyers and judges on overnight stays in places small and crude and in which any traveler counted himself fortunate to find something other than bare ground on which to pass a night. And while it is true that in the nineteenth century when men slept together it did not generally raise the issue of mutual erotic attraction, that is at least in part because the twentieth century's far broader societal understanding of homosexuality did not yet exist.

Lincoln could certainly have afforded alternative sleeping arrangements long before four years had passed, just as Speed could have indicated a desire for his bedmate to make other arrangements. Sleeping together was clearly a mutual choice rather than a necessity. By the time the lodging relationship broke up, both men were on the verge of marriage, leading one to believe that no other cause came between them to end the arrangement. And marriage was the only realistic life for either man: For Speed, it meant a life partner in whatever field he chose; for Lincoln, bachelorhood in a budding political career would have been a bizarre choice and impaired any nineteenth-century man's social aspirations. Neither Speed nor Lincoln would have framed any relationship between themselves—whatever its sexual nature or lack thereof—in terms of a life preference. Such a thing would simply have been almost beyond imagining in their time and place.

Though Lincoln's letters to Speed exist, the opposite correspondence does not. Robert Lincoln may have destroyed the letters from Speed after his father's death, or Lincoln may have destroyed them himself. Those from Lincoln to Speed don't add much to the argument one way or another, except that no other letters from Lincoln to anyone else reflect nearly the same degree of dreamy warmth. The communications from Lincoln to his friend can be said to present a profound depth of caring for Speed, but their supposed "nineteenth-century floweriness"—especially the effusive greetings—isn't particularly relevant to anything. As for the supposed impossibility of being both president and homosexual, the notion is on its face absurd.

With Lincoln's well-documented fear of marriage and his hesitation around women during his courting days, it isn't surprising that he would wish to engage the services of a prostitute, a woman with whom he could discover something of the physical necessities of marriage before actually getting married. The most famous incident in this regard had him supposedly begging off from a waiting prostitute because he discovered he wasn't carrying enough money to pay the woman's fee—and then continuing to turn her down even though she said she would allow him to complete his business with her and pay up when he could.

To repeat, sexual orientation was an unknown (or, at least, undefined) state in Lincoln's day. No one would have described physical love between men (or women) in such terms. If two men had been discovered in some degree of public sexual activity, one assumes such a scenario would almost certainly represent a career-destroyer. But short of such a commotion, it's hard to see how a private, unknown relationship between any two men could have become a public issue. Lincoln could talk about "sleeping with Speed for four years" without such a comment entering the public consciousness as an admission of sexual abnormality (as sex between males would then have been regarded).

In their courting years, the subject of marriage—each other's—consumed Lincoln and Speed's friendship just as it did their wider lives. In early 1841, the friendship was seriously strained when Speed sold his half-interest in the Springfield store and returned to his native Kentucky. By this time, Lincoln was trying to decide about his on-again, off-again relationship and possible marriage to Mary Todd. Speed's departure dismayed Lincoln, who critically needed his friend's presence for support during his period of marital uncertainty. And soon after returning to Louisville, Speed, too, found a young woman he regarded as a likely wife.

In what may well have been the most joyful interlude in Lincoln's life—"joyful" meaning unalloyed with the fear of performance or meeting a fiancée's expectations—in the late summer of 1841 he went for an almost monthlong visit to Speed's home near Louisville. For a Lincoln painfully feeling the want of his friend since Speed's departure from Springfield earlier that year the sojourn proved blissful. For one thing, he had never before experienced such personal luxury, sumptuousness entirely foreign to his own experience of the world. Farmington, the Speed mansion in one of the prettiest corners of the Ohio River valley, was ornamented with large and airy salons, high ceilings, and tall windows, and the house's grounds were peppered with outbuildings and gardens and walnut-tree-lined drives—and, of course, the little houses in which the dozens of black slaves owned by the Speeds passed their own exceedingly humble lives. In this paradoxical setting of luxury propped up by the labor of unfree humans, Lincoln was treated by the family as an honored guest. He was quartered in the large front bedroom just off the main hall and overwhelmed with all the courtesy and respect the Old South and its upper-class families were free to so bounteously supply— which bounty included a slave solely to see to a guest's personal needs.

Speed's relationship with Fanny Henning, a conventionally demure, bright-eyed fellow Kentuckian, seemed to concern Lincoln as deeply as did the course of his own bumpy courtship with Mary Todd. Though almost all of the correspondence from Speed to Lincoln has been lost, many of the letters in the opposite direction found their way into print. From these letters written by Lincoln—questions and answers, comments, often signed "Yours Forever"—later generations were allowed to see the depths of both men's fears about marriage, as well as recognize each man's commitment to the future well-being of the other.

During that month of shared happiness, Lincoln and Speed spent hours mulling over their love lives. Lincoln fretted about what to do with Mary when he got home. Speed fretted over what he should do about Fanny, the latter evidently expecting a speedy resolution on his intentions. On the men's long walks through the countryside, they possessed the entire range of this beautiful plantation to themselves. Sometimes Lincoln played with Eliza Davis, one of Joshua's nieces who was visiting at the time. Often he passed pleasant hours with the gentle and maternal Mrs. Speed, Joshua's mother, who graciously gave him a handsome Oxford Bible by which to commemorate his stay with her family. Though never overly taken with the pleasures of the table, Lincoln loved the bowls of fresh peaches with cream that the family kept in good supply for him. And Lincoln even assisted the growing Joshua-Fanny attachment by talking politics with Fanny's uncle-guardian so the lovers might have time alone. On one such stolen hour the two did finally become engaged, while Lincoln was still Joshua's houseguest.

When Lincoln's visit ended, Speed accompanied him back home, the two men traveling on a steamboat down the Ohio and up the Mississippi to St. Louis and thence overland to Springfield. Unsurprisingly, Speed remained in a lather over his new engagement, continuously pressing Lincoln for some kind of insight to help him decide whether he really loved Fanny. Speed especially worried over Fanny's health, but Lincoln suggested such concern was perfectly normal, saying, "It appears to me that you yourself ought to rejoice, and not sorrow, at this indubitable evidence of your undying affection for her." Lincoln was consumed with the same concerns about his feelings for Mary Todd and whether he could be successful in marriage and happy in a lifetime with the mercurial young belle of Springfield. Throughout their mutual orgy of indecision, Lincoln tried to persuade his friend that Fanny's "heavenly blue eyes" would sure enough capture his heart. He also told the young Kentuckian, "I shall be so anxious about you, that I want you to write every mail."

In February 1842, Joshua Speed and Fanny Henning married. Lincoln repeatedly wrote Speed that year to press him about the realities of marriage; in the letters, he seemed especially concerned about Speed's "success"—probably meaning in the marriage bed—just as he did about his own chances for marital "success." We don't know what words Speed used to assure Lincoln that all would be well—as it evidently *was* well between himself and his own new bride—but he must have assured his friend that marriage was at minimum endurable, and probably even pleasant. On November 2 of that same year, Lincoln and Mary Todd were wed in the parlor of Mary's older sister's home in Springfield. Both men accomplished what they persuaded each other had to be done.

As married men, Speed's and Lincoln's lives further diverged, now separated from each other by wives as well as by geography. The men nonetheless continued to write, mostly about marriage and its consequences. Speed's life progressed unspectacularly, he and his wife making a home on a farm in Pond Settlement, a few miles outside Louisville; their life together was pleasant though childless, and thus no son was produced to be named Abraham. Lincoln's life with Mary passed on a long, upward arc, at times gently and at times in fits, until politics finally launched it like a shooting star. Oddly, none of the four Lincoln sons was named for Joshua, possibly because of Mary's canny understanding that none of those sons could ever rise to the rank that Speed had achieved in her husband's life. Lincoln would perform legal services for Speed over the years, and Speed would always be available to buck up his old friend in times of need. Joshua Speed never importuned the president of the United States, despite being the one man Lincoln would have granted almost any favor at his disposal. When in

1860 the president-elect suggested giving a cabinet post to his friend, Speed declined the offer. Carl Sandburg wrote that the response pleased both men.[21]

But an intellectually unbridgeable gulf stood between the men. On slavery, their minds diverged unalterably. The mid-nineteenth century's overriding moral issue came between countless friendships, and it is not in any way unusual that it also divided Lincoln and Speed. Speed remained a man of a slave state, a product of a cultural phenomenon that was seen by him and millions like him as the economic bulwark of their region and a God-given gift from the white man to the infinitely inferior black man. Lincoln obviously saw it very much otherwise. This chasm between them surely caused Lincoln to forsake Speed as a close moral adviser in the great office to which he entered. But always, to near the day of his death, Lincoln savored Speed's physical presence near him. The memory of those four years in the room above the store gave Joshua Speed a stronger claim on his heart than any other friendship in the fifty-six years of Abraham Lincoln's life.

THE *TRENT* AFFAIR

With the worst of her fears behind her about paying off the overspending on the White House refurbishing, Mary resolved to simply enjoy her home's new splendor. The first lady did, though, continue to spend lavishly on her wardrobe and to travel around the Northeast in search of diversion from the pressures of White House life, and she generally acted as though the war shouldn't stop her from having the best possible time. Admittedly, McClellan's just constructed ring of forts around the capital lessened the concerns of a rebel invasion of Washington, and the war looked to be settling into a simmering standoff: In the autumn and early winter of 1861 there had not been another great set-piece land battle like Bull Run. Nonetheless, the conflict had already begun to fragment Northern society into quarreling factions, with seemingly as many people against Lincoln's war policies as there were in agreement with them.

The president passed the Christmas season buried in his work, sometimes coming dangerously near to being overwhelmed with the details of running a country at war. When Speed left after Thanksgiving, few pleasurable diversions remained for him aside from watching his sons run wild through the White House; with the Taft boys in tow, the youngsters continued to get up to every kind of exploration and imaginary war-making. At the beginning of December, Lincoln sent his formal annual message to the Congress, serving that body notice that "the Union must be preserved, and hence, all indispensable means must be employed," and prophesying that "the struggle of today is not altogether for today—it is for a vast future also."[22] Little question existed that Lincoln intended to see the struggle through to a federal victory.

During a dreary December, Lincoln became embroiled in what was called the *Trent* Affair, a menacing episode in the nation's relationship with Great Britain, the nation that reigned as the world's single superpower throughout most of the nineteenth century. Relatively little remembered today was Lincoln's responsibility for the conduct of the nation's foreign relations and of U.S. diplomacy, whose overwhelming aim during the Civil War was to ensure that other countries withheld diplomatic recognition from the "illegal" (as it was unwaveringly regarded by Lincoln) Confederacy. As Britain was the world's greatest imperial power, and therefore the nation most likely to serve as the model for other countries, its stance on this issue was critical to the North's vital interests. With the British ruling class's attitudes strongly sympathetic to Southern society and to maintaining the cotton supply the South sent to British textile mills, Lincoln well understood that American dealings with Britain had to be conducted with the utmost care—even if many of the North's more radical abolitionist politicians seemed to miss the subtlety in that conflation of interests. To raise the danger to the boiling point and flagrantly doing so in the face of American anger, in May Prime Minister Lord Palmerston's cabinet conceded "belligerent" status to the Confederacy, meaning that the Royal Navy would now grant to Confederate ships on the high seas the rights of any state at war.

The *Trent* Affair resulted from Jefferson Davis's decision to send two official emissaries to Europe: the Virginian James Mason to represent the Confederacy in Britain, and Louisiana's John Slidell to do the same in France. The two men successfully ran the Union navy's blockade of the Southern coastline and thereby made it to Cuba. From there they boarded another ship, the British mail steamer *Trent*, to carry them to Southampton. From that port Mason would go to London and Slidell to Paris. But on November 8 those plans went awry in the Bahama Channel. A U.S. man-of-war, the *San Jacinto*, fired a shot across the bow of the

Trent, the American ship's captain having been notified that the British vessel was carrying the two Southerners. The boarding officers from the *San Jacinto* demanded the surrender of both Confederates as well as that of the two secretaries traveling with them. With U.S. guns aimed squarely at the *Trent,* the furious English captain had no choice but to hand over the four men. The Americans immediately brought their captives to Boston's Fort Warren, where the Southerners were locked up. The legal heart of the situation was that the American ship was justified in inspecting the neutral British ship and, having found human contraband, in ordering its captain to sail into an American port for adjudication—but the intended diplomats themselves could not actually be legally removed at sea from a neutral vessel.

Though the American public was delighted with this high-seas kidnapping, most of knowledgeable Britain was, understandably, furious: The Union Jack was not to be sullied by any state under any circumstances, not even by the hard-pressed United States in its fight to the death with a rebelling slavocracy. Downing Street sent eight thousand troops to Canada (for that country's defense from any American incursion), an act implying imminent war and one that clearly stamped that intended impression on Washington. Though Lincoln had initially been as happy as were most Northerners about the coup at sea, he quickly came to realize the implications in what had happened and reminded his hawkish secretary of state of the prudence of "one war at a time,"[23] on which position Seward prudently concurred. The president nonetheless hedged a bit, looking for the most U.S.-friendly solution, while in London Palmerston furiously demanded that the diplomats be released and threatened war if they weren't.

Famously, this is when Queen Victoria's husband entered the picture. Already sick with the typhus that would kill him within two weeks, Prince Albert—who unofficially reviewed all government decisions presented to his wife for her pro forma approval—understood the stupidity of any war between the United States and the United Kingdom. In brief, the Prince Consort rewrote and softened a hard-edged cabinet memorandum directed to the American government. Albert's revised language offered the assumption that neither nation wished to engage in any conflict that would end their long and mutually beneficial friendship, held out the face-saving view that the American in charge of the *San Jacinto* had acted without direct orders (which was, strictly speaking, true), demanded that the men be released, and, finally, obliged the American government to apologize. To attach the necessary weight by which to encourage American acceptance of these terms, the British added that after seven days without a concurring reply from Washington it would break diplomatic relations with the United States. On Christmas Day, after four hours of his cabinet's discussions, Lincoln accepted the British formulation. The next day the four Southerners were let out of Fort Warren, where they had probably caused the American government more trouble than if they had been in London and Paris. The men proceeded to Europe aboard the British man-of-war HMS *Rinaldo*. The president relieved himself of a pressing and dangerous care, only to give himself leave to return to the countless new worries that continued to demand virtually every waking minute of his day.

A NEW YEAR

Even on the New Year's Day holiday in 1862 the war continued to slash the nation. For the soldiers in fields and encampments from Virginia to Texas, daily reality added up to little more than the hardships of military life and the prospect of sudden death or maiming. Though the weather in that first winter of the war had so far been unusually mild, that fact heartened few of the troops, most being both psychologically and physically unprepared for the unprecedented difficulties that faced all soldiers. The major actions on New Year's Day itself saw men in blue shelling Florida's Fort Barrancas, their opposite numbers in gray doing the same to Florida's Fort Pickens. General Jackson was initiating troop movements in the Shenandoah Valley with the ultimate aim of capturing Baltimore. General McClellan was recovering from typhoid fever while his army remained static, "training," which lack of enterprise was increasingly annoying a president who believed an army was meant for fighting. And in the White House, the first couple were spending the late morning and early afternoon of this national holiday attending to the president's annual reception for all and sundry able to get themselves halfway decently dressed and then make their way to the Executive Mansion.

Mary was, if not thrilled at the prospect of shaking innumerable hands, more than happy to show off her triumph to the people who, theoretically, owned the building. The free-for-all nature of the occasion didn't mean, though, that presidential protocol would go unobserved. The Lincolns stood outside the entrance to the Blue Room when the first visitors to present themselves—the cabinet members and their families—walked past them and shook their hands. Next in order of rank came the beribboned and gold-braided members of the diplomatic corps. The somber chief justice, Roger Taney of *Dred Scott* repute, and his flock of equally somber associate justices followed the diplomats. The capital's resplendently uniformed military and naval grandees concluded the special presentees and led one observer to comment, "If our soldiers could prove as useful as they are ornamental, nothing more could be desired of them."[24] At noon, the doorkeepers finally threw open the tall gates on Pennsylvania Avenue and permitted the general public to enter to pay their assorted respects to the besieged president of the United States, the latter's hand growing increasingly swollen from the enthusiastic pumping of those greeting him, though Mary managed to escape injury by restricting her own greeting to a polite and all-but-imperceptible nod of her flower-coiffed head.

While the Lincolns remained so occupied, the throngs of visitors availed themselves of their constitutional right to have a good look at the wonders the Lady President had wrought over the last few months. While the mob wandered, the Marine Band entertained, the uniformed musicians pumping out the most popular patriotic tunes of the day. The popular Hutchinson Family of abolitionist minstrels sang a few of their numbers as well. The East Room, the Red, Green, and Blue rooms, and the State Dining Room all looked splendid, Mrs. Lincoln having transformed these formerly dingy chambers into beautifully furnished and beflowered salons magnificent enough for the palace of any head of state in the world. The beautiful new carpet, sewn in one piece large enough to cover the building's biggest floor space in a single glorious sweep, was largely covered with a protective cloth, but still drew appreciative murmurs from many visitors. One attendee thought it gave the nation's chief drawing room the look of a "verdant park." Predictably, there were mishaps, among them Senator Orville Browning from Lincoln's home state finding that a thief had pocketed his wallet sometime that afternoon.

Though New Year's Day had brought with it glorious weather—Washingtonians said it was the most beautiful January 1 they had ever seen—everyone knew winter's howling storms would shortly arrive. For the Lincolns, the frigid blasts would bring with them the last of the family's joy. While greeting his visitors, every few minutes the president would be distracted from the faces of the anonymous citizens passing him in a blur, and he would see his young sons from the corner of his eye. Willie and Tad, hand in hand, ran shrieking and scampering among the legs and the crinolined hoops of the capital's citizenry. What the president couldn't see was the sickness that had already entered both boys' bodies.

FOUR

DEATH IN THE WHITE HOUSE

I N THE WAR'S FIRST WEEKS, MILLIONS OF NORTHERN-
ers had believed it would be over by Christmas. But now that the holiday was approaching, the conflict showed absolutely no signs of
resolution, either on the military front or in the political sphere. En-
gulfed by waves of criticism, Lincoln himself became the focus of the
country's disillusionment, with particular bitterness directed at the short
shrift he had given the Constitution in his flouting of its protections of
habeas corpus. The Democratic press—a large part of which was Copperhead and thus antiwar in its sympathies—blistered the president for
his arrogance, though Lincoln defensively rationalized his stand on the
grounds that it was better to immediately imprison the men who incited
soldiers to desert—those manipulators, of course, being the real targets
of the president's action—than simply to punish the young and pliable
soldiers seduced by such sedition.

While General McClellan gained the goodwill of his soldiers, mainly
for not sending them into battle "unprepared" and risking what he believed could be a repeat of the slaughter at Manassas, Lincoln evaluated
his top field commander by a different standard. The president remained a self-admitted neophyte in military tactics and strategy, but he
was proving himself a remarkably fast learner. What Lincoln wanted
was the destruction of the Southern armies and their leaders. What
McClellan appeared to want was the capture of trophies, principally

Richmond, prizes he believed would serve as the most useful psychological factor in defeating the enemy. But Lincoln was coming to see that nothing but the destruction of its armies would affect the Confederacy's will to make war and cement its secession from the United States. As the president tried to persuade the general of the logic of his viewpoint, the arrogant and hypersensitive McClellan simply ignored a commander in chief he privately and even sometimes publicly disparaged.

One night in mid-November 1861, McClellan committed a stunning act of military misconduct. The president, accompanied by his private secretary John Hay and Secretary of State Seward, stopped in for an evening visit at McClellan's home in a comfortable town house only a few blocks from the White House. It wasn't unusual for Lincoln to call on his subordinates unannounced, the usual purpose of such visits being to discuss some serious war matter on which he needed counsel or which he believed required his immediate attention. Even though such talks with McClellan had been fairly common, the general believed they overly taxed his own energy and served no useful purpose.

On this occasion, the general wasn't at home when the high-ranking guests arrived, so a servant directed the trio to the front sitting room to await McClellan's soon-expected return. About an hour later he finally did come home, but entered the house quietly enough to see the president without being seen himself. Knowing that he would likely be kept up for discussions on his plans for attacking the enemy, McClellan silently went up to his bedroom after directing the servant to announce that he had retired for the night. His conduct amounted to telling Lincoln to leave. This mind-boggling insult to the president outraged Hay, though Lincoln feigned to dismiss it with the often repeated quip that he would "hold McClellan's horse if he would win the war." Nonetheless, the president never again called on McClellan at his home, and his disenchantment with the general's military performance rapidly began to swell.

Sadly for the first family, it wasn't only the president whom newspapers and generals insulted. Lincoln could have, if he had chosen, read from press and military sources an ever-escalating barrage of censure aimed at the first lady, much of it savage. Though Mary's public behavior was widely seen as worthy of criticism, the target of most of the vitriol was of course the president, his administration, his policies, and *his* war. Yet given the nature of Mary's emotional balance, the assaults must have contributed in no small part to what would soon turn into a full-blown mental collapse.

Other difficulties, many of then grave, also plagued the White House's occupants. As if the army and its commanders and the press attacks on his wife weren't enough to thoroughly frazzle Lincoln, the president now found himself buried in woes in his *second* family, the official one with which he spent more time than he did with Mary and his sons. The biggest current difficulty concerned his war secretary, clearly a critical appointee given the country's status. In reality, Lincoln had been well aware of Simon Cameron's shortcomings when he chose him, the Pennsylvanian having been immersed up to his teeth in corruption as his state's governor. Yet the then president-elect believed Cameron was savvy enough about bureaucracy to make sure the War Department would work efficiently. But since the early months of the conflict, Congress itself had had its collective eye squarely fixed on the War Department's many and often egregious "irregularities."[1]

Much of the suspicion regarding Cameron—whose rudeness likely added to his disrepute—involved government contracts, in particular the shoddy state of military equipment purchased through those contracts. The new House special committee set up to investigate the matter uncovered a range of troublesome facts indicating that the secretary had abused his public trust. The matériel on which the army operated and for whose purchase Cameron was responsible unfortunately included flimsy uniforms that literally fell off the soldiers' backs, scores of diseased and dying horses, and dangerously flawed guns on which suppliers nonetheless realized enormous profits. Notwithstanding, the committee could find no evidence of the secretary himself being enriched by these matters.[2] Still, responsibility for these issues ended at Cameron's desk. Rather than letting the affair simmer by retaining Cameron, in January 1862 the president got rid of him. To assuage the secretary's pride, Lincoln named him minister to St. Petersburg, then a diplomatic posting regarded as more dazzling than substantial. One senator, clearly pleased that the disreputable Cameron was gone, mockingly advised the tsar that he should begin to lock up his valuables at night.[3]

What lent this controversy its lasting importance to the administration and to the war was the nature of the man who replaced Cameron in the War Department. Edwin Stanton, an Ohio Democrat who had up to now acted as Cameron's chief adviser, was a lawyer to whom the president ironically had ample cause to forgo extending any goodwill. Lincoln had encountered Stanton six years earlier, when the already nationally well-known attorney had meanly humiliated the future president in the famous McCormick Reaper case, in which Lincoln was acting as a junior counsel and both men were representing the same defendant. The self-important Stanton, McCormick's lead attorney, ignored Lincoln's presence at the trial, dismissing the Illinoisan as a "damned long-armed ape." Stanton's famously brutal tongue was probably at least partially founded in personal tragedy many years earlier. Within a short time following his marriage, he lost a cherished daughter to illness, then another sickness killed his wife, and finally a brother died of a self-inflicted throat slashing, horrors that almost felled the driven Ohio lawyer. But even after Lincoln was elected president, which achievement surely astounded Stanton, he didn't hide his ill will toward the new chief executive, referring publicly to Lincoln's "painful imbecility." Stanton's malevolent mouth and tendency to bully never greatly changed, but his opinion of his new boss *would* eventually modify—enormously so.

As in so many instances throughout Lincoln's life, his choice was not made on the basis of his own ego or sensitivities. Instead, he consistently picked men he believed could best serve his cause, that cause now being the United States winning the war. Stanton was a brilliant man—though admittedly a martinet prone to vituperate men he thought inferior to himself, which when he was appointed still included the president. But he was also incorruptible and would staunchly remain above any considerations of personal gain. Lincoln believed Stanton would be everything Cameron was not, an estimation that eventually proved to work to the benefit of the administration and the nation. Lincoln soon discovered another and unexpected advantage in his choice, finding that Stanton bore a pair of capable shoulders on which he could often lean. Sadly, the relationship between Stanton and the first lady did not turn out so well. Mary began her connection with the Stantons disliking the wife (the secretary had remarried after his first wife's death), a woman Lincoln himself admired for what he thought of as her sterling qualities of character. Given Mary's disposition, the first lady's dislike for

Mrs. Stanton soon grew into as great an aversion to the president's brilliant and committed new cabinet officer.

WILLIE

The New Year's reception having been esteemed a success by the capital's elite, the enthusiastic first lady decided the White House should now host a genuinely spectacular event, a splendid and exclusive party to celebrate the restored elegance of the seat of the nation's chief executive, a party that would coincidentally set the seal on what she believed to be her triumph as first lady. Unhappily, Mary's undertaking would turn into a quagmire, leading much of the nation to conclude that she had abandoned all good sense in her resolve to glorify the White House and her husband's administration by ignoring the reality that the nation was bemired in calamity. But closer still to Abraham and Mary Lincoln's personal story, this party would always be associated with the harshest testing the couple would be forced to endure in Washington.

Set for the first week in February, Mary's gala defied the spirit of the times, with much of the war-weary public bitterly criticizing the Lincolns for such frivolity in these hardest of days. Moreover, the magnitude of Mary's contemplated party violated the norms of protocol that had long governed official presidential hospitality. Further, not wanting her ball open to noninvited guests, Mary limited her affair to no more than five hundred people, frankly intending the guest list to be exclusive. Holding the invitees down to five hundred meant that many of Washington's self-important figures could not be invited and were severely unhappy at the snub. John Nicolay noted that "half the city is jubilant in being invited, while the uninvited half are furious at being left out."[4] After some tactical social recalculations, three hundred additional invitations were mailed out, with the final list expanded so as to make sure everyone who absolutely had to be invited *was* invited.

Though Senator Ben Wade of Ohio and his wife were included among the "original" five hundred invitees, the lawmaker—one of the most zealous abolitionists in Congress—responded to his invitation with an astonishingly boorish reply. "Are the President and Mrs. Lincoln aware that there is a civil war?" he wondered. "If they are not, Mr. and Mrs. Wade are, and for that reason decline to participate in feasting and dancing." Wade's unsubtle warning of the affair's political cost appears to have had no dampening effect on Mary Lincoln's party plans, though her husband must have flinched at such censure from so important and powerful a senator.

In weighing the pressures the first lady endured in the White House years, it is fair to wonder if it was a lack of either understanding or intelligence that drove her, or if, instead, it was merely a kind of giving-as-good-as-she-got defiance. If the latter, such bravado served her poorly. Perhaps Mary simply regarded making the White House happy and gay to be her own private responsibility, and she evidently meant to do her utmost to demonstrate to her husband that spending on "flub-dubs" hadn't been such a bad thing. Whatever motivated her, Mary's resolve could be unshakable, and in this case she meant to show that, despite a war overflowing the very threshold of her home, the Union and its president were getting along just fine.

The planning that went into the event was far-reaching, not least regarding the feast Mary wanted. The first lady was convinced that local caterers would not be able to provide a sufficiently luxurious midnight buffet (much less did she depend on the White House's limited kitchen staff), so Mary engaged the famous and costly New York City catering firm of Maillard and Company. The menu and presentation that Maillard came up with would, she hoped, draw admiring gasps from even the most jaded of the invitees.

To ensure that the first lady herself would shine as brightly as her beautiful home, Lizzy Keckly's sewing magic produced a spectacular costume. Lizzy created a wide-skirted and dramatically low-bosomed ball gown, its heavy white satin embellished with cascading flounces of black lace. Mary explained that the black-and-white motif for the dress represented a mark of respect for the British Prince Consort, who had died in December, and thus also of deference to Lord Lyons, Queen Victoria's minister in Washington and one of the invited guests.

Giddy with anticipation about her party, which was set for Wednesday evening, February 5—the event was, incidentally, being financed out of her husband's private funds—Mary wasn't overly concerned when her two youngest sons developed fevers after riding their ponies on the White House grounds. Willie was first to come down sick, and Tad followed a few days later. Mild illness was a routine part of nineteenth-century winters, and the physician who was called assured the parents that the boys had simply caught colds. But Willie's fever rapidly turned into chills, and with the chills came a much higher fever, one that quickly spiked from mild to dangerous. Before long, Nicolay and Hay could hear the brothers' cries coming from their bedroom at the other end of the long hall. Now, Mary's mild distress began to change to icy fear. Both president and first lady constantly looked in on the boys—especially the much sicker Willie, whose brow was constantly checked while at the same time he was assured everything was going to be all right.

With the invitations already having gone out for what was probably the most lavish White House party held to that date, Mary frantically questioned the doctors about whether to call the affair off. But the physicians continued to assure her that Willie and Tad would recover, that their illnesses were simply everyday occurrences, and that she and her husband should feel free to carry on with their schedules and social plans. Historians now are fairly certain that both boys were not suffering from colds but had actually contracted typhoid fever, a disease that even today kills some six hundred thousand people a year worldwide, even though it has nearly been eliminated in the developed world. The Lincolns' doctors perhaps failed to remember the boys' bout with measles some eleven months earlier, a disease that would likely have lowered its victims' future resistance to any new microscopic invaders.

In 1862, White House living arrangements were tragically conducive to the spread of typhoid fever. *Salmonella typhi*, the bacterium that causes the illness, lives only in humans, in whose intestines and bloodstream it is carried. Victims as well as long-term well-carriers shed their typhi bacteria in their stool. Ominously, the stream that flowed directly behind the Executive Mansion's south lawn served, in effect, as Washington's public sewer, and thus was filled with feces. At that time army camps had been set up along its banks, enclosures that lacked any latrine outflow other than ditches that ultimately emptied into the Potomac River, which supplied Washington's water. As a result, simply by drinking the water from any of the White House's faucets, the entire first family allowed typhoid bacteria easy entrance into their bodies, where the bacteria could multiply and finally breach the bloodstream.

Adding to the danger, a marsh used as a dump for both animal carcasses and human waste lay within the Lincoln boys' play range, and in it even more dangerous germs developed.[5]

A body reacts to the entry of such foreign bacteria by developing a fever and other symptoms of typhoid—weakness, headache, loss of appetite, a rash, and stomach pains, the latter likely causing Willie's ever more rending screams so clearly heard by Hay and Nicolay. In the unhealthy conditions of Lincoln's time, one can only wonder why the disease didn't kill everyone living in the Executive Mansion.

Mary allowed Bud Taft to stay in the sickroom throughout most of the long illness, Willie evidently being cheered by Bud's presence. The president stopped in several times a day, often finding Bud stroking Willie's hair or gently laying his arm over his friend's shoulder. On one occasion, Lincoln told Bud that he should go home, that it was getting late. Bud answered the president, "If I go, he will call for me." Julia Taft wrote that Lincoln came back later that same evening, picked up the now sleeping Bud, and carried him to a bed.[6] There was, of course, no real understanding of the danger Willie's disease presented to Bud or, for that matter, to the patient's parents.

In the early days of the Lincoln boys' illness, when there was still no suspicion that the disease was actually typhoid fever, the doctors continued to predict a recovery. Mary was thus led to believe it was safe to carry on with her intricately planned party. Yet some apparently did suspect the danger inherent in the president's sons' illnesses, and talk began to circulate as to the appropriateness of continuing with the party plans. Mary had hoped the affair would represent a day when she could once and for good prove the Lincolns' social acumen. Instead, the planned gala was bringing her only a mounting, and sickening, fear.

At around nine o'clock on the cold winter night of February 5, the Lincolns' guests began to arrive under the White House's massive portico, the carriages discharging Washington's notables, who quickly filled the impressive rooms and corridors of the Executive Mansion. Shining nearly as brightly as the gold-trimmed frock coats of the diplomatic corps were the dress uniforms worn by the generals of the Union army. Brightest among the latter was the splendidly turned-out George McClellan, against whom the president appeared to bear no grudge for the treatment the arrogant general had shown him a few weeks earlier.

At Lincoln's first inauguration, the country was on the verge of war and the ceremony was carried out under unprecedented military security arrangements. The Capitol looming up behind the temporary inaugural stand was still without its dome.

Four years later, security concerns had lessened considerably and, at the president's order, the Capitol's dome was now finished. Ironically, the man who would murder the president a few weeks after this photo was taken watched the swearing-in, buried in the crowd; an extremely agitated John Wilkes Booth stood above and behind Lincoln, to the president's left.

Flanked by the entirety of his executive staff, Lincoln was photographed on
November 8, 1863. John Nicolay and John Hay filled a function carried out today
by hundreds of presidential aides. Nicolay, seated here, and Hay, standing, remained
personally and professionally devoted to Lincoln throughout the first administration,
but both had by the second inaugural decided to leave the White House to take up
posts in the diplomatic service. Hay would remain a lifelong friend
to Lincoln's eldest son, Robert.

Military hospitals sprang up like mushrooms in the capital area, all filled with sick and
mutilated men from countless battlefields. This ward is likely typical of those that were
frequently visited by Mary Lincoln. The first lady brought gifts of fruit and candy from the
packages she and her husband constantly received at the White House as well as flowers she
tended in the Executive Mansion's greenhouse. Mary also read to the men and wrote
letters for them to be sent to their families across the North.

Treasury Secretary Salmon Chase constantly bedeviled Lincoln with his ambition to capture the presidency for himself. But he was a smart department head and capably fulfilled the demands of his critically important office. His daughter, Kate, looked down on the Lincolns as hicks and considered herself rather than the first lady the real queen of the capital's political society. Lincoln eventually disposed of Chase at the Treasury, but promoted him to Chief Justice, a move that redounded to the nation's credit and to Lincoln's legacy.

Ford's Theater, the saddest site on American soil: The tragic consequences of the assassination would immeasurably darken America's racial journey through the next hundred years. The theater is in far better physical condition today than it was in April 1865.

The president spent more time with his cabinet (this picture also includes General Winfield Scott) than he did with anyone other than his two secretaries. Many of his cabinet choices were men who openly considered themselves superior to their president, but Lincoln possessed the character to ignore personality differences and appoint men solely based on their ability to serve his administration.

This February 1862 ball, the grandest of all the Lincolns' White House parties, brought the family little other than grief. The party was widely and bitterly criticized for its unbecoming profligacy in the midst of a raging civil war. While the guests reveled and dined on expensive luxuries in the mansion's newly redecorated first floor rooms, the Lincolns' beloved son Willie was upstairs dying, his harried parents leaving their guests every few minutes to hurry to the sickroom to try to comfort the stricken boy.

Robert Todd Lincoln at the time of his marriage. Robert is widely regarded to have resembled his maternal grandfather far more than he did his father.

Willie Lincoln shortly after his family's arrival in Washington. Because of Willie's rapidly maturing personality and intelligence, his father happily anticipated a successful life for his third, and most loved, son.

Thomas "Tad" Lincoln with his father in February 1865.
After Willie's death three years earlier, Lincoln lavished vast love
and attention on this son, his fourth.

Mary Lincoln's photo overlaid on a
piece of the bloodstained dress she wore
on the night her husband was murdered.
The first lady's unfortunate hairstyle,
though archetypal for the period, had the
effect of hardening her plain, often
dour, features.

The Anderson Cottage on the grounds of the Soldiers' Home is a far cry from the taxpayer-provided luxury current first families enjoy at Camp David. But for the Lincolns, it represented a gigantic leap in comfort compared to the misery of summer life in the White House.

Lincoln's Tomb at Oak Ridge Cemetery in Springfield, Illinois. Eventually buried with him were all the immediate members of his family except the eldest son, Bob, who chose to be interred at Arlington National Cemetery in Virginia.

Evidence of the power of a smile, even a slight one. In fairness to Mary, studio photographs of the era required long exposures, and keeping a smile from turning into a rictus was difficult.

Robert Lincoln, sometime in the 1870s; the increasingly successful (and corpulent) lawyer would spend the rest of his life in the highest ranks of American industrial and political life.

The president and first lady greeting guests at their last White House reception, March 1865. The attendees included generals, cabinet members, and leaders of the Congress.

Lincoln and Tad, the pair looking at an album; the eminent Civil War photographer, Mathew Brady, took this picture (here rendered as a drawing) on February 9, 1864. Tad was the only family member ever to be formally photographed with Lincoln.

Looking far older than his actual fifty-six years, Lincoln was photographed (by Alexander Gardner) for the last time four days before his death.

Mrs. McClellan, on the other hand, made what was considered an unfortunate impression, having appeared in a seemingly "secessionist" dress, one trimmed with a band of scarlet velvet crossing her bodice from shoulder to waist; its off-putting "Confederate flag" effect was thought by many as merely accidental but nonetheless "unpardonable in the wife of the commander of the Union armies." With the White House's limited space, only part of the Congress could be invited, which meant the lordliest members of the Senate and House, many bearing names that were household words.

Vying with the uniforms and evening gowns of the guests was the livery worn by Mrs. Lincoln's domestic staff, servants clad in mulberry-colored outfits whose tint would, Mary reasoned, nicely complement her new solferino-edged china, dishes she put on prominent display at the evening's supper. The daringly low décolletage of the bodice Lizzy had made for her drew double takes as well as malicious comments. One senator later wrote to his wife that Mrs. Lincoln had put her "bosom on public display." Even the president himself slyly remarked just before the ball began that his wife might have been wise to move some of the dress's long train higher up to cover her exposed chest. For his part, the host was dignified-looking in a black swallow-tailed coat, which nicely set off his wife's black-and-white semimourning (for the departed Albert).

The Marine Band played charmingly for the crowd, the uniformed musicians dispensing the most popular tunes of the day. A new melody was even introduced, the "Mary Lincoln Polka," dedicated to the evening's hostess. Scattered throughout the state floor were richly scented flowers grown in Mary's beloved White House conservatory. Candlelight from the chandeliers and sconces shone on every surface, their yellow glow reflecting off the ladies' jewels and the equally bright medals covering the chests of many of the gentlemen. Small knots of the attendees chatted amiably after their long waits in the reception line to shake the president's gloved hand (when the famed war nurse Dorothea Dix passed in front of Lincoln, he asked her if she might assign one of her nurses to help out with Willie's care) and nod toward the first lady (Kate Chase, the treasury secretary's daughter, took a moment to warmly ask Mary about her son's condition). One topic on many of the guests' lips was the president's eldest son. Robert had joined his parents for the party, but unlike so many other young men his age, he conspicuously remained a civilian.

After all the guests had passed in front of the president and the first lady, everyone was at last invited to partake of the anticipated wonder of the evening—Mrs. Lincoln's much discussed supper. Though the hosts meant to have the doors to the State Dining Room opened precisely at midnight, the key had somehow gotten lost. Following a hurried search and the key's eventual recovery, the hungry guests, shepherded as gently as possible by the crimson-clad attendants into manageable groups so the tables wouldn't be mobbed, finally descended on Maillard's victuals.

For five days the caterers had been in Washington readying the dishes and culinary displays Mrs. Lincoln had ordered for the evening. Their labors produced almost a ton of beautifully dressed turkey, duck, venison, pheasant, partridge, and ham, first for the guests to briefly gaze at and then to eagerly consume.[7] Many of the main dishes were decorated in military themes—one dessert represented a frigate, as though the great sweetmeat were in full sail and about to depart on a faux sea of spun sugar from the anchorage of its nougat stand. A model of Fort Sumter was surrounded by roasted-and-refeathered game. The "Japanese" punch had been blended from a mix of fine vintages and came as a surprising exception to the Lincolns' customary teetotal hospitality.

The influential *Washington Star* trumpeted the party as "the most superb affair of its kind ever seen here."[8] But for the Lincolns the splendor was illusory. Throughout the evening many guests noticed the host and hostess's repeated absences from the State Floor. The reason they left the throng so many times over the evening was widely surmised; it had even been announced that dancing was not permitted because of "illness in the house." When the president and the first lady were able to briefly escape the guests' pitying eyes, a burden that was becoming intolerable for Mary in light of the drama upstairs, the couple would go to Willie's bedroom and gently stroke their son's forehead for a few moments, agonized by the reality that they could do nothing more to help the boy as he fought his affliction.

Lizzy tended the dangerously ill patient's sickroom throughout the evening, watching over a boy whose condition just since that afternoon had suddenly and alarmingly worsened. The doctors' earlier assurances aside, Willie's illness was by now life-threatening. Tad's milder attack caused far less anxiety, and it began to seem probable that the younger brother had escaped Willie's more dangerous state, perhaps because Tad's health had not in the last year suffered so greatly as his older brother's. Willie's measles and his scarlet fever of the prior winter are thought to have added to his present danger, the combination depriving him of some of Tad's relatively greater strength. Beyond that, Willie's earlier illnesses had probably damaged his kidneys and heart, increasing his susceptibility to the typhoid bacteria. Historian Jean Baker theorized that the most dangerous threat to Willie during the battle with typhoid bacteria was the internal hemorrhaging or intestinal ulceration that was likely to have affected him.[9]

In retrospect, the evening of the great party marked the beginning of the end for the boy. For the two weeks following, Willie lay in nearly unremitting pain and fever. Life could not, of course, come to a standstill for his father, the president being unavoidably consumed in the affairs of his office. But Mary remained at her son's side night and day, with Lizzy Keckly or Holly Taft occasionally giving the first lady a break for a short nap. Newspapers were now reporting that the president's sons were ill with "bilious fever," a bile disorder, but on February 12 misguidedly stated that the older and sicker boy was out of danger and would live. The Lincolns, though, continued to call in every expert at hand, physicians who they hoped might work a miracle. Dr. Robert Stone, one of the leading members of the capital's medical community, treated Willie with Peruvian bark, calomel, and jalap every thirty minutes when the boy was awake, and blackberry cordials were gently fed to him. Sadly, none of these "remedies" produced the smallest effect on the disease raging inside the boy's body, where bacteria were likely causing deadly fissures to his internal organs. Hope began to dissolve at midmonth. Word of the failure of treatment got out to the press, which on February 17 stated the president's son was "hopelessly ill" and the next day pronounced that recovery was "not expected."

In a chamber newly resplendent with its purple draperies held back by heavy gold cords, Mary's perfect son lay dying before her eyes, the boy seemingly so tiny in the elegant bedroom. The son whom she expected to act as the helpmeet of her old age lapsed into a coma on February 18. It isn't hard to imagine the panic the first lady was barely controlling in those last hours of Willie's life. Try as she might, there was simply no way to stop what was happening. Her husband was president, a man who could order armies to clash with other armies, who could save men condemned to death, who could change laws with his signature— but who could do nothing to save the one small life that gave her own life such joy and hope. By the morning of the last day, February 20, Mary teetered on the edge of collapse. In his last hour, Willie came suddenly awake and clutched at Bud Taft's hand. Mary experienced a moment of elation. But life was not meant to continue. At five o'clock in the afternoon, William Wallace Lincoln died. He had just turned eleven two months earlier.

The president was immediately summoned. When Lincoln entered the room, he went to Willie's bed and, after lifting the cover that had been pulled over the boy's face, murmured, "It is hard—hard—to have him die." Lizzy Keckly wrote of Lincoln's reaction, as he stood at his just dead son's side: "Great sobs choked his utterance. He buried his head in his hands, and his tall frame was convulsed with emotion. I stood at the foot of the bed, my eyes full of tears, looking at the man in silent, awe-stricken wonder. His grief unnerved him, and made him a weak, passive child."[10]

After several minutes of stunned paralysis, Mary began to alternate between convulsive wails and silent prostration. The president seemed unsteady on his feet, his beloved son's death too enormous a reality to grasp. He left the room and walked down the hall to Nicolay's office, where he found his secretary resting. "Well, Nicolay, my boy is gone, he is actually gone." The president then went to find Tad, still sick from his own battle with disease. Father and terrified son clung together, the man trying as well as he could to soothe the boy.

Lizzy remained with her client and by now friend. Later, the president remembered to ask that Bud Taft be brought to the White House to see Willie's face a last time. But when the boy was brought into the death chamber, the experience proved so traumatic for him that he had to be carried out of the room.[11]

Willie's body was taken to the Green Room, one of the main floor's three state parlors. Lizzy helped clean the body, after which it was embalmed. That evening the president entered the room that his wife had so recently and elegantly refurbished. Looking into his son's face, he said, "I know he is much better off in heaven, but we loved him so." The dramatic scene shocked Lizzy, who later wrote of her distress at again seeing the president in such evident grief. Sadly, the seamstress had been unable to soothe Mary, whose self-control was now all but gone. It has been written that Mary would never again enter the Green Room after the funeral because it was where her son's body had been prepared for burial, a story that is perhaps apocryphal but whose sentiment seems well matched to the first lady's personality gestures. After Willie's corpse was placed in its coffin, a sprig of laurel was laid on the boy's chest. The little rosewood and silver coffin remained on a bier in the Green Room while the funeral was set for the East Room, just down the hall. The first lady was too ill to attend. In the short term, Senator and Mrs. Orville Browning, the family's old Illinois friends, remained close at hand in the White House to comfort Mary.

On the day of Willie's funeral, even the weather conspired to reflect the turmoil that the boy's parents were enduring. As the East Room filled with mourners—officials and those in Washington closest to Abraham and Mary Lincoln—a violent storm shook the city, its heavy winds toppling steeples, tearing off roofs, and sending into gutters the many outdoor wreaths and black funeral hangings Washingtonians had hung on their homes to mark the presidential family's tragedy. At noon, the president, the first lady, and Robert came downstairs and there spent half an hour alone with Willie's remains in the Green Room. After the family's departure, the servants and nurses were allowed a few moments to see the boy for the last time. Throughout the two o'clock East Room service, Mary remained in her bedroom, frequently convulsing. She was unable even to care for Tad, who was not allowed to leave his room pending his own full recovery from the disease he shared with his brother. The first lady's one sign of recognition of what was occurring downstairs was her request that the bouquet in Willie's hands be saved for her.

In the mansion's greatest chamber, servants had almost completely covered the walls with black crepe, just as they had done with many of the building's exterior walls. Crowded inside, the large and distinguished throng of mourners gathered to listen to a service led by Dr. Phineas D. Gurley. General McClellan was there, and a journalist present noted that when during a prayer the military commander bowed his head, his eyes were wet with tears. At the end of the service, the children in Willie's Sunday school class went into the Green Room where their friend lay. After the grown-up pallbearers picked up the coffin, the children followed close behind. The coffin was taken to a hearse waiting under the portico at the White House's main door, whence two white horses pulled their light burden out to Pennsylvania Avenue and into the tempest still raging over the city. A carriage bearing the president, his eldest son, and two senators fell in close behind. The procession ended at Georgetown's Oak Hill Cemetery, where the president had arranged for his son to lie, sealed in a vault belonging to a family friend, to await the family's eventual return to Springfield, in which city the family knew that Willie would one day be reunited with them all. In the first days after the entombment, Lincoln twice went to the cemetery, alone, and lifted the coffin's lid to look on his dead son's body.[12]

MOURNING

In the weeks following the tragedy, the paths of husband and wife diverged sharply. Though the president's suffering was unassuageable, Lincoln still had a job to do. Because of his loss, in a way he came to better understand that his own anguish was but a small portion of the national sorrow that was the war. In the face of losing a son whom he loved beyond measure, Lincoln pressed on, burying himself in the numberless details of a war being fought with no end in sight for causes that deeply divided even the remaining loyal half of the Union.

Even though Mary was paralyzed with grief at having lost a beloved son, the barrage of criticism continued with the first lady's detractors yapping and snarling at her heels. Some actually blamed Willie's death on the party, fantasizing that had the Lincolns been minding their sick son rather than hosting the gaudy extravaganza, the boy might somehow have avoided his fate. Whatever her faults, lack of love and care for her children wasn't among them, and hearing this unjustified calumny could only have heightened Mary's agony. But the president was clearly frightened about his wife's health. When several weeks after Willie's death he saw no improvement in her depression, he told her that he would have to have her institutionalized unless she began to regain the mental equilibrium lost over the blow they had both suffered. Yet the feelings of loss and what-might-have-been so badly injured her that she would not fully or even in large measure recover during the remainder of the White House years. For Mary, whatever joy there had been in the Executive Mansion ended with Willie's death.

For many days after her son's funeral, Mary barely left her bed. The violent grief she endured gravely weakened her health, causing her among other afflictions eye damage from the unceasing tears she shed. At Robert Lincoln's urgent request, Mary's sister Elizabeth arrived from Springfield to stay at the White House, and not until March 2 did her sibling coax the first lady into getting out of bed and dressed—in the shroudlike mourning clothes that were in the nineteenth century compulsory for the class of women who could afford such relatively expensive symbols of grief. The mourning became her exclusive costume for most of the next two years: a heavy black dress over a crinoline, a thin line of white fabric showing at the cuffs and neckline, and a black widow's cap. Her first public outing—to church services—in this new clothing concealed her so completely that a fellow worshiper noted, "One could scarcely tell she was there."[13]

Gone into mourning with the first lady was the White House's social life. After Willie's death the mansion became bereft of the kind of entertainment the Lincolns had hosted in their first year. There would be no more grand fetes on the scale of the February party, and the rare parties and even Mary's informal gatherings of friends would from now on be conducted on a reduced level. Eventually, the mourning dresses Lizzy Keckly made for Mary assumed a highly luxurious quality, and mourning jewelry—often crafted of then popular tightly woven hair—decorated the first lady's fingers, wrists, neck, and ears. Probably in an attempt to brighten his wife's life, Lincoln ordered a set of seed-pearl bracelets and a necklace from New York's Tiffany and Company in April, their $530 price an eyebrow-raising sum for the time.[14]

The Taft children's presence came to an abrupt halt almost immediately after Willie's death, and with it vanished the sunshine the two brothers and their sister had lent the mansion. The first lady wrote to Mrs. Taft asking her to keep the youngsters at home, because their presence reminded Mary of what she had lost and was thus unbearable. In a stroke, Tad lost his only real companions aside from Willie, but the hurt to her son was clearly less important to Mary than what she perceived she could or could not tolerate. Yet in consideration of the first lady's actions at that time, Willie's loss wasn't the only Lincoln family death in these weeks. In April, Mary's young half brother Sam Todd was killed fighting for the Confederacy at the battle of Shiloh, but she was barred from uttering any public expression of loss for Sam, because to do so would risk inviting politically damaging public anger, and, worse, opening the administration to the onus of "traitor in the White House." And beyond these losses, there was still her son Tad's misery, the boy in a deplorable condition between the lingering effects of his own illness and his constant crying from losing a beloved brother.

Piled on top of Mary's miseries was the press persecution to which she—and, to only a slightly lesser degree, the president—was subjected in regard to the party, the continuing wake of which turned out to be a public relations nightmare for the Lincolns. Many influential people freely and loudly voiced their disagreement, indeed their disgust, with the "entertainment" given by the first family while such suffering was being borne by those in uniform and by the families those men had left at home.

The criticism was, to a large degree, understandable and perhaps even justifiable. But the vituperation descended into absurdly personal charges against the couple, especially against the first lady, whose well-publicized shopping sprees had already burdened her with a reputation for extravagance. Mary Clemmer Ames wrote that she considered Mrs. Lincoln's purchases "vulgar and sensational in the extreme." Another remarked on the "disgraceful frivolity, hilarity, and gluttony" the party represented. One opposition journal—the *Liberator*—viewed the White House revel as understandable in light of Mrs. Lincoln's sympathies being aligned "with slavery and with those who are waging war."[15] And, probably inevitably, another detractor contrasted the February ball with the state of the sick and wounded soldiers, publishing a poem expressing this repugnance:

> O God! For a cup of cold water
> From the Lady President's Ball.[16]

THE WAR

Though he lamented Mary's suffering, the president was extremely circumscribed in the time he could find to soothe his wife's agony, distress that in the late winter of 1862 turned into a full-scale nervous break-down. The day after Willie's funeral Lincoln was back at his desk, sur-rounded by the stink of stale air and tobacco spit and the grimy and often forlorn petitioners for everything from jobs to mercy. Aside from attending to the inevitable backlog of people seeking his attention, he spent that day discussing prisoner-of-war paroles with his cabinet and approving the issuance of the newly devised paper money, what came to be called greenbacks. To the president's immeasurable relief, on the fol-lowing day the doctors upgraded Tad's condition, removing the boy from the danger category. But beyond any other concern facing Lincoln—including even the well-being of his sick wife—lay the reality that the war was going poorly. To the commander in chief's dismay, the Northern forces weren't getting anywhere near to stopping the notionally weaker South's ability to create havoc.

In the Western theater of operations beyond the Appalachians, the still little known General Ulysses Grant had achieved major victories; his defeat of the Confederates at Tennessee's Fort Donelson shortly be-fore Willie's death represented a decisive and much welcomed (espe-cially by the Northern press) victory for federal arms, a success that put the North on a path to control of the vital Western rivers. Unhappily, the follow-up Union victory at Shiloh proved so costly—over thirteen thou-sand federal troops were killed or were missing or wounded—that any vestigial hope of imminent victory on Lincoln's part vanished like snow in the spring.

In the Eastern theater—particularly in Virginia, the war's so-called cockpit and the core of Confederate strength—the generals presented Lincoln with little progress that might reduce his daily despair. Many difficulties associated with waging this war weighed down the president, but he counted one of the heaviest to be the little general with the Goliath-size sense of self. George McClellan continued to build a force that, on paper at least, appeared insuperable, and his work also contin-ued on Washington's ring of defenses to keep the capital safe from at-tack. Northerners widely believed, probably correctly, that the fall of Washington would represent an almost unbearable political disaster, with one major effect being that Europe would greatly respect a Con-federacy capable of capturing the Union capital, likely so much so that Britain and France would recognize the South's legitimacy and assist it in its fight for independence.

Regardless of McClellan's rationalizing, Lincoln understood that an army, no matter how well trained, wasn't going to win *anything* if it wasn't unleashed against the enemy. Yet when pressed to attack, McClellan instead obstinately called for more troops and more supplies, though Lincoln believed the general already had enough of both. Meanwhile, the commander sat on his battle plans. The secretary of war agreed with the president: "If he [McClellan] had a million men, he would swear the enemy had two millions," Stanton wrote, "and then he would sit down in the mud and yell for three."[17] The timorous McClellan continued to put off a direct attack on the enemy army and went on planning instead for an attack on the Confederate capital from its rear, his rationale being that the fall of Richmond would represent a heavier blow to the rebels than would a field victory over its armies. Lincoln disagreed, yet lacking a better man to replace McClellan, the president reluctantly continued to give him his head. But he ominously wrote the general conveying his impatience: *"You must act,"* the president insisted, knowing the North desperately needed a major victory, and quickly, to reverse seriously sagging public support for the war. When in May McClellan still did not avail himself of an opportunity to possibly destroy a Confederate army in Virginia, the president wired the general, "You must either attack Richmond or give up the job and come to the defense of Washington. Let me hear from you instantly."

The next months the rebels came up with a heavy blow for the Union. Confederate general Joseph E. Johnston had temporarily been put out of service after being badly wounded at the battle of Fair Oaks in Virginia, but this unexpected gift to the federals was more than outweighed by Jefferson Davis's replacement for Johnston, a man who would far outperform even his respected predecessor. The brilliant if flawed fifty-five-year-old General Robert E. Lee took command of Confederate forces on June 1.

Lincoln didn't know it yet, but Lee's appointment—probably Jefferson Davis's most consequential decision as Confederate president—would shortly come to spell real disaster for the federal cause. For the time being though, other matters intervened for Lincoln. The president was being pounded on a front that would demand his attention fully as directly as did the fighting itself. Pressure was on him to bring forward the issue of slavery, the cause that lay at the epicenter of the conflict between North and South. And the loudest demands were coming from the other end of Pennsylvania Avenue.

LINCOLN AND SLAVERY

No issue in the sixteenth president's life is so subject to conflicting views as the relationship between Lincoln and slavery. Without slavery, there would have been no President Lincoln, the iconic, overarching hero forever enshrined in the nation's collective memory. The two extreme poles of how Americans look upon this president regarding slavery are widely separated, from the proposition that Lincoln purposely brought about a civil war to eradicate the system of white human beings owning black human beings, all the way to the notion that his sole concern was that the South be preserved as part of the Union irrespective of the preservation of the institution of slavery. The degrees of nuance between these positions are infinite. But whatever Lincoln's attitudes toward the "peculiar institution," few today seriously assert that the nation would ever have come to secession and civil war had slavery not existed in the American South. The real quandary about Lincoln is instead in the weighing and judging of his beliefs about the postslavery place of blacks in a majority-white society.

Slavery repulsed Lincoln from the time he came into his young manhood. The squalor of slave life and the misery of the trafficking in human beings that he saw along the Ohio and Mississippi rivers, probably most vividly in the South's great port of New Orleans, gave him an early and a lifelong animosity to what was beyond argument the preeminent evil ever committed in the nation's life. Where Lincoln differed from the vast majority of men and women who were equally repelled by slavery was in his extraordinary, nearly unparalleled ability to articulate the magnitude of slavery's injustice and how that injustice proved the hypocrisy of America's noisily expressed claim of national virtue. His prepresidential legal and legislative careers were filled with almost every imaginable issue affecting the mid-nineteenth-century frontier, but always coursing through Lincoln's public life was the question of slavery. As his became a well-known national voice on the issue, Lincoln vividly spoke against the institution spreading beyond the Southern slave states, into the new Western states and states-to-be. He surmised that if slavery could at least be contained in those states where it already existed, it would then eventually die out. But beyond this optimistic public voice, Lincoln deeply abhorred the ownership of one man by another, of those held in chattel bondage being denied the benefits of their own labor, denied the right to the food they produced, denied any hope whatsoever of improving lives constricted by reason of skin color.

However unremarkable Lincoln's moral loathing of slavery seems to Americans unacquainted with nineteenth-century mores, it flew directly in the face of the nearly universal attitude of his time toward the institution specifically and black human beings generally. In truth, the animus held in antebellum America by the overwhelming majority of its white citizens against black persons is almost impossible to overstate. The moral-based opposition to slavery on the part of white abolitionists—a group of people that at the outset of the Civil War represented nowhere near a majority of even the North's population—often rested less on democratic precepts or beliefs in human equality than it did on philosophical opposition to chattel ownership of human beings: Few abolitionists envisioned an America where blacks would partake of genuine equality. The seemingly contradictory belief that the institution of slavery should be ended while retaining the equally strong conviction that blacks were innately and unalterably inferior to whites was a mind-set held even by Lincoln. This did not, of course, make Lincoln's antislavery position ignoble. Instead it put it squarely within the norms of most of his white liberal contemporaries. The sad fact was that racial prejudice was profoundly ingrained and nearly universal in Lincoln's white America, an attitude that had been reinforced over countless generations by almost every cultural structure of Western society, including the family, the academy, and the church.

Though Lincoln could not, of course, re-create himself as a twentieth-century man, his resolution that chattel slavery should end is still more than enough to qualify the sixteenth president for the American pantheon. That achievement outranks even his saving of the union of North and South, a union that would unquestionably have failed at some future time in the absence of the destruction of slavery. Yet two poorly understood issues tend to confound Lincoln's role in both of these achievements. Lincoln *did* view winning the war and preserving the Union as more important than ending slavery—and did so for unimpeachable reasons. And he never believed in racial *equality*, although it can still convincingly be suggested that destroying slavery was the fire that fueled his presidential life.

From the time Lincoln began to publicly talk about the injustice of slavery, he rarely failed to make clear that he viewed the social integration of blacks into a white-controlled America as, if not impossible, certainly unlikely and undesirable. He often suggested the colonization of the country's black population, which amounted to that group's exile or deportation, options he thought desirable, even necessary, in a postslavery nation in which blacks would no longer be controllable by owners. Late in his life he explained his views to a group of African-Americans visiting the White House. "Colonization would be," he said, "a sacrifice . . . of your present comfort," but necessary "for the sake of your race."[18] Long after becoming aware that blacks had no interest in leaving the United States to begin their lives afresh in all-black colonies, Lincoln continued to hold out the possibility—at least in his public voice—of enforced deportation to places like Central America, the Caribbean, and Liberia. Such a scheme's domestic and foreign politics and logistics—let alone its moral implications—made little more sense then than they do now.

Lincoln's justification for black colonization was surely based on kindly motives, though the kindliness was meant as a balm more to white sensibilities than to black. In short, he simply did not see a nation in which whites would ever accept blacks as their equal, and he saw no possibility of enforcing such acceptance in the way that slavery itself *could* be destroyed by force. Equally, he saw blacks forever tormented by living in a nation in which they would remain barred from most of the blessings that nation bestowed on its white citizens. Again to his black visitors in the White House, Lincoln said, "You and we are different races. . . . Whether it is right or wrong I need not discuss, but this physical difference is a great disadvantage to us both, as I think your race suffers greatly, many of them living among us, while ours suffers from your presence."[19] Lincoln held no animosity toward blacks and never wished them anything but the human dignity he believed the ending of slavery would bestow on them. He simply did not believe it was possible for the black and white races to live together harmoniously in America and framed his policies based on that assessment.

Directly tied to the pressure on the president to emancipate slaves by decree was his refusal to undergird the moral framework supporting the war by affirming that such emancipation was, if not the sole reason for the conflict, at least equal to saving the Union. Lincoln knew that declaring black emancipation—or even promising future emancipation— would likely seriously jeopardize the war, and that black emancipation would be injured, likely fatally, if the war was lost.

The Northern abolitionists used strong arguments with which to frame their anger and disgust at Lincoln's policies. First came the matter of how European governments viewed the American war, the most important opinions being those of the leaders of Great Britain and France. Both nations were capable of rendering important assistance to the Confederacy, and strong voices were raised in both to do just that.

It wasn't the close social ties between the British upper classes and the Confederate aristocracy that most promoted British leanings toward the South, but rather economic factors. American cotton—almost entirely *Southern* cotton—helped make the British textile industry successful and Britain rich. With the Union navy blockading Southern ports, that cotton was no longer getting to England's textile mills. Even though the British had presciently stockpiled cotton in anticipation of an American war and a probable naval blockade, influential voices in Britain wanted a Southern win and an end to the threat to this element of Britain's industrial primacy. On the other hand, offsetting the cotton factor was the British people's nearly universal disgust with slavery, of which the United States was one of the last "civilized" practitioners in the world. American abolitionists had a hard time understanding why Lincoln refused to play this latter card, which in their view would have made an instant ally of Britain and its people.

Lincoln had intellectually sound and strategically powerful reasons for holding back from the abolitionists' pressure. The most deeply held tenets in his public life revolved around his respect for the law and legal procedure. Lincoln felt himself bound by the law, law that, among other things, made slavery legal in the Southern states. He abhorred the institution, wished it didn't exist, and spoke against it with the greatest public oratory in American history. But he believed it had to die a legal death, and thus as president he extended to the Southern states the opportunity to end the war without ending slavery. As his biographer David Donald points out, Lincoln's acceptance of slavery in the South did not necessarily reflect his own morality, but rather the requirements of his profession. He thought slavery could die through the exporting of blacks—shipping them to a place where they could create new homes for themselves, separate and away from the whites who hated them. He held out the hope that the institution could be killed through compensating slave owners to free their slaves, a notion that even the border states rejected as unworkable. Most of all, he believed slavery could and would slowly be extinguished by restricting it to the states where it was already legal and forbidding its export to new states and territories entering the Union. Southerners feared the latter notion the most. They had, after all, brought on the war not because they genuinely believed the new president, Lincoln, would actually force emancipation on them, but because they knew he *would* forcibly stop its spread outside the South, a development Southerners thought represented a supreme unfairness *and* an eventual death sentence for the institution standing at the heart of their own social order.

As we've seen, Lincoln knew that great barriers stood in the way of emancipation by executive decree. First was his justifiable fear that such an action would cause the rising of the border states against the Union. Delaware, Maryland, Kentucky, and Missouri, all slave states that had refused to join the rebellion, still made clear that any presidential fiat freeing their slaves was wholly unacceptable to them. Delaware's views didn't matter greatly, but those of the other three states did, and thus they remained crucial at least during the first half of the war. Had Maryland seceded, the national capital would have been surrounded by hostile territory, a militarily intolerable situation requiring substantial resources to bring the state back under secure federal military control. Had Kentucky or Missouri seceded and successfully sustained their secession, the Ohio and Mississippi rivers would almost surely have come under Confederate control (or at the very least become unacceptably hazardous for Union river traffic), a situation that in Lincoln's famous assertion would have just about overwhelmed the Union's ability to win the war.

Beyond the border state concerns, much of the Northern population remained in thrall to the Democratic Party's antiwar wing, men who would have been happy to make peace with the Confederacy and thereby allow the Union to split into two nations, one slave, one free, and each hostile to the other. Emancipation would certainly not have been a welcome development to that part of the Northern Democrats.

What was more, it was self-evident to Lincoln that any presidential emancipation decree would only be effective where the federal military could enforce it, which at midwar encompassed only a small part of the Confederacy. With the federal government failing to show itself able to win the war, least of all to defeat the enemy in the vitally important Eastern theater, emancipating blacks would amount to a largely symbolic gesture, one that was unenforceable as well as aggravating to a huge part of the North and a plainly dangerous move where the border states' actions were concerned.

Yet a shrill and ever-mounting call for a presidential decree of emancipation was growing. Swelling Northern opinion saw the freeing—if still only a symbolic freeing—of Southern blacks as a tool to both injure the Confederate planter class and increase the size of the forces opposing the rebel armies. By the latter logic, freed slaves would surely rise against their Southern plantation owners, something that had not happened so far in the struggle. If Lincoln were to free the slaves by executive order, Northerners hoped that such an action would instill in blacks the courage to make mini-rebellions against individual owners. But the concept was highly dangerous for the slaves concerned: Owners in the Confederacy remained watchful of any incipient rebelliousness on their slaves' part and, when confronted, quickly resorted to draconian means—including murder—so as to warn others against the same course.

As for utilizing blacks as soldiers in the federal armies, Lincoln remained far from persuaded that they could be turned into effective fighters. He also feared they would never be socially acceptable to white soldiers and officers. But mounting numbers of runaway slaves and Southern free blacks were reaching the safety of Union army lines, and not employing them to effective military purpose was becoming even more difficult to justify. Though Lincoln knew that the four million blacks in the South might if freed work to the Union's military favor, such a scenario could also end in a race war between Southern whites and blacks, one with the devastating social consequences of crippling the region for decades.

Meanwhile, Congress took it upon its own authority to free at least one small pocket of blacks. Though the fact is often overlooked, the nation's capital was just as much slave territory as was Alabama or South Carolina or anywhere else in the Confederacy. As though he were in

New Orleans or Atlanta or Richmond, when the president walked through the seat of the nation's government, he could expect to see slaves trailing in the footsteps of their masters. White persons legally owned three thousand of the District's inhabitants, black men, women, and children whose masters included senators and judges and the leaders of the city's society. In the spring of 1862, the Congress decided to change this state of affairs. It passed a bill providing for the mandatory, though compensated (at $300 per slave to their owners), emancipation of these human chattels. Unsurprisingly, the city's Southern-dominated white population vigorously denounced the move, and the city's newspapers ridiculed the $300 compensatory payment as insufficient. Though Lincoln advised Congress to proceed slowly, the legislature passed the District emancipation bill on April 12—with 95 percent of the Republicans voting in favor, 90 percent of the Democrats against.[20]

THE PROCLAMATION

Faced with this troublesome matter, Lincoln knew he had to take some decisive action on executive-ordered emancipation. The vitally important issue stopped, after all, with him. As president and commander in chief of the federal armed forces, he possessed the authority to grant freedom to slaves, doing so, if he chose, under the special war powers designed to protect the Union and thus allowing him to clothe the action in the mantle of a military decision to diminish the ability of the rebelling states to pursue their rebellion. As he succinctly put it, "As commander in chief . . . I suppose I have a right to take any measure which may best subdue the enemy."[21] The Congress did not at the time have the power to legislate emancipation against his wishes; any bill that body passed on the matter would require his signature, which if withheld could not be gainsaid given the body's political balance.

While the controversy stormed around Lincoln and the White House, the president remained silent as to how he would decide the question. More than anything else, what held his hand on emancipation was the lack of a great military victory by which emancipation might be seen as justified and undergirded. He understood that in the face of continual battlefield losses—a second great battle at Bull Run in the summer of 1862 ended in another substantial victory for Lee's Army of Northern

Virginia—any presidential decree freeing the rebels' slaves would be interpreted by many as little more than posturing, a move made hollow by the Union's clear inability to make it mean anything concrete. Lincoln called such a gesture something no better than "the Pope's bull against the comet."[22]

In the end, Lee gave Lincoln the opportunity he needed. The Confederate commander invaded Maryland in September, sending fifty-five thousand troops across the Potomac to cut the rail lines connecting Washington with the West. But the rebels failed. McClellan unleashed his army on Lee at a place called Antietam Creek. In the deadliest day of fighting the nation has ever known, some four thousand soldiers from both sides were killed in the single day of combat; another twenty-five hundred died of their wounds. Though neither army achieved a clear victory, the federals at least stopped the Confederates, pushing Lee back into Virginia. The North claimed "victory" at Antietam, even if it amounted to stopping Lee rather than destroying him or the threat he represented. Lincoln deprecated McClellan for letting Lee's army escape, but decided he could for the purposes of emancipation call the battle a "success." Lincoln shrewdly used this "victory" to give an emancipation proclamation the buttressing of federal military potency he believed it required.

The Emancipation Proclamation was not a document that all-out freed America's slaves. Neither was it one that spoke of such sentiments as the universal brotherhood of all Americans of all colors. The "freedom" it would give to enslaved African-Americans would be limited to those held in captivity in the seceded states only, which is to say the Confederacy. Slaves living in the unseceded border states were not included, which gave the document the ironic effect of freeing slaves the Union was incapable of freeing and leaving in slavery those it *was* capable of freeing.

Lincoln had been working on such a document long before he published it late that summer of 1862. Still, it would not come into effect until the following New Year's Day. To reflect his special wartime authority that he took as justifying the edict, he wrote it not in the majestic language typified by the Declaration of Independence, or even of his own great speeches delineating the injustice of slavery. Rather he framed the proclamation as if it were a lawyer's brief, stating in cold, clear language the straightforward facts of his action. Nonetheless, all parties—abolitionists, Copperhead Democrats, Congress, newspaper editors in both North and South—understood the Emancipation Proclamation for what it was. The edict changed the rationale for the war from that of saving the Union to instead one of eliminating the cause that had put the Union in need of saving.

FIVE

SHADOWS EVERYWHERE

AFTER THE UNBROKEN MISERY OF THE PAST MONTHS, in the summer of 1862 a bit of genuine pleasure finally came into the Lincolns' lives. In mid-June, the family got to move out of the White House and into an idyllic haven away from the grime, squalor, stench, heat, and disease-laden vermin of hot-weather Washington. Their new temporary home lay only a short carriage drive away from the Executive Mansion, but for Abraham and Mary Lincoln it was a paradise discovered—and for the next five months there they would live, grateful for the distance from the scene of their son's death.

The beginnings of what would become the Lincolns' presidential re-treat went back to the early 1840s, when a wealthy Washington banker named George Riggs rebuilt an old and dilapidated stone farmhouse into a country summer cottage. The villa was located three and half miles away from the city center, toward the northeast and the Maryland line, but within the District boundary. Riggs built his house atop a small range of hills, the elevation providing the occupants with cooling breezes as well as an absence from the exhalations rising from the Po-tomac and the filthy waterways flowing through Washington's crowded heart, its remoteness a blessing unshared by the people living in the city's summer heat and humidity.

Riggs called the house a "cottage," as the rich then understated their luxurious seasonal residences. In reality, it was a wealthy man's indulgence, a three-story stucco structure in the English Gothic Revival style and containing twenty-two rooms under its multigabled roof. Embellishing the facade was a vine-hung piazza, on which stood a bank of rocking chairs for the family's pleasure.[1] Gas lighting, running water, and indoor toilets made the house a modern marvel, and its capacious parlor with a view down through fields to the Capitol gave it a richness much appreciated by all who lived in it.

In the early 1850s General Winfield Scott acquired the property from Riggs and set it up, in conjunction with the federal government, in what was then an unusual and decidedly progressive home for the army's elderly poor and disabled veterans. Several more houses were built nearby—though none as grand as the Riggs residence—and the finished ensemble became collectively known as the Soldiers' Home. President Buchanan summered in one of the cottages throughout his entire presidency, obviously eager as anyone else of means to be away from the central city.

Two days after his inauguration, Lincoln and his wife separately drove out to the place to have a look around, possibly on the recommendation of Buchanan himself. They both must have been favorably impressed with what they saw, because the White House shortly thereafter let it be known that the presidential family would likely occupy it during the upcoming summer. Fort Sumter and war changed that hope when it became obvious that a country retreat so far removed from the safety of the White House was an unwise option for the president, especially with neighboring Maryland a virtual roost for dangerous secessionists and rebels. After Bull Run, Lincoln's attention was continually occupied with crises demanding his presence near his military commanders and the War Department's telegraph machine, and Mary was meanwhile busied with her shopping trips. So the couple stayed put in 1861 and likely looked forward to different circumstances in the following year.

Things didn't, of course, improve much in 1862 compared to how they had been in the prior year, with the military situation indeed becoming a good deal worse. But thanks at least to General McClellan's newly built line of fortresses ringing the District, Lincoln decided the Soldiers' Home was now a realistic option to alleviate the summer miseries suffered by everyone in the White House from the president down. Thus on June 13, 1862, the family packed up their clothes and other necessities of daily life and set out for the fresh air and cooling breezes of what was then the deep and rustic countryside.

Given the primitive communications of the time, it wasn't possible for the president to abandon the White House during the day, as modern presidents now do for weeks on end. So after breakfast on every week-day morning at his new summer residence, Lincoln would either ride on horseback or be driven in his coach-and-four into town, there to put in a regular day of work at the Executive Mansion. Through the summer Nicolay and Hay continued to share their combined bedroom–sitting room across the corridor from the executive office suite, and they to-gether with the president, in addition to a few other aides, carried on with their duties as usual. The family's move meant that for the sum-mer Mary was, of course, no longer at the other end of the corridor, which undoubtedly pleased Nicolay and Hay, the pair by this time hav-ing come to openly disdain any interference from the first lady in their boss's official life. No firm schedule directed Lincoln's official day, and its conclusion generally ranged somewhere between dinnertime and bedtime. But at whatever hour his workday ended, the president would get back on his horse or into his carriage and return to the Soldiers' Home.

Until the first family moved into their summer residence, presidential security had remained primarily a hit-or-miss proposition—probably, though, more miss than hit. Even during the first weeks at their "cot-tage," the Lincolns were often entirely without armed protectors. Such was the case not only in driving back and forth from the White House, but at night as well, when their only near neighbors were the elderly veterans who continued to live in the nearby buildings on the grounds. Washington's closely strung line of forts represented a fair measure of security, but rebel agents could easily have gained access to the com-pound and have just as handily murdered an ill-guarded president. It was, admittedly, an age when belligerents did not generally think assas-sination an honorable war measure, but that spirit of the times hardly meant that such an act was inconceivable. As with many American pres-idents, Lincoln adopted the fatalistic belief that if someone wanted badly enough to kill him, then that someone would find a way to do so. But given the danger in the immediate capital area, even Lincoln must have realized that such a rationalization was imprudent when it came to the safety of a very public head of a nation at war.

In September, this state of affairs changed. Pressed by the recognition that Confederate soldiers were ranging through western Maryland, the military governor of the District of Columbia dispatched two companies from a Pennsylvania Volunteers regiment to guard the presidential cottage, and at the same time sent a New York mounted regiment to ride alongside Lincoln on his daily commute.[2] Already known for his disdain for security, Lincoln nonetheless learned to live with what he thought of as an unavoidable encumbrance.

Mary regained her mental ability to function in public during that first family summer in the Soldiers' Home. She adhered, however, to the outward symbols of mourning that the Victorian age mandated, including dressing in the heavy black clothing that covered her body from head to foot, a costume in which middle- and upper-class ladies were expected to conceal themselves for a year after their loss. But the first lady was at least out of her bedroom and back among people, feeling well enough for a trip to New York to collect funds for military hospitals and to get Tad away from the dangerous smallpox and malaria then afflicting Washington. Probably equally important to Mary was the chance to visit Robert, now a sophomore at Harvard. She knew, too, that Tad desperately wanted to see his last remaining brother, Robert representing an admired and much loved figure to the small boy.[3]

Mary's absence left her husband without company in the evenings at the cottage, although the solitude perhaps soothed the president's spirits given his wife's still troubled state of mind. Workday pressures were now crushing Lincoln, already having transformed him into a man appearing far older than his fifty-three years. To relieve his mind of the responsibilities of the war, the president turned inward at the Soldiers' Home and sought out the company of the ordinary and unpolitical men who were guarding him. Particularly curious about the officer in charge of the guards, one Sunday morning Lincoln asked for that soldier to call on him at the cottage.

David V. Derickson turned out to be an unusual man. The forty-four-year-old captain was a Republican and a committed advocate for the Union cause and had once been a community leader in his hometown of Meadville, Pennsylvania. Given that many Civil War military units were made up of men from the same geographical area, it wasn't unusual that

Derickson's son Charles was a company sergeant in the guard unit and thus served under his father's direct command. The outfit was called the Bucktail Brigade, named for the fur pieces its members wore on their caps. And by the chance of having been chosen for their extraordinary duty, these fortunate men became a central part of the life of the president of the United States and, regardless of their undoubted courage, reaped the benefit of removal from the battles in which thousands of their fellow soldiers were being killed.

Years after the war, Derickson reminisced on his war duties in a story written for his local newspaper. What had struck him as most unusual about the president was Lincoln's easygoing demeanor. On Derickson's first day of duty, Lincoln asked the officer to ride along with him to the White House. For almost every day in the summer and fall of 1862 and right up until the presidential family moved back into the White House in November, he guarded his new boss on the journey between town and country. The captain recollected that the president invited him to accompany him inside the Executive Mansion, and being in the epicenter of the nation's military command undoubtedly astonished Derickson.

The duties borne by Derickson and his men were substantial and consequential. One of the Bucktails' principal concerns dealt with any possible rebel attack against the Soldiers' Home. The troops knew it wouldn't have been difficult for the Confederates to mount an assault on the exposed presidential retreat, and soldiers in the compound even wrote of hearing what sounded like nearby enemy cannon fire.[4] Moreover, rumors flew around that a Confederate spy had been captured while posing as an official messenger. After this scare, on Mary Lincoln's insistence, a full cavalry escort of fifty armed riders, detached from the Eleventh New York and known as Scott's Nine Hundred, began to surround the president on his daily commute, which—predictably— displeased a president disdainful of showing fear in public. Though he accepted the Bucktail soldiers as protection around the Soldiers' Home itself, he believed the cavalry unit that surrounded him on trips back and forth from the White House threw up an unnecessary barrier between himself and the public. More peevishly, he even complained that when the first lady joined him in the carriage, they "couldn't hear themselves talk" because of the noise made by the rattling cavalry. The responsible officer, General Henry Halleck, shrewdly dismissed the president's complaints as mere Lincolnian grumbling rather than as a serious objection to the necessity of men shielding him with their own lives.[5]

Mary and Tad left for another trip to New York and Boston in October, one that would keep them away from Washington for a month; part of the journey was dedicated to shopping and part of it to seeing Robert at Harvard, whose continuing student status and thus excuse for a military exemption greatly comforted his mother even as it irritated large sections of the public. Left alone at the cottage with only a few servants and the Bucktails, the president found himself unusually depressed and irritable at the dismal war tidings, not to mention the prospect of the personal showdown with McClellan that he knew couldn't be put off much longer. What was more, Lincoln knew that the November midterm elections were expected to bring disastrous losses to the congressional Republicans. Adding to all this gloom was Tad's absence, the boy's company since Willie's death having kept the president's worst psychological devils at bay.

Lincoln continued to spend every workday in his White House office, listening to the entreaties of the men and women who lined up in never-ending queues in the corridor, most pleading for jobs or mercy or whatever they thought the president could give them that they couldn't get anywhere else. His official company consisted in the main of generals and legislators and cabinet members, his principal business the unrelenting war. Only at night did he occasionally manage to escape these burdens. During the weeks when he was alone at the Soldiers' Home, the men of the guard often provided him with the kind of human companionship that came without obligations.

Lincoln often joined the soldiers around their campfires, happily sharing a plate of beans and a cup of coffee with them; once he even brought an important visitor to these informal encounters, a man Derickson later remembered as possibly having been a senator. The soldiers knew the president would listen to them, and sometimes they voiced their feelings about some injustice or another; one grievance was substandard socks, the troops hoping that if the president knew of the problem he would fix it by passing the complaint along to the War Department.[6]

David Derickson formed a special bond with Lincoln, the president often seeking out this especially articulate soldier. Derickson was a rugged-looking man, dark-haired and bearded, and shorter than Lincoln, as almost everyone was. Having been accompanied by Derickson on a four-day trip to the Antietam battlefield and, as we've seen, guarded by him every morning and evening on the drives in and out of the city, the president honored him with his trust. So intimate did the relationship eventually become that the captain was frequently invited to spend the night in the cottage itself. When Mary Lincoln was present at the Soldiers' Home, she apparently was sufficiently aware of her husband's friendship with Derickson that she would ask the captain to intercede on her behalf when she needed help getting something she wanted from her husband.

In the second week of November the first family moved back to the White House, having spent nearly five months living in their summer villa. It is difficult to gauge the couple's feelings about returning to the scene of their son's death, though it seems easy to believe Mary would have preferred to stay in the country had that been possible. She continued her official mourning at the White House, and the social life of the nation's most prominent residence was relatively dormant. As for the president, however he felt about giving up the privacy and peace of his temporary residence, he would at least have the pleasure of retaining his new, now much devoted, guard. Though Captain Derickson would soon be transferred to another unit, the Bucktails themselves stayed with the president throughout the war.[7]

GHOSTS

The mid-nineteenth century was an age of spiritualism, and countless war deaths brought the phenomenon into homes all across the divided nation. One of those homes was Mary Lincoln's White House.

Mary already knew something of spiritualism, having witnessed the rituals of her family's household slaves during her Lexington childhood. When she was still a young woman, "spirit conveyors" had appeared in Springfield, arousing the curiosity of all three Todd sisters living there. But during the summer and fall of 1862, Mary possessed far greater reason than simple inquisitiveness to turn to the metaphysical and the pseudoscientific: She was sick with longing for Willie, and she couldn't accept that her son's spirit couldn't somehow be made manifest for her. She believed that with help she would be able to reach out, feel, and even communicate with him. Lizzy Keckly, after having lost her own son in battle, had been converted to spiritualism, and the dressmaker told Mary that she had miraculously talked with his disembodied spirit.[8] As a result, the lure of spiritualism was more than the psychologically wounded first lady could resist, and she easily submitted to its promise of respite from pain.

Today the reality of Mary's immersion in the occult sounds sadly tawdry. And in truth the quacks and phonies who lured her into consultations and séances did use every kind of professional magician's trick to persuade Mrs. Lincoln she was truly in the company of her son. Mary likely knew she couldn't actually hear Willie's voice in the "encounters" arranged for her, but she accepted that in the sessions she was at least being watched over by his "presence." And if Willie couldn't speak for himself, then she took for truth the assurances offered her that he was "known" to be "happy."

Probably the most flagrant of these charlatans was the so-called Lord Colchester, a man who presented himself as a member of the British nobility. The self-proclaimed illegitimate son of an English duke[9] worked as a medium in New York City, where spiritualism enjoyed widespread popularity. The presence there of so many spiritualists was likely an important reason the first lady had been eager to visit the metropolis that summer. When Colchester later brought his wizardry to Washington, Mary invited him to conduct one of his séances at the Soldiers' Home.

Mary thoroughly persuaded herself that Willie did indeed make some sort of contact with her, and this belief ensured that Colchester remained lucratively welcome in the first family's home. The president, kindheartedly eager to indulge anything that might help ease his wife's pain of loss, nonetheless felt obliged to draw the line at what he saw as mining Mary's vulnerability and quietly asked the superintendent of the Smithsonian Institution to look into Colchester and his methods. It took little effort to find that at his séances the medium engaged in sham and tricks to call up the "spirits" of the dead. Noah Brooks, a close friend of the Lincolns and concerned about the first lady being hurtfully exploited, looked still further into Colchester's techniques. In the middle of a séance, Brooks caught the con man manipulating mechanical devices to create what he claimed were the vocal manifestations of the departed. Colchester was booted out of the presidential summer home and told that if found in Washington on the following day, "You will be in the Old Capitol prison."[10] The threat carried little real force, and Colchester continued his profitable trade in a Washington still much attracted to the dreams he was thought to be able to make reality—though from then on he at least kept away from the first lady.

Other charlatans continued to try to perpetrate such frauds on Mary, given her unrelenting hopes of being reunited with Willie, but by mid-1863 she seemed to have finally given up on achieving the impossible. Undoubtedly hurt by being belittled, she sadly accepted the proof of the conjurors' tricks when they were exposed. The likelihood remains that when she most needed comforting, her son's illusory visitations might have provided such contentment. If that is the case, Mary Lincoln was neither more nor less gullible than uncountable numbers of her fellow Americans who attempted to once more see their sons, lovers, husbands, and fathers, all dead far before their time on the Civil War's battlefields.

MERCY'S LAST RESORT

While Mary remained deeply depressed from the loss of her son, her husband had to face still another kind of torment in his official duties. As president, Lincoln bore the constitutional authority "to grant reprieves and pardons for offenses against the United States." The power could not be delegated to a subordinate. In Lincoln's hands alone rested one of the most consequential responsibilities any person can assume, that of lessening or even waiving punishments meted out by a federal or military court. At its most profound, the president could save any judicially condemned person from a sentence of death. This power, whether to diminish or to expunge punishment, was unlimited: Lincoln's decisions could not be reversed by anyone under any circumstances. What made this issue so staggering a weight on a wartime president's shoulders was that it encompassed the authority to change the sentences of innumerable military courts—most significantly, of course, *death* sentences. Abraham Lincoln conscientiously and invariably employed this prerogative with his fullest commitment.

Why the sixteenth president expended so much energy and compassion on his reprieve and pardon authority can probably never be fully understood. The best we can surmise is that Lincoln exercised this power so painstakingly and with unparalleled humanity for the same reasons he habitually looked for the good in people and overlooked the not-so-good, or that he instinctively shrank from cruelty, or that he so deeply abominated slavery at a time when it represented a social norm. The greatest irony of Lincoln's life is that a human being of such consummate decency found himself in the position of presiding over, indeed of ordering, a slaughter of his fellow citizens the equal of which the nation hasn't yet seen.

With millions of men engaged in America's first modern, total war, the rigid requirements of military discipline inexorably expanded. Never before in its history had the country experienced a military establishment such as that which arose during the Civil War, and the scope of the theretofore little-experienced crimes peculiar to military life came as a shock to the nation. Insubordination, willful disobedience, desertion, cowardice, striking an officer, sleeping at one's post—all were "crimes" peculiar to military life, and the penalty for each could be death, "shot with musketry" or "hanged by the neck until dead" in the pitiless words of the court. Commanders dispassionately regarded these trespasses as seriously damaging order and discipline, sins that if left unpunished could undermine the efficiency required to pursue and win the war. Thus with the start of the conflict, firing squads and hangmen began their grim labors of dispatching offending soldiers, and even in the capital city itself people began to hear the sharp report of synchronized rifles on the army's execution days.[11]

Beginning with the first weeks of the war, Lincoln made himself extraordinarily available to almost any soldier who wanted to see him. If a man was in uniform—enlisted or officer—he enjoyed the right to go to the White House, join the queue, and see the president. Sometimes it took days to get to the head of the line, but as long as the soldier had permission to be absent from duty, he knew that the odds of his talking to Lincoln were in his favor. Even those who couldn't reach the commander-in-chief in person could write to him, and they could expect to be heard as a result. Many of these soldiers' complaints were unimportant or trivial, such as seeking a leave, correcting an error in pay, or requesting transfer to another unit. But Lincoln held firm to the principle that if he remained the final resort of redress for his soldiers' grievances, then he must be available. And because the president was accessible for the small things, soldiers instinctively understood that he was also available for the big things. And there wasn't anything any bigger to a fighting man than to be facing a firing squad or a hangman's rope.

In the fall of 1862 Lincoln created the new position of judge advocate general of the Union army, whose primary function was to help him decide whether to extend clemency to the soldiers whose pleas were sent up the chain of command for his review. Lincoln ordered that no military execution was to be carried out without his personally having weighed the merits of the sentence against the facts of the crime. In cases of crimes that could draw a death sentence in civilian life—rape, murder, treason, dealing in slaves—the president generally withheld clemency and allowed the executions to be carried out, though he occasionally granted a temporary stay to permit a condemned man a short time to arrange his affairs before being put to death.

But Lincoln found it nearly impossible to accept that some of the capital offenses of military justice—desertion, sleeping on duty, and the like—equaled capital "crime," at least in the sense that he understood the word. He was not in any way ignorant of the reasons that justified harsh military discipline, fully understanding his commanders' desires to make examples out of such cases as the most efficient means to discourage others from following their lead. Many commanders deeply disagreed with lenience, believing that to pardon a deserter only led to more desertions, or that a sleeping picket potentially endangered many men's lives. Some even told the president to his face that his policies were wrong. General Daniel Taylor wrote to Lincoln, "If we attempt to shoot a deserter, you pardon him and our army is without discipline." And General William Sherman wrote his view of the matter to the judge advocate general: "Forty or fifty executions now would in the next twelve months save ten thousand lives."[12]

Lincoln simply didn't agree that the men convicted of these offenses ought to be put to death, irrespective of the effect his clemency might have on other soldiers' behavior. "Let him fight instead of being shot," he would tell the sentencing court when pardoning or dispensing a lesser sentence to such offenders. About a death sentence for a minor offender he wrote, "What possible injury can this lad work upon the cause of this great Union. I say let him go."[13] Another principle clung to by Lincoln in capital cases was to reprieve or pardon nearly all sentences involving servicemen under eighteen, of whom thousands served in the Union forces.

In the second year of the war, Lincoln was determined to avoid a miscarriage of justice in a military incident that ended in the mass judicial condemnation of 303 Minnesota Sioux Indians. A deadly clash between opposing cultures and ways of life had led to this astonishing legal decision. On one side were European Americans who had settled Minnesota and had seized the land and destroyed the livelihood of the indigenous people. On the other hand, those indigenous people were justifiably bitter at the horrific loss they had suffered. Friction between the sides finally escalated into a Sioux uprising against the people they saw as invaders, a conflict ending in the deaths of 350 white Minnesotans, the worst such massacre of whites by Indians in the nation's history. The army suppressed the rebellion, and a military court condemned 303 of the captured Sioux warriors. When informed of the sentences, Lincoln immediately asked that the court records be sent to him for his personal review.

Like nearly all white Americans of the mid-nineteenth century, Lincoln regarded Indians as an inferior race in just about every way that ugly judgment implies. His few official meetings with Indians had not been models of tactfulness. In one White House gathering, he told a group of Indians, "We [whites] are not, as a race, so much disposed to fight and kill one another as our red brethren," this when Union and Confederate armies were slaughtering each other in the thousands. Notwithstanding, the notion of a mass hanging of 303 people in the name of the United States was more than Lincoln could either stomach or allow. Even though he was immersed in the events surrounding the terrible battle then being fought at Antietam, he took up every one of the Minnesota court records and carefully sifted through them for evidence of real capital guilt on the part of the individual Indians concerned. Knowing that to pardon even a single Indian would earn him the enmity of the white settlers—every adult male among them a potential voter, of course—he narrowed the list of condemned to thirty-nine names, each one of whom he concluded had actually been responsible for the deaths of the whites. On December 26, 1862, thirty-eight Sioux men (one man had been reprieved at the last moment) were hanged from a great square scaffold in Mankato, Minnesota, in what was the largest mass execution in American history. But a shameful incident had been saved from becoming a great deal more shameful through the intervention and justice of the president of the United States.[14]

One can conclude that Lincoln's actions in respect to military clemency probably helped discipline: The president became widely beloved by the ordinary fighting man, a regard for the commander in chief that surely heightened battlefield morale in a war notorious for the horrendous hardships it demanded of the men in the front lines. The president was aware of the moral ambiguities of his policy. In no way naive about the negative effects of desertions on military morale, Lincoln still reasoned that it was indefensible to shoot young and impressionable deserters when the antiwar agitators and politicians whose sophisticated arguments egged those men to desert remained free to speak as they chose, one of the reasons for his controversial suspension of the writ of habeas corpus. Rather than do that which was demanded by military "requirements," throughout his presidency Lincoln weighed the higher question of justice as the overriding factor in his decisions. He believed he was dispensing justice rather than simple mercy and suffered few qualms when authorizing the hanging of a murderer while at the same time barring the shooting of a deserter. His friend Leonard Swett said after Lincoln's death that the president "would be just as kind and generous as his judgment would let him be—no more."[15] It should be kept in mind that 267 Union army executions *were* carried out during the Civil War, many of them punishment for the 520 Union army murders that occurred during the conflict.

Because throughout his presidency Lincoln remained so conscientious on this issue, the sheer work involved in these reprieves and pardons weighed on him as did no other routine presidential duty other than the overall conduct of the war. On one April day in 1864, he reviewed sixty-seven cases, sitting with the judge advocate general for hours deciding which death sentences he would permit. Occasionally he wanted more information before deciding, the delay giving the commanding officers fits but keeping the cases "in soak," in Lincoln's apt phrase, rather than being rushed into faulty and potentially irreversible judgments. As General Holt put it, "In every case he always leaned to the side of mercy. His constant desire was to save life."[16] His secretary Hay thought him "the tenderest of men," though Lincoln himself once said, "Doesn't it seem strange that I should be here—I, a man who couldn't cut a chicken's head off—with blood running all around me."[17]

In time, Lincoln became known to thousands of Union soldiers as Father Abraham, surely in large part for this quality of caring and his insistence that these men receive justice *and* mercy. Few knew how much this burden cost the president in the hours he gave to it and what strain he bore in saving the lives of so many Americans in uniform.

ROBERT

One member of the presidential family tried, with less than perfect results, to stay clear of the public eye. A comparatively distant figure in the Lincoln family drama since his father's election, Robert had been living at Harvard since before the inauguration, and he seemed cheerfully settled in the pleasant academic life of the country's foremost college. The only cloud darkening the eldest son's sky was the growing grumbling, especially in the newspapers, about his remaining out of uniform when so many men of his generation were serving their country, liking it or not.

Having joined the class of 1864, Robert was immersed in a world of privilege the likes of which his father had never known. Civil War–era Harvard was more of an advanced high school than what we think of today as an upper academic institution of self-discipline and inquiry—in the 1860s students did and thought pretty much what they were told to do and think. The notion of "electives" remained virtually unknown. So did the concept of studying modern languages for credit, meaning those tongues actually spoken by large bodies of people. Instead, students pursued Latin and ancient Greek, both of which were required through three years. The roughly nine-hundred-member student body (during Lincoln's years) followed a single given course of studies each year. For freshmen it consisted of composition, Greek, Latin, mathematics, and elocution, with a half year of religious education and a half year of history. Robert would later study French, an undertaking that pleased his French-speaking mother. The faculty was made up of forty teachers, a group then (as now) distinguished by famous names and that in 1860 included such luminaries as Louis Agassiz, Oliver Wendell Holmes, and James Russell Lowell.

The tightly knit, all-male student body at Harvard came disproportionately from well-to-do Eastern families. As a Westerner, Robert started out at a disadvantage in social status, his father's position notwithstanding; one writer wrote that his parentage gave him "celebrity," but called it "a very insignificant factor in determining his essential importance."

His physical characteristics sharply distinguished Robert from his father. Robert was husky in the Todd manner as well as being far shorter than his Lincoln genes might have made him. He was also conventionally good-looking, the son bearing absolutely none of the president's famous gauntness. In these years, Robert's face still bore the softness of boyhood, with only a touch of the exotic found in his sloe eyes. By the time of his graduation, the softness had begun to morph into a round, mustached solidity that distinguished his appearance for the rest of his life.

Academically, Lincoln ranked just above the center of the ninety-nine men of his class who would graduate in 1864. By later standards, Harvard's grading of that era seems irrational. There were no examination marks as such. Instead, teachers subjectively graded students according to their "scholarship," with deportment demerits weighing equally with classroom performance. None of this much mattered to Robert, however, who simply wished to be regarded as a "gentleman," which status among his classmates his middling grades did nothing to diminish.

As much as Lincoln and his peers archly pretended to ignore his special political status, the general public would not allow the president's son to forget that his father was running the country, directing a war, and gradually shifting the fundamental motivation for the war from simply that of saving the Union to instead ending slavery. Regardless of his having distanced himself from the White House, being Abraham Lincoln's son during the Civil War in fact represented a large burden. Still widely referred to by the press as the Prince of Rails, Robert unquestionably generated significant public interest, and he found his actions frequently reported on, whether he liked such intrusiveness or not.

That his mother much sought out Robert's companionship did much to keep him in the public eye. The first lady was eager to have her son spend his holidays and vacations with the family in Washington. But failing to tempt him to visit the capital, she—usually with Tad—would instead go north, there to escape Washington's various oppressions in addition to basking in the company of the son who brought her great pride with his achievements at Harvard. One unusual but annoying factor affected his disposition: More than a few marriageable young women saw in him the perfect mate. To Robert's probable amusement, a young Indiana woman even informed him that she had named her baby after him and politely asked him to send her a "baby dress or a pair of boots."[18]

Robert's achievements at Harvard put him far ahead of his father in formal, classical knowledge, which probably widened the emotional gap between them. Regardless of his problematic relations with his father, Robert could exhibit great caring for his family if such help was needed, as when after Willie's death he wrote his aunt Elizabeth Todd Edwards in Springfield imploring that she come to Washington to take care of the dangerously unhinged first lady; Mrs. Edwards did hurry to Mary's side and stayed for months, during which time she wrote of her own desire to escape the gloom of the White House to return to her own happy family in Illinois.

The rift between the president and his firstborn left a poignant mark on Lincoln's White House years. The father seems never to have shared with his eldest son the same closeness Willie and Tad achieved, a disadvantage that wounded Robert. In the privacy of John Nicolay's bedroom, Robert told the story of a "great row" he had just had with the president over the way his father spoiled Tad, a matter that caused the elder son hurt.[19]

A subtle barrier evidently kept Lincoln from the deepest part of Robert's life. Nobody can ever know entirely why this was, why the paternal relationship assumed such different forms for the three sons. But during the war Lincoln likely put aside or else hadn't yet achieved any substantive expectations for the two youngest boys, the president never knowing Willie and Tad in the same near-adult light in which he saw Robert. Yet the strains went beyond that. From Robert's boyhood, it appears that Lincoln kept Robert at a greater distance than he ever would the younger boys, as though he hadn't perhaps yet learned how to remove the barrier between the expectations of an adult and the reality of a still limited child. More lately, Robert had assumed the cultured, educated class attitudes of Harvard, sentiments in striking contrast to Abraham Lincoln's frontier frame of view.

In the White House years Lincoln appears not to have made significant overtures to narrow the gap with Robert. Consequently, Robert later admitted that his relationship with his father in those last years of the president's life was, at best, distant. The younger man would write that during the war "any great intimacy between us was impossible—I scarcely ever had ten minutes' quiet talk with him during his presidency, on account of his constant devotion to business." During his visits to Washington, Robert did however develop a close friendship with his father's two private secretaries, particularly with John Hay. Nearly the same age and similar to each other in personality, Hay and Robert Lincoln formed their own mutual admiration society, although it irked Mary Lincoln because of the tense and often unpleasant relations she herself suffered with her husband's two secretaries.

For the public, the most serious issue hanging over Robert was that he remained a civilian and did so until the last weeks of the war. In contrast, many of Robert's Harvard classmates left their studies before graduation to join the services. Had the president insisted that his own son face the same dangers as those being encountered by innumerable American parents' sons—dangers faced by those sons at Robert's own father's orders—Robert, too, would probably have joined up. But Mary remained adamantly against it, particularly after Willie's death, fearing that she could lose another child. Lincoln admonished his wife on the issue: "The services of every man who loves his country are required in this war. You should take a liberal instead of a selfish view of the question, Mother."[20]

In the final accounting, Robert's continued civilian status came not as a favor to him, but really to the president—and, by extension of course, to the first lady. The death or even serious mutilation of her eldest son after the overwhelming loss of Willie would almost certainly have driven the mentally shaky first lady into true insanity. Lincoln understood that and accepted the criticism of his son's civilian status rather than risk his wife's collapse and the strain that such an incapacitation would almost surely have lent his presidency. Whether he was justified in this stance is left to every American's own judgment.

PHYSICAL LINCOLN

As 1863 began, almost every sign pointed to a great deal more disagree-ableness in the new year for Lincoln and the Union cause. On New Year's Day, the president at last signed his Emancipation Proclamation, putting the controversial executive order into legal and moral if worryingly unen-forceable effect. From that historic high point, though, Lincoln could see—as could most of the nation—that the federal forces were not de-feating and seemingly *could* not defeat the Confederacy. The future Supreme Court justice Oliver Wendell Holmes, then a young soldier re-covering from battle wounds, wrote that he had made up his mind that "the South have achieved their independence," a sentiment that looked to many as though it were coming true. With all the depressing battle losses, countless citizens all across the North shared the fear. As for the man in the White House and at the center of it all, one visitor to Wash-ington gloomily assessed the situation, "The lack of respect for the Pres-ident in all parties is unconcealed. . . . If a Republican convention were to be held tomorrow, he would not get the vote of a state."[21]

To Lincoln it seemed that almost everything was going wrong. The recently fought battle of Fredericksburg had handed a great victory to the Confederacy and a correspondingly horrendous defeat to the Union; in that futile encounter, the North lost thirteen thousand soldiers (as op-posed to five thousand for the South) around the small Virginia town where the federal army of the incompetent General Ambrose Burnside was overwhelmed by Lee's legions in gray. Americans were horrified by the mounting deaths and by the flood of men fed up with the carnage who deserted to return home to attend to fragmented families and foundering farms. Furthermore, Lincoln's proclamation angered count-less Northerners who were willing to sacrifice for a continued Union but not for the freedom of faceless Negroes. The mid-February passing of the Conscription Act, in which Northern men found themselves liable to being drafted, was detested virtually everywhere, especially and justi-fiably in light of its provision that the well-off could escape enlistment merely by paying for the services of a substitute.

In the midst of all this bleakness, Lincoln spent every waking hour at his desk. Working to put out fires before they became conflagrations was dangerously depleting his energy, to the point where his closest associates worried about his continued health. Though he was still in his early fifties, exhaustion, depression, and the disease-fraught environment of wartime Washington were scourging the president's body. Unfortunately, few ways were available to Lincoln to keep exhaustion at bay. Though he was directing a struggle the likes of which the nation had never before experienced, as with all nineteenth-century presidents the era's miserliness denied him an adequate staff with which to run his office. The demands on Lincoln's time as the first president governing during a modern, total war but still being forced to operate under the same primitive staffing conditions as those of his predecessors are almost impossible to grasp today.

Intensifying this plight was the president's strong belief that he was morally obligated to make himself available to ordinary citizens suffering with commonplace, though often tragic, troubles just as he had to be accessible to the generals and politicians with their gargantuan problems. That he continued to interview the office seekers who infested the White House was, of course, a problem of his own making, but one his secretaries eventually talked him into paring down to a less burdensome level. Midway in his presidency, he finally permitted Nicolay and Hay to shield him from a portion of even the benign seekers of presidential attention, though access to Lincoln still remained, by later standards, mind-boggling. The downside to his zeal to make himself approachable was the physical toll it took. So worrisome was this wear on the president that Horace Greeley alarmingly remarked, "When we last saw Mr. Lincoln, he looked so weary and haggard that he seemed unlikely to live out his term."[22] Nearly everyone who now studies presidential photographs taken during his four years in office is stunned by the rapid progression of Lincoln's aging, from 1861 when he was a man who looked his actual age, until 1865 when he could easily pass for a quarter century older than his true years.

Lincoln's mental state imposed an additional burden on this president's wartime health. Depression had been his constant companion from youth. At thirty-one, he wrote about it to his law partner: "I am now the most miserable man living. If what I feel were equally distributed to the whole human family, there would not be one cheerful face on the earth." Guessing his own prognosis, he added, "Whether I shall ever be better I can not tell; I awfully abode I shall not. To remain as I am is impossible; I must die or be better, it appears to me."[23] William Herndon said of him that his "perpetual look of sadness was his most prominent feature." This deep melancholia had almost surely interfered in his courtship with Mary Todd, perhaps to the point where in only slightly altered circumstances their seesawing marriage plans might have been abandoned.

Lincoln's depressive personality, which marked him as far back as his youth and which some historians surmise was related to his unpleasant relationship with his father, may have been exacerbated by his adult addiction to blue mass. Most of this nineteenth-century patent medicine's ingredients were inert: licorice root, rosewater, rose petals, honey, and sugar. One wasn't inert, however. The amount of pure mercury added to blue mass pills made them potentially lethal, though at the time mercury's toxicity wasn't understood because the heavy metal doesn't kill immediately. Rather it invades the body and does its damage, often enormous in scope, slowly and (in Lincoln's day) without obvious connection to the mercury itself. One of the insidious effects of mercury is the neurobehavioral damage it causes, including depression or worsening of preexisting depression. The then standard daily dosage of two blue mass pills put one at serious risk from mercury poisoning. Lincoln ingested an unknowable but surely enormous number of the tablets over many years.

Besides exhaustion and depression, Lincoln's health was damaged by physical disease from the pervasive filth and germs that blighted life in the Civil War era and the rapid aging that came from the illnesses he endured. Among his relatively minor problems was presbyopia—causing a need for reading glasses—which hit him, as it does many people, in his forties. He bought his first pair of spectacles for thirty-seven and a half cents at a jewelry store in Illinois. Six and a half diopters strong, they were probably three times the strength he needed, which would tend to explain the headaches of which he complained after reading for long periods.[24]

Lincoln's other medical troubles in the White House presented considerably more serious consequences to his family as well as to himself. From the time the family entered the Executive Mansion in March 1861, germs and microbes causing a wide range of diseases assailed them all. Some of these illnesses were then thought of as simply an unavoidable and even a normal part of life. One was malaria, which in its milder form affected Tad. The boy constantly took quinine, the medicine cut with sweet syrups but whose bitterness was undisguisable.

Naturally, the president's son hated to take the stuff and refused it from anyone but his father, who sometimes had to be called out of meetings to talk Tad into swallowing it.[25]

The White House and its grounds became a kind of zoo during the Lincoln years. In every presidency of that era, horses (and, unfortunately, their abundant dung) were, of course, a part of the Executive Mansion's surroundings. But in the Lincoln White House, the younger presidential sons kept just about every kind of tame pet they were given or could catch. Besides dogs and cats, which even the president enjoyed, domesticated goats and rabbits roamed the building. A turkey presented to the family for a holiday dinner became instead, thanks to Tad's tears, a pet after receiving a reprieve from the president. The manure from all these creatures attracted flies in hot weather, thus drawing even more disease into the family circle. In all weather, visitors tracked animal feces into the building, adding to the pungent smell that characterized the nineteenth-century Executive Mansion. And in winter, the drafts that entered the aging White House's innumerable crevices kept the colds that every Lincoln caught raging and which the president tried to ward off by habitually draping a woolen shawl around his shoulders.

Among the almost unending health dangers occasioned by White House life was that of diseases borne by the many people constantly milling about the building. Even in the evening, strangers were able to fairly freely make their way anywhere on the main floor. But in daytime, the mansion could be mistaken for a crowded train station. Not only were there the office seekers and importuners trying to get to the president, but there were the squadrons of tourists and even people simply escaping the cold outside and who kept the building well supplied with every imaginable kind of germ. For example, well-carriers of typhoid and diphtheria, themselves immune, uninhibitively if inadvertently spread their deadly ills in all directions. Of course, many of these free-ranging germs made their way into the bodies of the presidential family. This was possibly the scenario that occurred shortly after the inauguration, when Willie and Tad came down with the measles. The disease so weakened Willie (he was already run-down from the effects of an attack of scarlet fever two years earlier) that less than a year later he died from an illness that Tad was concurrently able—just barely—to survive.

To add to these blows to Lincoln's assaulted body, dental problems also plagued him. In line with the same thinking that made amputation almost automatic for soldiers suffering from major limb injuries, so dentists of the era simply yanked out decayed teeth. In some places in the country by the early 1860s, anesthesia—generally chloroform—was used for extractions, but it evidently wasn't widely available in Washington. Lincoln had known of it in Illinois, and when in 1862 he visited Dr. G. S. Wolf's office near the White House complaining of an aching tooth, the president brought along his own vial of chloroform.[26] Nonetheless, Lincoln retained a well-founded fear of visits to a dentist. During an anesthetic-free extraction in his Illinois years, the practitioner had pulled out a piece of Lincoln's jawbone along with the tooth.

MARY'S LIFE

Beyond these afflictions besetting the Lincoln family, the first lady's mental problems at times dominated life at the White House. After Willie's death, Mary became an eccentric. At least, that was the assessment made of her by part of every level of society she touched—her family, the Executive Mansion's staff, official Washington, and the nation at large. The presumption was that her very presence in the president's life placed an additional burden on Lincoln, one he could not easily bear while running a war and at the same time trying to sustain his own mental equilibrium. In spite of history's current understanding of the adversities Mary faced, the widespread dislike and disapproval of Lincoln's wife during the White House years was comprehensible. Glossing over Mary's shortcomings in a spirit of retroactive kindness would not give an accurate portrait of how she was perceived during her husband's presidency.

To history, Mary's behavior is not important because of the woman herself but because of the man to whom she was married. She was not a political figure during her husband's administration, though not because she didn't try, often with fervor, to influence political events. After his election Lincoln simply ceased paying Mary much attention, politically speaking. As a helpmeet in Illinois, she *had* played a vital role in Lincoln's career, most crucially in pushing him forward on the public stage, eventually all the way to the presidency. But her role had never been large in the realm of policy advice, even if she did buck up Lincoln's vacillating spirits at critical times in his climb to national prominence.

But the political affairs of the presidency were entirely beyond Mary's capability to be of any use to her husband. As first lady she could have been detached or simply unremarkable, as were nearly all presidents' wives until well into the twentieth century. Had she wished, she might have played the role of national hostess-in-chief with skill and graciousness and have thus gained a large measure of historical respect for helping a put-upon president during a time of unprecedented national turmoil and danger. But she did neither—at least she did neither *well*. She was rarely graciously quiet in the manner of the nineteenth century's womanly ideal. From the very beginning of the Lincoln administration, Mary's bluntness and rudeness, the latter intentional or not, earned her legions of enemies and detractors. As we've seen, her wartime spending on luxuries, her extravagant White House decorations, her account juggling, her lavish travels, her Southern connections, her many and expensive gowns, and above all, her seeming interference in her husband's business, all represented to the American people a woman who could neither be liked nor be simply quietly ignored. And even in the privacy of their married life Mary was unable to provide her husband with a dependably calm harbor, which for a stressed and beleaguered president would have represented a profound treasure.

The marriage did retain the outer garments of normality. Lincoln habitually deferred to his wife's whims and demands, at any rate where they didn't involve politics. He understood his wife's pathological jealousy of other women, the latter ironic in the sense that Lincoln never demonstrated the least interest in the opposite sex or in betraying his marriage vows. Though bereft of any foundation, her jealousy was nonetheless a leitmotif in their marriage, especially in the White House years when she feared he was or might be tempted by the constant parade of handsome females passing through the presidential orbit. Most important, Lincoln was unquestionably aware of the fragility of his wife's mental state and feared that to confront her over it would be to risk knocking her completely off her mental foundations. He even risked his political standing in this regard, perhaps most visibly in accommodating her wish that their eldest son remain out of uniform, steadfastly believing that Robert's loss would be beyond her capacity to accept—and that a disabled Mary would be beyond *his* capacity to bear.

WAR RIOTS

The biggest and bloodiest battle of the entire conflict was fought that blisteringly hot summer of 1863 in the hitherto peaceful country-side of south-central Pennsylvania. Over the first three days of July, scores of thousands of men flung themselves at each other in and around the town of Gettysburg, killing each other in a slaughter of bib-lical proportions. When the shooting stopped, a staggering twenty-three thousand soldiers in blue and a like number in gray were dead or maimed. If one side or the other was the "winner," it is said that the Union came out on top because it stopped Lee from cutting off Wash-ington from the rest of the North and from moving the Confederate army into federal territory. Lincoln, though, declined to view Gettys-burg as a victory, instead regarding the battle as a disaster for federal arms. It was not his objective to merely run Lee out of the North, but rather to destroy the rebel army. When at the battle's conclusion Gen-eral Meade, the Union commander, let Lee escape rather than pursuing the Confederacy's biggest army and destroying it from its rear, Lincoln believed that his commander's failure caused the war to be significantly and unnecessarily prolonged. When one of the president's generals noted that the rebels had been driven back into their "own" territory, Lincoln's response was sheer fury. In stinging irony, the president icily noted that Confederate "territory" *was* the United States. The moment was one of the lowest points in the war for Lincoln, who in anguish over the failure said, "We had them within our grasp. We had only to stretch forth our hands and they were ours."

But the Confederate cause, too, suffered a crushing strategic defeat at Gettysburg. By failing to best Meade, Lee lost his chance to strike a heavy blow to Northern morale, a wound he'd believed a Southern vic-tory would achieve. And he lost any hope for another serious incursion into nonrebel states. Finally, the Confederacy forsook virtually its last chance to persuade Britain or France to lend their support to the South: London and Paris could now unequivocally see that Southern arms would not, over any foreseeable time, prevail against the North. At the same time of these events in the Eastern theater of the war, in the West the Union army finally captured the last Confederate strongholds on the Mississippi—Vicksburg and Port Gibson—assuring the federal forces of complete control over the nation's most important river and opening the Confederacy's back door for the Union army to pour through.

Adding to the president's general wretchedness was that summer's rioting that made a charnel house of a large swath of New York, the country's largest and most crowded city. With the vastly increased need for human cannon fodder on the Union army's many fighting fronts, the draft had of necessity been sharply ratcheted upward. Manhattan's poor Irish immigrants were ripe pickings for induction, but these men believed their present economic misery should not be converted into death on the battlefield. Irish anger was heightened by the horrendously unfair provision permitting the affluent to pay a draft substitute to take their place in the army. Such furor further translated into hatred and loathing of African-Americans, whom the Irish newcomers saw as the cause of the war given the president's recently promulgated Emancipation Proclamation. The result was one of the worst civil uprisings in American history, a race riot in which blacks—including wholly innocent children in a New York City orphan asylum—disproportionately became the victims.

SOLDIERS' HOME

The president, the first lady, and Tad left the White House in June 1863 to again take up summer residence at the Soldiers' Home. Mary and Tad had just returned to Washington from a trip to New York and Philadelphia, presumably for shopping and recuperation from Washington's hardships. With several wagons of White House furniture sent to the presidential villa, the house was once more turned into a comfortable home for the Lincolns. A few alterations had been made to the arrangements at the summer residence, most noticeably that of moving the soldiers' encampment about a quarter mile away from the house. The separation was great enough to afford the family real privacy, though it had become less convenient for the president to wander out to talk to the soldiers when Mary was away. Sadly, Captain Derickson, the guard commander, had been transferred in April, denying the president a man who the prior summer had become almost a companion.

Presidential social life had diminished nearly to the vanishing point since Willie's death and Mary's unwillingness to face throngs of guests. The couple had, however, hosted one fairly festive event in February when fifty people came to the White House for an evening reception honoring General Tom Thumb. At forty inches tall, the small but gregarious "general"—so dubbed by his exhibitor, P. T. Barnum—was a national sensation. When he married Lavinia Warren, a lady near his own size, the country went wild with romantic ecstasy in its eagerness to get its collective mind off the war. While on their honeymoon to Washington, the general and his wife received an invitation to the White House from Mrs. Lincoln. Greeting them with his wife at the north entrance, the president bent his enormous frame over the small guests in a gracious and friendly greeting that left the onlooking guests swooning in admiration. Son Robert, home on leave from college, turned out to be less gracious. Invited by the first lady to join the festivities downstairs, the proud university man refused, informing his mother, "I do not propose to assist in entertaining Tom Thumb. My notions of duty, perhaps, are somewhat different from yours."[27] The snub may have been the result of travel weariness, but it's likely that Robert long regretted his arrogance.

The Lincolns started out their second summer at the retreat in the company of a full security detachment of mounted soldiers. A new cook also came with them, this time a white woman to replace the black cook of the previous summer. But a little over a week after arriving, on what was coincidentally the second day of the battle of Gettysburg, an incident occurred that greatly worsened the first lady's troubles.

Driving into the city from the Soldiers' Home, Mary's carriage suddenly began to collapse, throwing off the driver and frightening the horses so that they ran out of control. The driverless vehicle quickly gained enough speed to pitch the first lady backward, flinging her over the side. On landing, the back of Mary's head hit a sharp stone. Outriders got her to a hospital, where her head injury was bandaged, and then she was driven back to the Soldiers' Home. An investigation of the incident found that the screws fastening the carriage's seat had purposely been undone in what looked to be an attempt to assassinate the president.

The newspapers reported the mishap, describing the first lady's injuries as minor. The president even wired Robert at Harvard to assure him that his mother was "only very slightly hurt by her fall,"[28] which was what Lincoln as well as the public believed. Transfixed by the events at Gettysburg, the president could only hope that his wife's spill had not, in fact, been serious.

But Mary's continuing poor condition proved worrisome. Eight days after the incident, Lincoln again wired Robert, this time tersely ordering him to "come to Washington," and when after three more days his eldest son hadn't arrived, he again wrote, asking, "Why do I hear no more of you?" This second request finally brought Robert to Washington, where he found his father sunk in depression from both the first lady's situation and the army's failure to capture Lee's army after Gettysburg. Robert went to his father's room to find him "in tears with his head bowed upon his arms."[29] In one of the few known instances that Lincoln confided in Robert regarding substantive military matters, he told his son, "If I had gone up there [after Lee's fleeing army], I could have whipped them myself."[30]

Unfortunately, Mary's injuries were now seen to be unambiguously grave, the blow to her head and the shock of the fall much worse than first believed. What was more, the nurse engaged by Lincoln to tend to Mary ominously reported that the first lady's wound wasn't healing properly. When the infected area of her skull started suppurating, a doctor finally opened the damaged area and drained it. In a time when infection killed far more soldiers than did actual blows on the battlefield, and when the power of germs was a long way from being understood, Mary was in reality in extreme danger. It took three weeks for the wound to finally heal and for her immune system to overcome the infection, and the ordeal left her weakened and worsened. What was more, her chronic migraine headaches, which had harassed her for many years, grew worse than ever as a result of the accident.

Increasingly subject to wanderlust, Mary now wanted simply to get away—from Washington and its miserable weather (the summer of 1863 was one of the most awful on record, the temperature peaking at 104 degrees and the humidity turning the city into a steam bath), from the people, including her husband's official family, whom she disliked or simply found annoying, and from the constant din of soldiers in the streets and the topic of war in every conversation. She worried about her youngest child, too, fearful that the summer miasma in the capital would bring another disease to the frail boy. At the beginning of August, accompanied by Robert and Tad, she departed for the cooler weather of New England, leaving her husband alone to execute his daily trek from the Soldiers' Home to the White House and back, as commander in chief unable to even think about a vacation for himself by leaving the capital and his responsibilities. Mother and sons ended their journey in the

White Mountains of New Hampshire, with Mary and the president constantly telegraphing back and forth to assure each of the other's well-being. Though Lincoln knew Tad was thriving in the cooler air of the Northeast, he sent his wife a wire on September 23 telling her, "I would be glad for you to come [home]. Nothing very particular but I would be glad to see you and Tad."[31] After a few more days browsing through the shops of New York, the first lady and her youngest son returned to the president at their Soldiers' Home cottage.

While still in New York, Mary had endured another bolt of pain from her birth family. On September 24, Lincoln wrote his wife to tell her that her youngest sister, Emilie, had been widowed by the battle of Chickamauga. There Emilie's handsome thirty-two-year-old husband, Ben Helm, was killed along with six fellow general officers of the Confederate army of Tennessee in the demonic battle's carnage. The news of the death hit both the president and the first lady hard, though because Ben had been an enemy officer the Northern public's attitude forced both to hide their grief. Lincoln had offered Ben a safe federal army posting in Washington, not only because he wanted Mary's sister close at hand but equally because he had come to love and respect his young brother-in-law. Few battlefield deaths, either Union or Confederate, were more painful to the president than this one, the victim a man whom Lincoln had once regarded as almost a son. The president's friend David Davis wrote that when Lincoln learned of Ben's loss, he said in anguish, "I feel as David did of old when he was told of the death of Absalom." The biblical passage he was referring to concludes, "Would to God that I had died for thee!"[32]

That summer, Mary's half brother David, an officer who had became notorious for the brutality he'd displayed while commanding a prisoner-of-war camp in Richmond, had been mortally wounded in the fighting at Vicksburg. And only a month before Ben Helm's death, the first lady's youngest half brother, Alexander, was killed in a skirmish in Louisiana. Though she hadn't known David well—he had left his Lexington home when still a boy—young Alexander was a sentimental favorite of Mary's, one for whom her feelings were probably as much maternal as sisterly. When given the news of his death, Mary was deeply saddened, crying out, "Oh, little Aleck, why did you have to die?" These family tragedies badly injured the first lady. Yet Mary had long braced her emotions with the understanding that her brothers were enemies to her nation; she chillingly told a friend that they would "kill my husband if they could and destroy our government."[33] Nonetheless she couldn't help but grieve, the difference between her and other relatives in the same position being that she could not expect sympathy from her countrymen for her losses. And paradoxically, this obligatory hiding of her sorrow left the Southern public convinced of Mary's indifference to the suffering of the very people from whom she herself had sprung.

Ben Helm's death soon brought unexpected consequences for the first family. Governor Helm of Kentucky, Emilie's father-in-law, wrote to Mary Lincoln's stepmother, Mrs. Robert Todd, in Lexington, asking Mrs. Todd to use her influence with the first lady to secure a pass through the lines that would permit Emilie to return home to Kentucky from Atlanta, the site of her husband's burial. President Lincoln accordingly sent his mother-in-law a letter to be forwarded to Emilie, allowing her to cross from Confederate to Union territory. But when Emilie reached the crossover point—Fortress Monroe, Virginia—federal officials demanded that she take the required oath of allegiance to the United States. Emilie refused, believing that would amount to treason against her dead husband. Concerned because the letter had come directly from the president, an officer telegraphed the White House for instructions. A return wire was soon received from the president's office: "Send her to me. A. Lincoln."[34]

The pregnant Emilie, accompanied by her older daughter and covered from head to foot in the black crepe of a widow's mourning, arrived in the federal capital on a November evening. By far the prettiest of the Todd girls, the sweet-faced Emilie looked more to be Mary's daughter than her sister. With genuine respect and affection, both the president and the first lady greeted their beloved relation at the White House, the three embracing in silent tears in light of the many losses the family had suffered. After her fraught journey to Washington, the new widow desperately needed the refuge and kindness Mary tendered this favorite of the Lexington family, who had nearly been lost to her because of the war. The first lady ordered the mansion lit up on the night of Emilie's arrival, apparently in an effort to cheer her, and after dinner the flames of candles enlivened the East Room and the state parlors. The two sisters walked around the building together, stopping in particular at the portrait of George Washington that Dolley Madison had saved from British flames decades earlier, noting proudly that Mrs. Madison's first husband had been a Todd.

The next day, their first full day together, the sisters rode through the city, an outing that ironically ended in near-tragedy when a small boy jumped in front of the carriage and was hit before the driver could stop. A doctor passing by checked the child, after which the first lady insisted on returning the boy to his home. For days afterward, Mary sent fruit, flowers, and toys to the boy to help him in his recovery from a broken leg.

Just as Mary found Emilie's situation heartbreaking, so did the younger sibling worry about the elder's supernatural beliefs about her dead son. Stopping by Emilie's bedroom late at night, Mary told her sister how Willie came to her: "He lives, Emilie! He comes to me every night and stands at the foot of my bed with the same sweet, adorable smile he always had." But it wasn't only Willie who Mary said returned. The first lady continued, "He does not always come alone; little Eddie is sometimes with him, and twice he has come with our brother Alec[k]. . . . You cannot dream of the comfort this gives me." The younger woman described Mary's eyes as "wide and shining and I had a feeling of awe as if I were in the presence of the supernatural." Emilie wrote that her sister's behavior frightened her and said these actions were largely due to the fear of Robert joining the army.[35]

Tragically, the sisters' differing loyalties could not be ignored, and their reunion's joy did not last. A few days after Emilie's arrival at the White House, the president and first lady were entertaining New York senator Ira Harris and General Daniel Sickles. The chief city of the senator's state had just gone through the vicious draft riots set off by the president's conscription order. A former congressman and, like Harris, a New Yorker, Sickles was perhaps best known for having murdered his wife's lover—the victim, Philip Barton Key, was the son of the composer of "The Star-Spangled Banner"—and having subsequently been acquitted on the basis of the "unwritten law" that excused a cuckolded husband from killing his cuckolder. The general had also lost a leg at Gettysburg, which likely contributed to his outrage at the sight of a Confederate general's widow living in the White House. Although the Lincolns had halfheartedly attempted to hide Emilie from public view, she had nonetheless joined her sister and brother-in-law for the evening's get-together.

The president might have known that Emilie's presence together with the subject of war—a topic guaranteed to be on his guests' lips—would make for a volatile mix. Sometime during the evening, Emilie responded to a comment made by either Harris or Sickles to the effect that "we have whipped the rebels at Chattanooga, and I hear, madam, that the scoundrels ran like scared rabbits." Ben had died near Chattanooga, and this insult to her husband's honor stunned her. "If I had twenty sons," she spit at them, "they would all be fighting yours."

The retort must have shocked the men, because later they confronted Mary Lincoln—their hostess and the president's wife—complaining that they couldn't understand why *her* son wasn't in the army, Harris stiffly adding that *his* one and only son was serving his country in uniform. Writing about the evening's events, Emilie noted that her sister's face went "white as death," but that she tried hard to keep control of herself. The first lady quietly responded to the affront, "Robert is making his preparations now to enter the army, Senator Harris; he is not a shirker. . . . If fault there be, it is mine. I have insisted that he should stay in college a little longer as I think an educated man can serve his country with more intelligent purpose than an ignoramus." The senator then turned to Emilie and threw one last insult in her direction: "And, madam, if I had twenty sons, they should all be fighting the rebels."

The outcome of the sisters' story added yet another layer of tragedy to the saga of the Lincolns in the White House. Emilie and her children could have remained with the first family; her brother-in-law was amenable, despite the political difficulty of a Confederate general's widow living in the nation's Executive Mansion, Lincoln knowing the value of Emilie's presence to his wife in her depressed state. But in mid-December Emilie decided to return to Lexington. Months later, in the fall of 1864, she came once more to the White House, but this time with motives beyond a mere family reunion. Emilie asked the president for a license to sell six hundred bales of her plantation's cotton, a commodity embargoed from slave states during the war. Lincoln asked only that his sister-in-law formally abjure her loyalty to the Confederacy as quid pro quo for granting the favor. She refused, again on the grounds that to do so would defame the memory of her dead husband.

After Emilie stormed back to Kentucky following this second visit, she wrote the president a sharp-tongued, denunciatory letter very much in the Todd family's characteristic "quick-rising, bridge-burning temper," as historian Jean Baker described it. She ended by stating that her family's deaths and its current misfortunes were due to Lincoln's minié balls—a particularly injurious type of ammunition used to murderous effect during the Civil War.[36] The slander was more than the Lincolns deserved or could stomach. Mary neither saw nor corresponded with this most beloved sibling again, the woman she and her husband had called Little Sister now dead to them both.

THE POX

Not only did seemingly endless family tragedies mark the last weeks of 1863, but also during those days the president contracted a disease that could well have killed him given the era's mist of medical ignorance. On the heels of his moral triumph at the Gettysburg battlefield in mid-November, Lincoln fell ill with a form of one of the deadliest diseases in history.

Following the almost incomprehensible butchery at the battle of Gettysburg a few months earlier, the federal government sought that fall to offer some form of solace to the families of the dead. Its answer was to turn the scene of their slaughter into a national cemetery. To underscore and solemnize the occasion, the organizers invited the president to deliver "appropriate remarks." Lincoln was not, though, to be the principal speaker, a role allotted to Edward Everett, the nationally known politician, diplomat, and scholar—he had been president of Harvard University—whose oratorical skills had for many years left his adoring audiences mesmerized. The official hoped that with the commander in chief following Mr. Everett with a few appropriate words, the dedication of the cemetery would end in a perfect balance.

On the night before the November 19 ceremony, Lincoln found himself, as often, depressed. One cause was Tad's poor health. At breakfast the next morning the boy was still too sick to join his parents. While merely worrying to the president, it caused the first lady to become nearly hysterical. The doctor told the boy's family that their son had most likely contracted scarlet fever, though in reality Tad was in the beginning stages of smallpox, then (as now) an extremely dangerous disease.

Since first being invited to the Gettysburg dedication, the president had been deeply engrossed in writing his remarks. Lincoln knew the occasion presented him with a not-to-be-missed opportunity to plainly express his reasons for waging the war, and by doing so to diminish the widespread criticism of his leadership that was seriously threatening his reelection. But the words came with difficulty, and as the dedication day neared, he had finished writing no more than half of what he wanted to say. Only on the day before leaving for Pennsylvania did he strike on the final and most important thoughts, and he needed but a short time to work out the remainder of the speech. The whole of his remarks came to 272 words.

Lincoln hardly ever left the District of Columbia during his presidency, his few brief absences from the capital having mostly been visits to his commanders in the field. Though physically he needed the quiet of a New England vacation fully as much as did the first lady, his sense of duty and the press of the war kept him nearly continuously at his desk. On the morning he was to leave for Gettysburg, he considered canceling the trip, with Tad's illness and Mary's disquiet over it troubling him, but in the end Lincoln judged his purposes at Gettysburg so important that he turned aside his wife's pleas that he stay at home. Accompanied by a few members of his administration—most notable was Secretary of State Seward—the president left Washington by train at noon. The commander in chief seemed in good temper at the trip's outset, even cheerfully accepting a bouquet of roses from a girl on the platform. His words to her were noted. "You're a sweet little rosebud yourself," Lincoln thanked the girl. "I hope your life will open into perpetual beauty and goodness."[37]

On its big day, disorder reigned in the town of Gettysburg, its streets strewn with piles of filled coffins awaiting reburial. But the weather was fine and the crowds hospitable, all seemingly eager to see and hear their president. Before Lincoln could speak at the ceremony, though, he had to sit through Everett's two-hour oration. General Meade had provided Everett with lengthy notes describing the battle's details, and with skill and vigor the orator painted a word picture of the clash, the address fortunately pleasing the crowd with its blow-by-blow description that seemed not to omit a single musket shot.

The president, though, *was* the honored guest, and the huge audience accorded him a respectful silence when he rose to speak. Fortunately, Lincoln's high and reedy voice had if not the virtue of beauty at least that of clarity, and as amazing as it seems for that pre-microphone age, his address was reportedly clearly heard by those gathered in the huge field, no matter how far one was standing from the speaker. Many of the fifteen thousand attendees were also watching as a photographer, hopeful of capturing the president in full flight of speech, wrestled with his equipment. As it turned out, so brief were Lincoln's remarks that the surprise was palpable when the president sat down seemingly before he had really even gotten started. The address's few dozen words had been delivered in a mere two or three minutes—minutes, though, that history would remember as the most profound in Abraham Lincoln's phenomenally brilliant oratorical career.

The president's thoughts as he put them into words that day became, of course, immortal. Stating that the war was creating "a new birth of freedom," the nation's chief executive was also tacitly admitting that America's *first* birth some eighty-seven years earlier had not been entirely successful, and that it had taken a war to correct the shortcomings. Though most of the audience likely did not recognize the supreme articulacy of the unadorned phrases, Lincoln did in fact miraculously encapsulate the meaning of this civil war to America's freedom and what that freedom in turn meant to the country's people—*all* of them, black *and* white. After Gettysburg, "the United States" became an expression understood not in the plural sense, but rather in the singular, a distinction of subtle but transcendent weight.

When Lincoln boarded the train that would carry him back to Washington, he was feeling headachy and tired, and he lay down in his drawing room and asked to be given cold compresses for his forehead. Arriving at the capital's station a few minutes past one o'clock the next morning, he probably already recognized that he was seriously ill and thus, when he reached the White House, immediately took to his bed, weak from malaise, fever, and head and back pain. His doctor first thought the president had simply caught a cold, but later changed his mind and diagnosed scarlet fever. The physician would probably have given Lincoln quinine and calomel, the only effective medicines then available for the disease.

Within two days, Lincoln's body was covered with small, widely scattered blisters, which looked to his doctor to be a kind of smallpox called varioloid. Varioloid differs from its big cousin smallpox only in the seriousness of its danger; the virus of smallpox and varioloid is basically the same, and each virus may cause one or the other of the diseases. Thankfully, varioloid was less severe and less likely to kill Lincoln. Under the worst scenario, though, the blisters could have become infected, mortally endangering the president with blood poisoning.

As soon as the news of the president's diagnosis got out to the press, interest in the theretofore nearly invisible vice president increased substantially, the *London Spectator* conjecturing on what course the war would take under a President Hannibal Hamlin. Lincoln remained in isolation in the White House for three weeks, which ironically gave him a much needed respite from the job and pardon seekers who still harried his working hours. He even managed to find some humor in the situation, joking, "Now *I* have something I can give everybody."

SIX

VICTORIES

O N NEW YEAR'S DAY, 1864, THE LINCOLNS WERE CON-
ducting their annual open house. But both knew that this year was
going to be different, in fact critical to their continued presence in Washington. In November, Northerners would decide whether to retain the
president or throw him—and his wife—out of the White House. The
first lady was clearly aware of the need to do everything she could to ensure her husband's continuance in office. So Mary resolved to finally put
aside her personal grief in the interests of promoting the president's
chances of winning a second term, a resolution that meant 1864's White
House social season was going to be busy, with the couple's official entertainment calendar just as full as she could make it.

In fact, Mary succeeded that winter in managing a pleasant social life
in the mansion. By now, the old slow-moving Washington had become a
city transformed, forsaking its onetime lassitude to become the nation's
genuine nerve center, the town's previous peaceful life having given
way almost entirely to the crisis that gripped the nation. Thus, most of
the White House's socializing revolved, in one way or another, around
the war. Many high-ranking military officers and their wives, for example, found themselves attending the first lady's Saturday receptions. In
late January, the Lincolns took a box at the capital's Grover Theatre for
a benefit performance of Tom Taylor's *The Ticket of Leave Man*, performed in aid of the Ladies' Soldiers' Relief Association; the president

loved almost any theatrical performance and likely considered this duty far more a pleasure than a chore. On the night of January 26, a White House reception in which eight thousand people passed in front of the Lincolns unsurprisingly exhausted both the president and the first lady, though the *Washington Star* noted in its next day's edition that Lincoln looked to be "in better health than ever."

In mid-February Robert arrived home for a visit with his parents, bringing along a group of his Harvard friends. On the evening of the fifteenth, all of them joined the first lady at a tableau at Willard's, the hotel having become the city's brightest social center in lieu of a White House long subdued in respect of the first family's difficulties. The tableau was performed by members of the city's social elite in aide of the Sanitary Commission, the Civil War's Red Cross–like organization, and was then a popular entertainment in which costumed people assumed elaborate poses that theoretically represented historical events or allegorical visions, holding the positions for a minute or two to give the audience the opportunity to appreciate the ephemeral spectacle.

One highly visible aggravation had been vexing Mary. The first lady was wounded by the deteriorated condition of her once beautifully decorated White House. Mary had, as we've seen, used her refurbishing allocation—and then some—to achieve results that were, by general consent, thoroughly successful. Though the rooms had been decorated in a fashion that most people today would regard as cluttered, they fit exactly with the prevailing taste of the 1860s—heavy, dark, and fussy, with copious bric-a-brac crowding every surface and anything that could be stuffed ending up overstuffed. The building might have stayed in good condition if Willie's death hadn't fatally undermined the first lady's spirits two years earlier. But now everyone in official Washington could see that the mansion was beginning to revert to the mess it had been when the Lincolns had entered it nearly three years earlier. The chief cause was neglect and sheer misbehavior, a constant hammering from around-the-clock crowding.

There would not, of course, have been a beautiful White House in the first place had the president been a bachelor. So preoccupied was Lincoln with the war and its direction that he cared little for his surroundings. But Mary had, at first, done her utmost to make the president's house one worthy of a great nation, as she framed her motivation.

That the country was fighting for its continued unity made the matter all the more important to her. But when she sank into near-seclusion upon Willie's death, care for her home sagged along with her morale. As a consequence and in the absence of a professional staff to look out for the house, guests and strangers alike began to pick it apart, indiscriminately chopping little pieces out of carpets, pulling damask and brocade "souvenirs" from the draperies and furniture, whacking tassels from elaborate window dressings, and pocketing the odd knickknack from an occasional table. All was done with the casualness of professional thieves. And without the stressed first lady's vigilant supervision, the floors of the corridors and formal salons quickly became stained with tobacco spittle, and dirt that fell from filthy boots got permanently ground into the mansion's expensive rugs.

Because of the debts Mary had incurred in remaking the residence, she was obliged to scrimp on staff and cleaning people, and the servants who did remain through the last years of her husband's administration don't appear to have made any great effort to preserve Mary's initial maintenance efforts. Though four metropolitan policemen had been assigned to keep an eye on the White House, their chief duty was not watching out for the house's contents but rather guarding the president. By 1863, the press had started commenting on this state of affairs, the *Washington Star* describing one lady of apparent means who suddenly fainted when confronted with her larcenous pinching of a valuable bit of White House decor.

Though Mary's passion for beautifying her home subsided over her husband's first term, her fervor for spending remained an almost neurotic obsession. A few days after the 1864 New Year's reception, the first lady left Washington for Philadelphia, the stated reason for the trip being "business," which to her usually meant shopping. Although she now tirelessly sought the lowest prices for the things she bought, that did not mean she looked for inferior merchandise. As she was the president's wife, whenever she visited a salesroom, the proprietor inevitably presented her with the most lavish articles at his disposal. Mary's lack of self-control meant that she would usually pass up, for example, an ordinary wool shawl for one made of cashmere. Far worse, she sometimes led proprietors to believe that if they would lower their price, the shop would benefit from continued White House business. What opened these practices to public comment was that she made no efforts to hide them, conducting her business with guileless transparency. The newspapers were, of course, eager to reveal the snowballing volume of her purchases.

Mary had always been attracted to the shining baubles of life, a trait that in itself is neither unusual nor discreditable. Nor is it difficult to understand why in her case she was so inclined. Raised in a home where luxuries were taken for granted, she ended up marrying a man who couldn't provide for her on the same level as her father's means had allowed. Beyond that, living in a tight-knit community in which her two older sisters were perched at the top of the local social ladder while she sat several rungs down surely made Mary eager to have what they had, if only to prove to herself and others that her birth rank hadn't fallen because of marriage to a relatively poor husband.

In the purely business end of her shopping and purchases, Mary possessed a steely will. The following letter to a merchant about a hat she was buying exemplifies the exacting and peremptory tone she took with the sellers of the goods she wanted:

Dec 11th, 1864
My Dear Madame:

Your last note has been received—I sent the velvet—which you will doubtless receive today—I did not wish *any lace* on the outside—therefore the bonnet must cost but $25.00 which is more than I expected to pay for a bonnet—furnishing the velvet myself—the feather must be long & beautiful—lace trimmings very rich and full; the outside you can arrange to your taste—

You can certainly procure black velvet ribbon—of the shade of the velvet of the bonnet—for strings—a finger length wide—very rich. I saw some in N.Y. when there—I do not think the edge *inserted* on the ribbon would look well. Qu'en pensez-vous? It is a bonnet for *grand occasions* & I want it to be particularly stylish & rich. Very especially, blk velvet is so *expens[ive]*, do not fail to turn in the sides of the front, more than an inch of course, it will some day, have to undergo, a new foundation—I am sure, you will not fail me in this. Another favor, I have to request. Can you have my bonnet, sent to me Express, on Monday next, leaving N.Y. on that day, and will you, send down to Tiffany & Co—for a blk velvet headdress, which he has as a measure, & enclose with the bonnet. Some of the narrow blk velvet ribbon, which you sent as a sample, with white edge, would look well, on one side of the front trimming. My strings must be one yard long each—*Do* have my bonnet got up in exquisite style.

> Very sincerely your friend
> Mary Lincoln

Two weeks later she followed up to the same merchant:

Madame Harris

I can neither wear, or settle with you, for my bonnet without different inside flowers—As to inside flowers of black & white, I saw some beautifully fine ones, in two or three different establishments in N.Y.—By going out, for them, you can procure them—I need to wear my blk velvet bonnet on Wednesday next. Do send me the flowers—By a little search you can procure them—I cannot retain or wear the bonnet, as it is—I am certainly taught a lesson, by your acting thus

> I remain and
> Mrs Lincoln[1]

Mary saw her advancement to the top formal social position in the country as entrance to a magic treasure cave, where her wishes would become reality and her status revert to that of the young lady of quality she had been in Lexington. But missing in Mary's psychological and mental makeup was recognition of this attitude's inappropriateness as wife to a president serving during a dire national emergency. In the 1860s the nation expected a circumspect first lady, one who would, for example, remain at her husband's side rather than escaping Washington's summertime discomfort by "vacationing" at cool and luxurious New England resorts and parading through the expensive emporiums of the war-rich Northeast.

Regarding Mary's pridefulness, various biographers have often noted the expensive shawls she bought. Shawls were common in the era, for both men and women, and most were, of course, fairly ordinary wool wraps. But Mary almost invariably chose the most luxurious and exotic models available; if she couldn't decide between competing colors, she would take one of each, and at prices that at today's values would sometimes run into four figures. Perhaps the strangest irony in the first lady's behavior was her rationalizing that these purchases helped the economy or, as one historian suggested, represented a "patriotic obligation" to bring money into the Treasury.[2] But heightening public exasperation with Mrs. Lincoln's prodigality remained the unalterable fact that the nation was fighting a war, one in which millions of wives were suffering the absence of husbands and taking on men's chores in addition to their own tasks, and who were losing those men in the slaughter for which Mary Lincoln's husband was widely held to be responsible.

Astonishingly, Mary was permitted to indulge in this politically damaging conduct by a husband who, if he wasn't aware of the exact costs of her purchases, must (or should) have been informed of the perilous heights of his wife's spending. Since newspaper accounts of her conduct were available to the White House, it is difficult to understand the president or his staff doing so little to confront it. For whatever reasons, the president chose to ignore his wife's buying and the ethical issues associated with it, and Mary evidently drifted into serious debt without her husband's full knowledge. The most logical explanation for Lincoln's tolerance of such impolitic behavior was that he reasoned it would relieve him of the greater consequences of his wife's being constrained. But putting aside the unknown extent of the president's knowledge, the probability remains that he would likely have considered the problem trivial compared to the truly critical political and military issues he was dealing with every hour.

Whatever the qualifying circumstances, the pressures besetting Mary were intense—from an unkind press, from critical Washingtonians, from the battlefield slaughter of her family—and the uninhibited buying might well have helped to maintain the balance she required to carry out her social duties as first lady. But the other side of the ledger was written in widespread criticism of her, by extension of her husband,

and ultimately of the Lincoln administration. Politically speaking, it was normal for her husband to be vilified by the press. Many newspapers, especially those associated with the Copperhead cause, reveled in calling the president an "imbecile," a "gorilla," a "tyrant"—one even came up with "Illinois beast." But it was decidedly not normal, politically or otherwise, for the chief executive's wife to be so insulted, and many administrations would pass before another first lady would receive even a fraction of the abuse the American press heaped on Mary Lincoln.

As happens to most presidents and first ladies, Americans sent the Lincolns thousands of gifts large and small in their White House years. Different from today, in Lincoln's era anything sent to the first family belonged to its recipients; the modern matter of actual or perceived bribery or influence peddling wasn't then a legal issue, and Mary Lincoln made no effort to hide her belief that anything sent to her rightly belonged to her. Most of the gifts were innocuous and well-intentioned—fruit, jams, baked goods, small knit or embroidered items. Many of these things Mary bigheartedly gave away, particularly to hospitals and to the needy. But gifts of substantive value, baubles that were glittery enough or costly enough to appeal to her blackbirdlike affinity, were likely to be kept by her. Mary received bolts of luxurious silks and textiles, jewelry and books, and even sewing machines. Someone sent her a gold brooch with forty-seven stones set in it. It went straight into her jewelry box—and the name of its donor, one William Mortimer, went as quickly onto her list of those benefactors to be "remembered."[3]

As the November 1864 elections neared, Mary told Lizzy Keckly that her personal debts to merchants exceeded $27,000 (the equivalent of perhaps a quarter of a million dollars in today's money), an enormous sum and one exceeding her husband's annual salary as president. One merchant—New York department store owner A. T. Stewart—was now actually threatening to sue the first lady if her debts to him weren't paid (Stewart did not carry out his threat, even though Mary's bills went uncollected). The first lady's fear of this situation, a dilemma having become indisputably grim, began to consume her. In October 1864, an article in the *Illinois State Register* entitled "All About the Domestic Economy of the White House" reported on her immodest buying and called her the most talked-about woman in America.[4] It is little wonder that during the 1864 social season she concentrated on acting as a conscientious hostess in the Executive Mansion in an effort to change this perception and thus to help ensure her husband's reelection.

The first lady's psychobiographer, Dr. W. A. Evans, concluded that Mary's alleged "insanity" in reality represented the mental inability to exercise normal judgment only where it came to money.[5] He noted that the inappropriate buying of unneeded merchandise or articles that she could not afford or that she thought she could finagle other persons into subsidizing for her was bad enough in the White House, but would reach truly astonishing levels only in her seventeen-year-long widowhood.

Other aspects of Mary's personality could be markedly unattractive and brought her understandable if not always justifiable disrespect from many quarters. Her tongue was often as sharp as an adder's, and her jealousy where the president and other women were concerned neither knew limits nor, as we've seen, was in the least justified by Lincoln's consistently faithful behavior. Yet in many respects Mary often acted as the embodiment of civility and kindness, as exemplified by her care for wounded soldiers. Because of its closeness to many of the war's biggest battles, Washington became a city of hospitals during Lincoln's administration. Covering great swaths of the district, enormous cantonment-type infirmaries were filled with thousands of injured and sick men, soldiers who had miraculously managed to get taken from battlefields to the hospitals that provided the era's primitive medical treatment. In many cases, these men were simply put onto cots where their recovery mainly depended on their own body's ability to fight off the infections from which so many of them died. The first lady's greatest wartime acts of benevolence were directed to these bed-bound men.

Occasionally with a friend but usually alone, Mary spent numberless days visiting such patients, most of whom could not receive family visitors because of cost or wartime transportation difficulties. The first lady was not in any sense a trained nurse, her connection with the men consisting merely of a motherly visit to express her concern for them. In many cases, the men did not even know she was the president's wife; Mary made little effort to reveal that, though neither did she hide it. She brought to the sick and injured many of the food packages strangers had sent to the White House, passing out candy and fruit, luxuries the patients were unlikely to have tasted since going to war. She also took baskets of flowers grown in the White House hothouse, gifts that ended by inserting small dashes of color and fragrance into grim wards filled with terrible sights and saturated with the smells of illness and death. Predictably, Southern newspapers mocked Mary's efforts by cuttingly referring to her as "the Yankee nurse."

Few people in the North ever learned of the first lady's hospital work, principally because she would do almost nothing to make it known. The humility she showed in maintaining that her acts of kindness were entirely private is, in the abstract, admirable. But given the flood of negative reporting that described Mary's life, her husband's secretaries were remiss in not seeing that Northern newspaper and magazine readers were presented with her behavior and thus able to judge her wartime actions in a more balanced and charitable light.

Testimonials to Mary's behavior were not uncommon. Shortly after her death, one of the hospitalized soldiers who had been a recipient of her kindness wrote of the first lady's visit: "At the first battle of Fredericksburg I received a painful wound in the face. . . . Among the many who came to the hospital to speak cheering words to the afflicted none was more kind or showed a nobler spirit than the wife of the Chief Magistrate of the Nation. She lives in the memory of those whose agonies she soothed with loving words. Frank G. Thompson."[6]

Another aspect of Mary's that has largely gone unmentioned was her attitude toward African-Americans. In her early life she believed servitude was the natural and right state for black people; as late as 1856 she even apologized to her sister Emilie for her husband's attitudes against slavery. In someone raised in a slave-owning home, such opinions are probably to be expected. But by the White House years, Mary's views had changed strongly to the side of abolition. Perhaps some of this change came because she finally saw a black person—Lizzy Keckly—as a fellow human being and friend rather than as a servant or an unfree possession. Certainly she shared her husband's wartime task in persuading his countrymen to recognize the human worth of black people, and she needed to validate the constant and heavy deaths from a war being waged for emancipation as well as for continued national union. In the end, Mary extended many kindnesses to African-Americans, as when she once urged her husband to contribute $200 for blankets for destitute escaped slaves living in Washington, assuring him that "the cause of humanity requires it."[7]

Many who encountered Mrs. Lincoln during the White House years must have been struck by the paradoxes in her behavior, as was her husband's assistant William Stoddard. For all the negative—sharp, sarcastic, impatient, selfish—faces she showed, her humanity and consideration often shone through. Stoddard wrote of these inconsistencies: "It was not easy, at first, to understand why a lady who could be one day so kindly, so considerate, so generous, so thoughtful and so hopeful, could, upon another day, be so unreasonable, so irritable, so despondent, so even niggardly, and so prone to see the dark, the wrong side of men and women and events."[8] Yet such was the case. Numerous tributes to Mary Lincoln's charity of spirit exist, but many begin with the proviso that the first lady's personality and actions *could* be hard to understand and charitably conclude that no one could have succeeded totally under the demanding circumstances that marked her years in the glare of national publicity. Stoddard allowed that Mary was often "authoritative" in her dealings with people, and that she was quick to judge negatively and to make her negativity known. Yet he admitted that she was "always ready to listen to argument and to yield to plainly put reasons for doing or not doing, provided the arguments come from a recognized friend."[9]

Her contemporary, the then well-known journalist Ben: Perley Poore (a name recognized today mostly for its strange orthography), wrote that the White House had not before been "graced by a lady as well fitted by nature and by education to dispense its hospitalities as it is by Mrs. Lincoln. Her hospitality is only equaled by her charity, and her graceful deportment by her goodness of heart."[10] In her duties as hostess of the president's house, by and large Mary was—primarily excepting the period after Willie's death—a commendable consort to Abraham Lincoln. Even in public affairs unconnected to her role as first lady, she would speak out when she saw the need. To the governor of New York Mary wrote about a woman convicted of manslaughter who had been incarcerated in Sing Sing prison. "I think *her* entitled to your clemency. She must have acted under the influence of a mind, distrait, besides there is but little evidence, that she contemplated or committed the deed, she is punished for. Pray, let me know, if my signature to a petition for mercy, with other names of respectability, will induce you to remit her sentence." Whatever the merits of her appeal, it was surely sincere, and she made it while mourning the loss of her own son.[11]

GRANT

Excluding only Willie's death, for Lincoln the first half of 1864 represented the most devastating days of his presidency. Francis Carpenter, an artist who was painting Lincoln's portrait in those weeks, remembered that "he hardly ever slept at all" and found him one morning with "great black rings under his eyes, his head bent forward upon his breast, altogether such a picture of the effects of sorrow, care, and anxiety."[12] The war with its simultaneous battles was now total, with pitilessly lethal combat occurring somewhere nearly every day. The Confederate armies weren't winning the war, but neither were they yet showing an inability to keep fighting. Nor, despite increasingly desperate conditions in the South, particularly growing famine in the cities, were Jefferson Davis's people pressing their government for a peace that they know would amount to the loss of their independence and the ending of the slave system. In the North, the draft had become ever more onerous: During February the president ordered up a half million additional inductees, men taken from ploughs and lathes and ledgers, not to mention from their families. Moreover, the new draftees lent the peace factions enormous moral weight. Closer to home, Lincoln was plagued by the machinations and ambitions of his cabinet, particularly Treasury Secretary Chase's virtually transparent attempt to run for the presidency by capturing the Republican nomination for the fall election. And even though the president had gained a brilliant new general, one who he believed would succeed where other commanding generals had failed, the spring campaigns would prove to be the worst and most dispiriting catastrophes for Northern arms since the conflict had begun.

A few festive occasions at the White House lifted some of the gloom. One of the brightest came on March 8 with the Executive Mansion's most anticipated social event of the season. That night Lincoln received Ulysses S. Grant, his newly created lieutenant general, the lofty three-star rank unused since being held by George Washington himself. The general promised that he could not be persuaded to run for president (McClellan was preparing to do just that on the Democratic ticket, and Lincoln didn't want another commander embracing such ambitions), and with Lincoln's mind thus relieved he appointed the astonishingly successful West Pointer to head the Union's armies. On the night of the party, Grant was without a dress uniform (he had supposedly lost the key to his trunk) and arrived at the White House to be shown off to the cream of Washington society in his grimy traveling uniform. The underdressed general turned his appearance into a kind of coup de théâtre by dazzling the well-fed crowd in a uniform still infused with the tang of war.

The diminutive Grant entered the crowded reception room through a heavy throng that parted for him as he walked forward to greet his host. When Lincoln saw him, he happily exclaimed, "Why, here is General Grant! Well, this is a great pleasure I assure you." After the president introduced him to the first lady and the secretary of state, he led the diminutive but handsome general into the East Room. There he asked Grant to climb onto a sofa so the crowd that quickly gathered could more easily see the star of the evening. The next day Lincoln formally presented Grant with his appointment as general-in-chief of the armies, the president clearly pleased that the Union's prospects of eventual victory seemed to have just taken a giant step forward.

Grant was not, as it turned out, to find immediate military success. Throughout May and June 1864, the new commander led federal forces in a quartet of vast and blood-spattered clashes in Virginia, with losses so great that they threatened to extinguish Lincoln's chances in the upcoming presidential vote. Fighting at the Wilderness, Spotsylvania, North Anna, and Cold Harbor represented killing on a nearly genocidal level. Under Grant's dogged direction in May, Union armies began a massive push southward into Virginia in an effort to destroy Lee's great Army of Northern Virginia. Though the North's superiority in numbers should have led to victory, the South's greater determination kept it from doing so. In a thickly wooded tangle called the Wilderness—the terrain was so clotted with trees and brush that the clash was described as "a battle which no man saw or could see"—Grant suffered twenty-six thousand men killed or wounded in a single week, the number greatly exceeding Lee's losses. The grown-over Wilderness battlefield actually caught fire from the concentrated musket flashes, a holocaust killing off many men who were only injured and consuming countless already dead bodies trapped in woods that had been transformed into a gigantic open oven. When Mary Lincoln learned of the circumstances surrounding the battle, she castigated Grant because of his profligacy with human life, calling him "a butcher . . . not fit to be at the head of an army." Even the president was appalled at the losses; one observer during these days described the distraught Lincoln as "pacing back and forth . . . great black rings under his eyes."

But Grant re-formed his forces and pushed on against the general he knew would have to be destroyed to defeat the Confederacy. Thus the next killing stop was Spotsylvania, where the campaign's slaughter continued. With both sides fighting tenaciously, the federals remained unable to defeat Lee's men, though Lee was equally incapable of stopping Grant's southward progress through Virginia. The bloodbath at Spotsylvania cost the North an additional eighteen thousand casualties, the South somewhere around two-thirds of that figure, with this immense carnage generated in just eleven days. As after the fighting at the Wilderness, countless numbers of ambulance wagons turned back toward Washington, bearing down on hospitals where they would debouch thousands of maimed men who could look forward to having limbs cut off or seeing festering abdominal wounds morph into always fatal gangrene.

The competing armies met again only two days after the fighting at Spotsylvania stopped, this time at the North Anna River, south of Fredericksburg. Unshakable in his resolve to destroy Lee's army, Grant tried again to overwhelm Lee's defense, but again failed. Yet Grant continued on. Elements in blue and in gray kept skirmishing until the Northern forces captured a little crossroads town called Cold Harbor, near the Chickahominy River and just ten miles outside the Confederate capital of Richmond, a city whose capture Grant knew would represent a symbolic victory of incalculable magnitude.

It was in this nearly anonymous Virginia backwater where Grant's brutal campaign to defeat Lee reached its climax. At Cold Harbor the fighting lasted through the first three days of June, with Grant trying once more to overpower Lee's seemingly undefeatable army. The violence at Cold Harbor was unparalleled. On June 3, the last day of fighting, the rebels killed or wounded twelve thousand Union soldiers in a single eight-minute spasm. Still Grant failed. Cold Harbor was his costliest clash, and it brought the total casualties in two weeks of fighting to defeat Lee to fifty-four thousand Union dead and wounded, a figure that just about equaled the size of Lee's entire army.[13]

THE CONVENTION

Desperate for news of success, Lincoln sat in the White House receiving instead reports of these staggering losses, profoundly aware that responsibility for them ended at his own desk. To add to his troubles, he was now widely blamed for putting a butcher in charge of the federal offensive against Lee's forces. And deeply politically worrying for the president given the horror of Grant's casualty lists, the Republican Convention was about to convene in Baltimore.

Seen in retrospect, Lincoln's renomination was probably never in serious peril. Most members of his own party felt they had already paid too high a price in blood to see the war effort jeopardized by another president. But the splinter Radical Republicans, who witheringly regarded Lincoln as weak and a bumbler, nonetheless attempted to choose a candidate more to their liking. Knowing they stood little chance of dumping Lincoln at the real convention, they instead met in a faux convention at Cleveland and there chose John C. Frémont to oppose Lincoln in November (and, of course, an as-yet-undetermined Democratic candidate). The Radicals pressed for, among other things, a one-term presidency and a constitutional amendment prohibiting slavery—and, most extreme of their demands, a confiscation of Confederate property and distribution of all such captured loot among the veterans of the victorious federal army. Though the majority of Northerners viewed Frémont and this platform without much seriousness, the Radicals did their utmost to smear the president by emphasizing the "fractured" state of the Republican Party.

Lincoln prevailed easily at the authentic Republican Convention in Baltimore, despite some underhanded machinations by Salmon Chase, his own ambitious treasury secretary. Chase tried to put his own name forward by not very quietly endorsing the view that his boss was unqualified to remain as president. But the real story coming out of the Republican powwow revolved around the vice presidency. Lincoln had never had much to do with Hannibal Hamlin, yet neither had he had any real trouble from him. About the worst that the president could say of his vice president was that his views were considerably more radical than his own when it came to slavery and how reconstruction would be structured in the defeated South. But the Republicans believed they would fare better in the fall election by installing a "war Democrat" on the bottom of their ticket, an arrangement not as strange as it sounds given that the Republicans were, after all, touting themselves as a Union party that was, in theory, meant to embody the entire pro-war range of Northern political sentiment.

The convention managers sounded out Lincoln about dumping Hamlin, and the president's lukewarm response effectively ended his vice president's chances of remaining on the ticket. Lincoln wired the convention, "Wish not to interfere about V.P. . . . Can not interfere with platform." With that, the delegates went ahead in mulling over a successor to Hamlin, the most eligible possibility seeming to be the Democrat Andrew Johnson of Tennessee, that seceded state's military governor and the only Southern senator who, because he believed his state should have remained in the Union, declined to vacate his seat in the Confederate exodus from Congress in 1861. But Johnson *was* unambiguously a Southerner and believed Lincoln was wrong to change the war's emphasis from preserving the Union to freeing the slaves. His Tennessee roots naturally gave him a deep sympathy if not for the South's secessionist cause then at least for the region's misery. That sympathy would within a year come up against a Radical-dominated Congress whose pity for *anything* Southern was just about nonexistent. But in the summer of 1864 Johnson's supporters had little trouble persuading the convention that he would make a better—or, at least, a more valuable—vice president than Hamlin, and on the third round of voting the onetime tailor from Tennessee won the nomination for the Republican ticket's second spot.

Lincoln's part in his vice president's "deselection," as it were, proved controversial to history. Some at the convention wrote that Lincoln had "ordered" Johnson to be placed on the ticket, though no one ever produced any conclusive proof of the allegation. Hamlin's grandson would later blame it on the efforts of Charles Sumner, one of the most radical of Republican senators, and carried out against the president's true wishes. More likely, Lincoln simply didn't greatly care about the man who would fill the second office. He had, after all, never included Hamlin in his inner councils and would probably not have done so with Johnson either (assuming he had lived longer than the one month after Johnson's swearing in as vice president). What many historians believe is that if Lincoln had been intent on keeping his original vice president, then Hamlin would have remained on the ticket in his second term. And history would, undoubtedly, have played very much differently than it did under President Andrew Johnson.

THE SOUTH

While Lincoln was bedeviled with concerns over his top commander's staggeringly costly failures in Virginia and what the country would do about a second term, Southern society and infrastructure were starting to crumble into dust. The North's overwhelming matériel advantage was flowing over the South like an unstoppable sea of mud, sucking the breath from its cities as well as from its backwaters. Granted, the North was winning principally because it was bigger, and not because its fighting forces were better or its morale greater, notwithstanding Grant's tenacity in the East and Sherman's brilliance in the Western theater and more lately in Georgia. Yet despite Davis's armies remaining the match—indeed often the superior—of Lincoln's forces, life could now unambiguously be seen flowing without cease from every corner of the Confederacy.

By mid-1864 a large part of the South's determination to press on with the war was built on the fervent hope that the North would turn Lincoln out of office in its fall election, with a "peace" candidate being elected in his stead. The Copperheads and other factions opposed to the war controlled many of the North's newspapers, and most had become particularly opposed to Lincoln since he had shifted his justification for the war from union to emancipation, with such journals forcefully demanding a change of administration in Washington. The phenomenon was, of course, music to desperate Southern ears, giving the rebels hope for a negotiated peace with Lincoln's successor, permitting the breakaway states to leave the Union. With Lee's extraordinarily dogged defense against Grant in northern Virginia, Lincoln's defeat still seemed a rational hope to at least a part of the Confederate leadership.

Reality was a different thing. In the West, the forces in gray were being eaten alive by Yankee armies, with more avenues continually being opened through which to pierce the Confederacy's defenses from its Western flanks. But it was the North's naval blockade that represented the most immediate threat to the rebellion's future. All along the coastal margins of the South (and more lately along the Mississippi River as well), the North exercised a nearly unimpeded capacity to stop the Confederacy from being resupplied with anything. Most critically for the life of the Southern people, that meant food. And that reality translated not only into starvation for much of the region's population—though people in the countryside remained somewhat better fed than did city dwellers—but also, with the scandalously high prices being paid for black-market staples, monetary inflation and the quickening destruction of the Southern currency and thus of the Confederacy's economic foundations. Even Lee was now admitting that collapse was "only a matter of time."[14] Most stunning, the South's own "peace movement" had begun to gather momentum, particularly in North Carolina and Georgia, adding one more complication for President Davis in warding off the disintegration facing his collection of disparate states.

Like so many families in both halves of the war-immersed nation, the Davises—Jefferson, his wife Varina, and their young children—drew on their home life for the strength to get through the trial. After endless days and nights micromanaging the war from the study in his Richmond presidential mansion, a residence known on both sides of the Mason and Dixon Line as the Southern White House, Davis looked to the warmth his family provided to gird himself for the stresses of his position. Only this past February, the president had survived a Union army attempt on his life.

But tragedy entered even the family's private space. That spring of 1864, with Grant bearing down on Lee with the might of an avenging horde, the Davises faced in their own home a portion of the misery confronting their Southern "nation," a misfortune that had, in a sickening coincidence, struck the Yankees' own first family just two years earlier. In April, with his wife seven months pregnant and his commanding general still barely preventing the federals from capturing the capital, much of Davis's spirit and morale miraculously remained intact. On the last day of the month, all that changed. That Saturday Varina Davis left the White House shortly before noon, her errand the thoughtful gesture of taking a homemade lunch to her husband at his downtown working office. Soon after Varina's departure, the Davises' five-year-old son, Joe, did what most five-year-olds do at one time or another and got himself into a perilous position. Joe thought it would be fun to balance himself on top of the porch balustrade surrounding the mansion, something he had been strictly warned against because of the long drop to the garden below. According to a witness, he appeared to be taking slow and careful steps so as not to lose his balance, but his footing failed him and he fell. The boy landed on his head and shoulder, breaking his neck, and within the hour was dead.

Like Mary Lincoln after Willie's death, Varina mourned deeply, pressed down with grief. And President Davis, who had himself taught his second child to ride and who had spent what few off-duty moments he could spare playing with his son, was equally devastated at the family's loss. Joe Davis's funeral attracted thousands of congregants, becoming one of the most poignant such gatherings in the short history of the Confederacy. The mourners paraded from the Southern White House to St. Paul's Church, ending at the burial in the city's Hollywood Cemetery. Flocks of children from the neighborhood carried tree boughs in Joe's memory. A woman remarked of the president's appearance that he looked to be "the saddest man she had ever seen,"[15] much the same that was said of Lincoln at Willie's funeral. Though later the pregnant first lady safely gave birth to a daughter, whom the couple named Winnie, the family tragedy and the declining fortunes of the Confederacy made the Richmond White House a dismal home. To mark Joe's death, the president wrote a note to his wife apologizing for the misery they had suffered over such a long part of their marriage. "This is not the fate to which I invited [you] when the fortunes were rose-colored to us both," he said, "but I know you will bear it even better than myself."[16]

THE PRESIDENT'S DAYS

With the army under Grant's new and forceful command (though the general's staggering casualty rate made his leadership widely unpopular), Lincoln felt freer to return to the everyday minutiae of the presidency.

Despite Nicolay's and Hay's efforts to protect their boss's time and energy from the supplicants who had long beset Lincoln, a daily flow of visitors still filled the corridor outside his office, and the president continued to regard it as an unshirkable duty to see as many as possible of the people who had business with him. Serious issues remained concerning Lincoln's security, most pointedly the ease with which dangerous persons were able to approach the president. On March 28 a man named Francis Xavier reached the president's office through, presumably, the normal process of simply presenting himself. But once in front of Lincoln, Xavier immediately launched into a harangue, attempting to prove that he himself was the real chief executive, since he had duly been elected to the office in 1856.[17] The unambiguous peril was, of course, the risk of such a troubled person being armed.

A part of the president's time was still spent on formalities, such as officially marking red-letter days in the lives and dynasties of foreign leaders, a social obligation that Lincoln believed helped the United States remain in other nations' good graces. On one typical day in August 1864, Lincoln signed a proclamation of congratulations to King Charles XV of Sweden and Norway on the marriage of Prince Nicolas Auguste; offered written condolences to Emperor Francis Joseph I of Austria on the death of the archduchess Hildegarde; congratulated King Leopold of the Belgians in writing on the birth of a granddaughter; and did the same for King William I of Prussia on a daughter born to Princess Antonie. Later on that same day, he interviewed the president of the North Western Railroad, after which he gave instructions to a number of cabinet officers. Probably most important in his mind was his next task of writing a letter to Grant suggesting that "putting our army south of the enemy," the course the general had followed that spring in the Wilderness, Spotsylvania, and Cold Harbor campaigns, "will neither be done nor attempted unless you watch it every day, and hour, and force it."[18] There were, undoubtedly, many more such items of business that day that went unnoted in the official diary of his presidency, but these provide a sampling of what he was constantly facing in the White House.

Happily for Lincoln, Tad intimately shared his father's life in those troubling months of 1864, excepting only when the first lady took the boy on one of her trips northward to shop or vacation in the resorts of New England. The president happily allowed his son nearly unlimited access to himself, unself-consciously opening his arms to scoop Tad onto his lap whether the president was greeting visitors, planning strategy with his generals, or working on policy issues with cabinet officers. Few who saw father and son together failed to notice the extraordinary mutual love between the two, and only the most self-important of visitors begrudged Tad's sometimes noisy presence.

On a personal level, on February 10, 1864, the Lincolns suffered another enormously hurtful shock to the family, reviving the heartbreaking memories of Willie's loss. The president's private stables, a brick structure standing between the White House and the Treasury building, caught fire. When Lincoln saw the flames from his upstairs window, he immediately realized the danger to the pony that had belonged to his dead son. The president ran outdoors, jumped over a boxwood hedge between the mansion and the stables, and tried to open the burning building's door. But the flames and heat drove him back, and it was sadly too late to save the animals trapped inside the building.[19] The family lost not only the horses that pulled their carriage, but Tad's ponies and John Nicolay's bay as well. But the loss that most affected Lincoln was Willie's pony, which had delighted his son in the early days in the White House. Lincoln was later seen standing in East Room looking out the windows at the still smoldering ruins, tears rolling down the deep furrows on his face.[20] A coachman who had been dismissed that day was arrested and charged with starting the fire, but the man proved his innocence. The ruins of the stables were immediately swept away, and a replacement was built farther south on the White House grounds.[21]

SOLDIERS' HOME

On Independence Day, the first family arrived at the Soldiers' Home to begin their third—and last—stay in their summer residence. The first lady had just returned from New York, bringing back her soon-to-be graduated son for a family reunion. Mary was likely happy to be taking up residence once more in the gingerbread cottage set among the shady trees and elderly veterans, having earlier in the year ordered a freshening up of the house at a cost of several thousand dollars. Eight of its fourteen rooms were repapered, the floors and windows cleaned and repainted, new lace curtains hung, and a matting of coconut-husk grass laid, the latter expected to keep the house cooler than did the old carpeting. In addition, some of the worn furniture was spruced up with new covers.[22]

On the first evening at the Soldiers' Home, Robert accompanied his father into Washington for a nighttime bill-signing session in the Capitol in what was surely a pleasant chance for the pair to draw nearer to each other's life. But despite such visits with his parents, Robert and the president remained distant. The Harvard student was now a man fully capable of living on his own and thus away from his family, though his mother continued to look forward to his visits and was grateful for his company. With his commencement from Harvard coming up shortly— for which Robert very much wished, in vain, that his father would be present—the son had to decide where he would go as an independent man and what he wanted his relationship with his family to be.

The issue of army service stood foremost in his mind. Robert continued to be subject to public disapproval for remaining a civilian, criticism that he realized would only increase now that he was finally finishing at Harvard. Robert could, of course, have joined the service at any time, even without parental permission. Yet he abided by his mother's wishes, while at the same time understanding the reality that if he was killed or badly wounded, it would represent an almost mortal blow to his father, making the president's arduous life even harder. Robert discussed his family situation with a friend, recalling a brief conversation with his father in which the president had asked what Robert was going to do after college. According to Robert, he replied, "As long as you object to my joining the army, I am going back to Harvard to study law." "If you do," the president answered, "you should learn more than I ever did, but you will never have so good a time." Robert commented that it was "the only advice I had from my father as to my career."[23] Evidently the president was still willing to sustain criticism rather than have his son go into uniform.

Much later in his life Robert remarked on another factor that could have governed Lincoln's reluctance to have him join the army. Referring to his civilian status, in 1915 Robert wrote that "something might happen to me [if in uniform] that would cause him more official embarrassment than could be offset by any possible value of my military service."[24] Robert was referring, of course, to being captured by the enemy. It could be surmised, however, that such an eventuality might have brought the president substantial sympathy, as opposed to Robert's continued civilian status, which provoked an unmeasurable but surely substantial degree of public hostility. But Lincoln himself in all probability believed that his wife's feelings really decided the issue. Assigning the responsibility to Mary, he reportedly once snapped at his wife in exasperation, "Many a poor mother, Mary, has had to make this sacrifice and has given up every son she had—and lost them all." In truth, of course, Robert's civilian status was a gift to both his mother *and* his father.

Less than a week after the family had moved into the Soldiers' Home cottage, their private difficulties were subordinated to a threat to the president's security. At the insistence of Secretary Stanton, at ten o'clock on the evening of Sunday, July 10, the Lincolns were made to quickly pack up and return to the safety of the White House. Stanton's urgings were based on intelligence that Washington's northern suburbs—including the grounds containing the Lincolns' summer residence—had suddenly come under a serious Confederate threat. Although the unexpected dislocation annoyed the president, he accepted his trusted war secretary's assessment.

The Confederate mischief maker was General Jubal Early, a corpulent, aging, and astonishingly shaggy-bearded Virginian. What he was missing in comeliness was, however, more than compensated for by personal bravado. Early believed the capture of Washington lay within his power, since the Army of the Potomac had left the federal capital wide-open when it pulled out of the city to chase Lee into Virginia. Indeed, most of Grant's army was now besieging Petersburg, leaving Washington with only light protection against attack, a substantial threat to the capital given the enormous value that capturing the city still represented to the Confederate cause. Early might also have seen an attack on Washington as a good way to induce Grant to dispatch a few of his units northward, thereby taking some of the federal pressure off Petersburg, a development Washingtonians had worried about since Grant's main army had headed south in the spring. To be sure, since the beginning of July rebel units roaming around the isolated northern perimeter of the District had kept many a Washingtonian awake at night. Early's presence near the capital infuriated the president, who believed it would embarrass the government coming so soon before the elections.

As mentioned earlier, because Washington's safety had been considered a matter of incalculable importance, the army had been ordered to build a barrier of forts around the city. Frequently strengthened, the fiftysome wooden citadels forming a thirty-seven-mile-long necklace were connected with one another by lines of trenches and provided the District with probably the most secure fortifications on earth. On the surface, it seemed foolhardy for Early to believe he could break the chain and seize the enemy's greatest prize. But Washington did still contain a few breaches of safety. Not only did the departure of Grant's forces into Virginia contribute to the danger—most of the best units were with Grant—but the supposed absence of rebel troops north of the Potomac had long lent Washingtonians a sense of complacency regarding the Confederate threat to the city. Even the Potomac bridges into the capital remained in iffy hands; the officer in charge of the Chain Bridge "thought" the bridge was mined and could be blown up if threatened, but wasn't really sure.

When one Union officer at Baltimore—General Lew Wallace, who would a decade and a half later become famous as the author of *Ben-Hur*—got wind that some twenty thousand Confederate soldiers were menacing areas of Maryland north of the District, he went out to meet and engage them. The clash came on the Monocacy River, where the rebels got the best of the federal force, compelling the latter to withdraw. But the Union effort achieved one saving grace in that it delayed Early for a day, a precious twenty-four hours allowing the District's defenders to strengthen their forces. Ignoring the small reprieve for his enemy, Early's troops went straight from the Monocacy to follow the Georgetown Pike, forming what amounted to a loaded pistol aimed directly at Washington's heart.

Thus the situation stood that Sunday when the secretary of war sent the carriage out to the Soldiers' Home to bring the Lincolns into the city and the safety of the heavily protected White House. John Hay later wrote of the unusual commotion the move brought, recalling when shortly after midnight his friend Robert Lincoln awakened him as he entered his room. Noah Brooks also wrote about the danger, noting that Assistant Secretary of the Navy Augustus Fox ordered a ship to be kept ready for the first family's evacuation.[25] Ominously, even the presidential guards were ordered to report to the fortifications, where they would face actual hostile fire for the first time in their service.[26]

Although the Confederates managed to get within sight of the Capitol dome and frightened thousands of Washington's residents with their gunfire, the threat to the city was short-lived. The rebels had centered most of the action on Fort Stevens, the northernmost of the string of defensive fortifications surrounding the city and the one closest to the Soldiers' Home. On Monday morning, elements of Grant's Sixth and Nineteenth corps disembarked from steamers on the Potomac wharves, the officers immediately forming their units of fresh troops and sending them up Seventh Street toward Early's reported positions. Scores of civilians followed along behind Grant's soldiers, eager to see what was going on and maybe even catch a glimpse of real fighting. At around four o'clock that afternoon the president himself appeared at Fort Stevens, impatient to check out the action and to personally inform the men that reinforcements were on the way. When Lincoln popped his head over a parapet for a better view of the battlefield, he was immediately reproached by a nearby officer, who yelled at the commander in chief, "Get down, you fool!" Legend has it that the officer was Lieutenant Colonel Oliver Wendell Holmes, the future Supreme Court justice.

Three more federal brigades arrived in Washington the next day, ending all real danger to Washington. Still, Early had been able to create a small firestorm, and his cutting of the telegraph wires between Washington and Baltimore gave the city's inhabitants a brief but frightening sense of isolation, as did the disrupted rail lines, which for a short period prevented mail and newspapers from the north getting into the city. Expecting that Early's "siege" might last longer, some Washington merchants disgraced themselves by marking up their prices on flour and potatoes to famine rates.[27] About the only part of the population that found anything agreeable in this affair were the "secesh," the Southern sympathizers who remained in Washington and gloated over every Confederate victory and kept their hopes alive that Lee's army would yet come riding triumphantly down Pennsylvania Avenue.

Lincoln may have commanded the federal armies in the constitutional sense, but he hadn't yet personally seen any fighting except for his brief visit to Fort Stevens the prior day. So late on Tuesday afternoon, he and a small but distinguished group of guests—some cabinet members and congressmen, as well as the first lady and a few of her women friends—rode out to Fort Stevens. Long-range elements of

Early's forces were still firing in and around the fort. A general gave an order for his men to charge from the parapet in the direction of the firing, the exciting scene causing the civilian notables to clap and shout in delight.

Early and his men faded off into the Maryland hinterland before crossing the upper Potomac and escaping back into Virginia. In August, Grant ordered his subordinate General Philip Sheridan to seek out and destroy Early's force. The episode was not free of tragedy: Significant numbers of federal soldiers died as a result of Early's audacious maneuver, especially at General Wallace's fight at Monocacy Creek. Probably the most lasting negative effect from Early's raid was the blow to the North's growing hope that the war's end was imminent. On the positive side, however, the rebels were no longer seen as able to threaten truly important Union targets.

A chilling souvenir of the rebel assault on Washington was found in the flyleaf of a book near Early's headquarters at Blair House, in Silver Spring, Maryland. It was a note addressed to the president: "Near Washington, July 12, 1864. Now Uncle Abe, you had better be quiet the balance of your Administration, as we came near your town this time to show you what we could do. But if you go on in your mad career, we will come again soon, and then you had better stand from under. Yours respectfully, the worst rebel you ever saw, Fifty-eighth Virginia Infantry." We don't know if Lincoln ever received the message.[28]

CHASE

It wasn't only the war and Mary that continued to challenge Lincoln's days. Since the beginning of his presidency, the cabinet had probably given the president more grief than it had useful counsel. And now, in the fourth year of his term, no cabinet officer distressed Lincoln more than did his treasury secretary, Salmon Chase.

Vastly annoyed at having been pushed aside for the 1860 Republican nomination by the young upstart Lincoln, Chase, or "Salmon the Solemn" as wags called him for his puritanism and passionate religiosity, spent considerable time and effort in devising ways to demonstrate his superiority over the chief executive. In the first half of 1864, Chase believed he stood a good chance of besting Lincoln for their party's nomination at Baltimore and barely tried to hide his politicking to gain the candidacy. In any administration, undermining the chief executive is, of course, regarded as disloyalty to the president, and so it was by Lincoln, in spite of his inclination to ignore untoward behavior in the name of cabinet solidarity. After Chase's latest wave of defiance came to the president's attention, the secretary attempted to avoid responsibility by blaming his friends' "overzealousness," claiming that he himself was merely a "reluctant candidate." There is little doubt, though, that had Chase been able to snag the nomination, he would shamelessly have done so. In the meantime, he made an effort to keep in Lincoln's good graces by asking for his name to be withdrawn from consideration at the convention. The power of a president's incumbency proved insurmountable, regardless of the widespread disapproval of Lincoln's direction of the war *and* for the president's "dictating" of social policy. In the end, Chase failed to even come close to unseating Lincoln. Senator Benjamin Wade of Ohio remarked on the treasury secretary's misplaced self-confidence, calling Chase's "theology unsound—he thinks there is a fourth person in the Trinity."[29]

Earlier that spring Chase had lost much of the political capital that had likely prompted the president to, at least temporarily, swallow his secretary's backstabbing. The federal paper money (popularly called greenbacks) the treasury secretary had instituted for the first time in history took the place of gold, a maneuver that importantly allowed government spending on the war without its having to pay its debts from the federal gold reserves. But because of inflation, greenbacks were losing their value while the price of gold was skyrocketing. On top of this brewing inflationary crisis, cases of Treasury Department corruption resulted in several of that agency's officials being put away in the Old Capitol prison. And though unconnected with Chase's own unblemished private life, another investigation exposed unseemly relations between male Treasury employees and the department's female clerks. Though Congress was able to squelch the latter findings (the least it could do for Chase given that the legislature had been responsible for inflation by failing to raise sufficient taxes to pay for the staggering costs of running a war), some of the odor from the scandal's publicity rubbed off on the secretary.[30]

Though Chase offered the president his written resignation, Lincoln refused it—but he didn't give the letter back. Instead, he care-fully stashed it in his desk against the day he *would* see fit to accept it. After the summer's nominating convention, the president finally did see fit. In effect, he fired his troublesome Treasury chief. On June 30, Lincoln wrote Chase a letter that was, by the president's standards, uncharacteristically blunt: "You and I have reached a point of mutual embarrassment in our official relation which it seems cannot be over-come, or longer sustained, consistently with the public service."[31] Though Chase's friends tried to persuade the president to retain Chase, Lincoln no longer believed that removing this burr from under his saddle would cause any damage to either the country or his admin-istration. He moved quickly to name a replacement. After a misstep in nominating and then withdrawing a hard-money man who the presi-dent discovered wanted to get rid of the inflationary greenbacks and take the country back to gold, Lincoln swiftly chose Maine senator William P. Fessenden. Fessenden said he would rather have remained a senator than become a political department head, but he loyally ac-quiesced to the president's wishes and said he would accept the office. The Senate confirmed the legislator in the probably record time of two minutes.

Ironically, Chase's future bore a great prize, the most glittering gift the nation has to bestow on a citizen other than the presidency itself, and one given him by none other than his nemesis. Lincoln may have been disgusted with Chase's inconstancy as a cabinet officer, but that didn't mean that he would ignore his undoubted intelligence and the service he was still capable of rendering the country. Following the Oc-tober death of Chief Justice Roger Taney, Lincoln forwarded Chase's name for chief justice of the United States, which position the former treasury secretary would hold, with untarnished probity, until his death from a paralytic stroke in 1873. Nicolay commented on this instance of Lincoln's generosity in a letter to his fiancée: "Probably no man other than Lincoln would have had . . . the degree of magnanimity to thus for-give and exalt a rival who had so deeply and so unjustifiably intrigued against him." The president's secretary called it "another most marked illustration of the greatness of the President, in this age of little men."[32] It wasn't *entirely* magnanimity that argued for Chase's new appointment. Lincoln astutely reasoned that as a probably long-serving chief justice,

Chase, a political Radical, would likely uphold two of Lincoln's administration's most important accomplishments should they someday be constitutionally threatened: the issuance of paper money as legal tender in place of gold and the emancipation of the slaves.

THE PRESIDENT IN THE WHITE HOUSE

"Everything is darkness and doubt and discouragement," Nicolay worryingly wrote in late August. And so depressed had Lincoln become at the war situation and his chances for reelection that he echoed his secretary's fears in the following letter: "This morning, as for some days past, it seems exceedingly probable that this Administration will not be re-elected. Then it will be my duty to co-operate with the President elect, as to save the Union between the election and the inauguration; as he will have secured his election on such ground that he can not possibly save it afterwards." He asked each cabinet member to sign the envelope in which he secured the document, though he allowed none of the men to actually read it, then put it in his desk to await the nation's decision in November. Fortunately for the nation, the gloom that prompted this painful letter was about to evaporate in an almost miraculous turnaround.

Lincoln didn't know it, but that summer his reelection prospects were really being settled in Georgia. While Grant had set siege to Petersburg as the prelude to eventually capturing the nearby Confederate capital, and while doing so had found the task both slow and deadly, the general's chief subordinate was preparing to seize the Deep South's most important commercial and transportation metropolis: Atlanta. William T. Sherman had cobbled together an army of some one hundred thousand men and, at the start of the Atlanta campaign, said to his quartermaster, "I'm going to move on Joe Johnston [the Confederate general he faced] the day Grant telegraphs me he is going to hit Bobby Lee. And if you don't have my army supplied, we'll eat your mules up sir; eat your mules up!"[33]

And that was pretty much how General Sherman fought the battle that would finally portend a foreseeable and certain end to the Confederacy. It had started out badly for Sherman when a Union attack at Kennesaw Mountain near Marietta, Georgia, was brutally repelled by the rebels at great cost to the federals. But at headlong speed and with hideous casualties on both sides, Sherman fell like an avenging angel on his heavily defended main target. Jefferson Davis wanted his army to save the Georgia capital at all costs, in the same way he demanded Lee save Richmond. In the Southern president's still searching mind, a pair of Confederate victories in these cities would so demoralize a war-weary North that the federals would finally allow the South to go its own way and end the war. Just as Lee appeared to be succeeding against Grant, so at first it seemed the rebel armies might well defeat Sherman. But by the beginning of September, the onslaught of Northern strength proved to be unstoppable against the brave but exhausted Confederate forces. On September 2, Sherman wired Washington, "Atlanta is ours, and fairly won." Together the opposing armies lost about forty thousand men in the struggle for the city.

The historical importance of Atlanta's loss was that it ensured Lincoln's reelection, and *that* ensured the continuation of the war and the end of any question of a negotiated peace that would either meet Confederate goals or fall short of the Union's peace requirements. Until Atlanta's fall, a chance remained—its degree is unknowable, though it was probably never large—that the Democratic candidate would defeat Lincoln in the November election. In such a happenstance, the South would probably not only have been cheered on to one last great push, but the new president in Washington might also have been forced by the constituency that had elected him to reach some kind of "arrangement" with the Confederate "nation." Such a compromise could possibly have meant an end to war if the South were accorded a "special" status in the Union permitting slavery to continue (at least for some specified additional number of years, likely to be measured in decades). All this ended when the rebellion lost Atlanta.

These late-summer events at last began to take some of the overwhelming pressure off Lincoln. The move into the Soldiers' Home cottage had gotten him away—at least, in the evenings—and acted as a balm to the president's harried spirits, relieving him of the constant interruptions by those who looked to the president for relief, even though most of such people did bear problems that were tragically real. Whatever additional pleasure he derived from his wife's company, though, would be denied him for a large part of this climactic wartime summer. In early August Mary took Tad, left her husband, and again boarded a train for the Northeast, this time bound for Manchester, Vermont, and its soothingly peaceful Equinox Hotel. She remained in New England for nearly a month and a half, declining to return to Washington until September 18.

Since Willie's death the Lincolns' marriage had grown dangerously frayed. Lincoln was so utterly immersed in the war, and so totally indifferent to his wife's pathetic concerns about status and standing and clothing and perceived snubs and raging hatreds, that he simply no longer turned to her either for empathy or for sympathy. Mary's growing mental instability had tragically distorted her own life, making her distrustful of many of those in her husband's political orbit and wounded by the hateful press criticism she continued to endure. All of this—the deaths of so many of the people she loved and the constant worries about her debts—clouded her mind to the degree that she couldn't see that her behavior had become a significant obstacle to her family's happiness and to her husband's political well-being.

Nicolay and Hay continued during the summer to live in their second-floor bedroom at the White House, and after Mary left for New England, Lincoln relied more than ever on these two men for companionship. They did not accompany the family to the Soldiers' Home, though, an intrusion Mary would have found intolerable given her strained relationship with the pair. Helped by the secretaries, Lincoln often worked late evenings at the White House rather than return to the country house he occupied alone in his wife's absence. Though the secretaries were far from universally popular with the president's official visitors—Nicolay was regarded by many as particularly irksome because of his cold attitude and overeagerness to shield Lincoln from what he considered to be "unimportant" callers—they seemed to form a perfect fit with their boss. Because the draft-age Hay was touchy about remaining out of uniform, Lincoln saw to it that he was given a commission as a major, rank that was socially helpful to the young secretary in performing the many sensitive duties the president assigned him. The physically fragile senior secretary might well have been exempted from service even had he wished to take up uniform. Lincoln often sent Nicolay around the country on delicate political errands, with the implication that his trusted assistant was to some extent to view the trips as vacation time in which to recoup flagging energies.

In the president's mind, probably the single greatest quality the two men bore him was their loyalty, an absolute, unqualified allegiance to a boss both secretaries had long since come to worship. During Lincoln's life, the things he told his young assistants in confidence were never divulged, or leaked, by either. Undoubtedly Lincoln was emotionally closer to both than he was to his eldest son, whose counsel or advice scant evidence suggests Lincoln ever solicited. The president depended on his secretaries' closeness and their ability to understand what he needed from such extremely critical servants, so much so that Lincoln would sometimes even discuss the impulses behind his own actions with them. Lincoln biographer David Donald wrote that Hay noted in his diary that the president spoke of his innermost views on the deepest questions of the war. Hay remembered Lincoln as saying, "I consider the central idea pervading this struggle is the necessity that is upon us, of proving that popular government is not an absurdity. We must settle the question now, whether in a free government the minority have the right to break up the government whenever they choose. If we fail it will go far to prove the incapability of the people to govern themselves."[34] What Lincoln said to Hay is about as clear an explanation of his mission to save the Union as the sixteenth president ever uttered.

The one significant area in which the secretaries served their master less than properly was in matters concerning the first lady. Throughout the White House years, the relationship between Mary and the Nicolay-Hay team went from cool but correct to frankly unpleasant. Both men mocked the first lady, though not, of course, in their boss's presence. Their references to her between themselves were childishly disrespectful, with constant references to the "hellcat" being a mild example. Had they been older, they might have recognized the strong mental currents that were all but drowning the first lady and may thus have been less judgmental and sarcastic about her demands and what they saw as her "interference" in matters they believed were best left to their own unimpeachable wisdom. Such an attitude would not only have been right, but it would have shown far greater respect to their boss.

Happily for the president, Joshua Speed visited his old friend during that last summer in the Soldiers' Home cottage. Spending the night, the Kentuckian looked in on Lincoln in his bedroom, where he found the president reading from the Bible. Undoubtedly recalling the religious skepticism Lincoln had espoused in their long-ago days together in Springfield, Speed said, "I am glad to see you so profitably employed. . . .

If you have recovered from your skepticism, I am sorry to say I have not." Lincoln's views on religion had changed in the White House as a result of his exorcism by war; given his responsibility for directing the titanic conflict, it would have been surprising if they had not. He responded to Speed's gentle revelation by putting his hand on the younger man's shoulder and remarking, "You are wrong, Speed; take all of this book upon reason that you can, and the balance on faith, and you will live and die a happier man."[35]

Yet not even at this point in his epoch-making life had Abraham Lincoln become a regular churchgoer, still not accepting that all the doctrine and ceremony of the church experience was necessary to him; as Mary later put it so well, he was not "a technical Christian." But he found solace in the Bible and, one hopes, justification for what he was required to preside over daily, which is to say slaughter and misery and heartbreak in pursuit of what he surely held to be goals shared by God. If he didn't think religion in the formal sense was necessary to his life, he had found nonetheless that the "Great Book . . . is the best gift God has given to man."[36] It seems almost unavoidable that any man put in the position of directing a war needs to exculpate his actions in the sense of remaining at one with his God. So, apparently, did Lincoln. He appears to have nicely summed up his attitude in a letter he wrote in September 1864: "Surely He intends some great good to follow this mighty convulsion, which no mortal could make, and no mortal could stay."[37] To the best of our knowledge, not included among Lincoln's many physical problems was the inability to sleep, soundly and straight through most every night.

HEADING INTO THE ELECTION

When Mary returned from Vermont in mid-September, the first lady did what she could to continue fostering her husband's reelection chances. One of her first tasks was to write to her new friend Abram Wakeman, who had worked his way into her orbit in hopes of promoting his patronage advancement from New York City postmaster to the more lucrative position of New York port collector. An unctuous lawyer, Wakeman found that his flattery worked well in gaining access to the first lady's circle of admirers and hangers-on who frequented her Blue

Room social evenings. That he presented himself as a spiritualist only added to his attraction to Mrs. Lincoln, who still hoped to make contact with her dead son. The influential Wakeman had personally helped to persuade New York State's Central Republican Committee to endorse Lincoln for the nomination at the Baltimore convention, which made him welcome company for the president as well as the first lady. Soon he was putting himself forward as Mrs. Lincoln's champion whenever she came to New York. Not unnaturally that meant that she began to regard him as a confidant, especially as an adviser on the pesky and ever-growing accounts with the city's most expensive merchants, men whose bills she knew would instantly come due if her husband lost the election.

Mary probably wasn't aware of the exact details of her husband's finances, but she knew enough to realize that her debts would wipe out a significant part of the family's savings. To Lizzy Keckly she succinctly explained the frightening corner into which she had painted herself: "If he is re-elected, I can keep him in ignorance of my affairs, but if he is defeated, then the bills will be sent to him and he will know all."[38] Keckly wrote that the first lady admitted she would "be clever" to even unscrupulous men if it would be useful in getting her husband reelected—adding, though, that she would "drop every one of them, and let them know very plainly that I only made tools of them."[39]

Conveniently for Lincoln, the Democrats made life considerably less perilous for his reelection chances when they crippled themselves by adopting an over-the-top party platform. To run against the president they chose the same General George McClellan who had trained a great army and then failed to use it to advantage. Still counted as a hero by many, McClellan made an attractive candidate, an honorable and capable man who would probably have turned out to be a more successful president than Andrew Johnson, Lincoln's actual successor. But at the Democrats' Chicago convention, the party saddled McClellan with a platform that he neither approved nor agreed with, one that was almost impossible for him to support in the campaign. The Democrats advocated a "cessation of hostilities" to end what they viewed as an unwinnable war, basing such peace on a so-called Federal Union of the States. Their appeal for an end to the war sounded disturbingly like a lack of allegiance to the Union, handing the Republicans a devastating campaign slogan to use against their opponents: "the Chicago Surrender." Giving credit to McClellan, the general did reject this peace plank in the platform, saying it besmirched his "gallant comrades of the army and navy . . . and tells them that their labors and the sacrifice of so many of our slain and wounded brethren had been in vain." But accepting the nomination of a party whose philosophy he could not fully support badly damaged the general's reputation and, with it, his electability.[40]

All of this became virtually moot after Sherman's gift to his president of a captured Atlanta. In fact, Lincoln's pre-Atlanta brooding subsided significantly with the Union's greatly improved fortunes on the battlefield. In his evenings at the Soldiers' Home he seemed more relaxed than usual, and the closer Election Day came, the calmer he appeared.[41] Mary did, though, continue in her nervous concern about the results of the vote, seemingly mostly for reasons that had less to do with the voters' national political wishes than with assuaging her financial worries.

In the run-up to the election, presidential security took on greater importance. One night a few weeks earlier, a shot was fired toward the president on the grounds of the Soldiers' Home—though whether it was deliberate or accidental was never determined. One of the soldier guards reported having heard the report of a gun, and then seeing the bareheaded president riding fast on horseback toward his cottage. Lincoln made an effort to minimize the incident's significance, saying someone had merely fired a gun, the sound of it scaring his horse and causing it to bolt—which thereby "jerked his hat off." The president said he wanted the matter "kept quiet."[42] But his high silk hat was found the next day, with a bullet hole through its stovepipe-shaped crown.

That incident led to a substantial heightening of presidential security. Where before Lincoln himself retained the final say as to whether he wanted an escort on any of his journeys between the Soldiers' Home, the White House, and the War Department, Stanton now demanded that all such trips be accompanied by a guard contingent—irrespective of the president's wishes. A detective chosen from former Washington Police Department officers now accompanied Lincoln at all times as a bodyguard, and Lincoln's old friend and bureaucratic factotum Ward Lamon took to sleeping on the floor outside the presidential bedroom door. Furthermore, Lincoln's late-night strolls around the Soldiers' Home grounds increasingly concerned the men who tried to keep him from harm. One night a young lieutenant crossed his path in woods around the cottage. The unusually late hour of the chance encounter led the officer to ask the president if such a stroll might not be risky. Lincoln was nonchalant: "Oh, I guess not—I couldn't rest and I thought I'd take a walk." The president reversed direction though, presumably heading back to the safety of the house.[43]

ELECTED

In the final weeks before the election, the president devoted a large part of his time to winning another four-year term. But the way a chief executive then worked toward his reelection was dramatically different from the way it's done today. Lincoln didn't participate in the Baltimore convention, he didn't crisscross the country making campaign speeches, he didn't make public statements on the campaign issues, and he rarely commented even on the accusations the Democrats made against his administration, some of which were unambiguously scurrilous. Appropriate to the times in which he lived, among the most damaging in the latter category were those touching on race. Lincoln had made clear to the electorate his belief in the postwar necessity of a constitutional amendment abolishing slavery.[44] But the political opposition distorted the president's tenet into a stand favoring black-and-white intermarriage, of which Lincoln did not speak favorably; whether he would ever actually have condemned such marriages is unknowable but unlikely given his beliefs in personal liberty. His opponents widely labeled him in the crude racism of the day as a "nigger lover" and with similar epithets and even nicknamed him "Abraham African the First" in mockery of his emphasis on defeating slavery (opposition candidate McClellan was running as a forthright anti-emancipationist). Lincoln just ignored the opposition's desperate and absurd charge that he aided his relatives in defrauding the government.

But more than mere personal slurs concerned Lincoln that fall. Taxes and inflation were continuing to rise, and the government's credit (and thus its borrowing ability) was nearly drained. Furthermore, the president made no secret that more draftees would be needed to finish off the rebellion, which angered the countless Northerners who had already seen their families decimated, their farms gone to ruin because of the absence of men to work them, and who despised the unfairness (of the rich being allowed to buy replacements) that had touched off the deadly New York draft riots.

Lincoln involved himself mainly behind the scenes toward continuing his tenancy of the White House. The president mediated local political disputes to help the Republican candidate come out looking as good as possible. He wrote to newspaper editors, as when he persuaded the editor of the *New York Herald* to soften his newspaper's antiadministration stand. And, famously, he saw to it that as many servicemen as possible were given furloughs to go home to vote—the presumption on Lincoln's being part that soldiers and sailors would cast their ballots for an administration promising to finish the war, thereby ensuring that the thousands of their dead comrades had not died in vain. Even more to the point, common wisdom among the troops had it that a Lincoln victory would so demoralize the South that the Confederacy's surrender would come sooner. In fact, Lincoln did speak informally to many of the soldiers passing through Washington that election season, emphasizing the importance of a Union victory. "It is not merely for today," he said on one occasion, "but for all time to come, that we should perpetuate for our children's children that great and free government which we have enjoyed all our lives. . . . The nation is worth fighting for, to secure such an inestimable jewel."[45] Many more thousands of soldier votes would likely have been cast had not some states refused to extend absentee ballots to troops in the field.[46]

Another useful election tool for Lincoln in the 1864 campaign was the reverential biographies published about the president. Seven were dispensed that year, including the Beadle Dime Library biography that wrote of the chance any American hardworking boy had to "climb the heights."[47] Many of the country's most respected magazines openly favored Lincoln's reelection, including the wildly popular *Harper's Weekly*, *Leslie's Weekly*, and *Godey's Lady Book*. *Leslie's* mocked the opposition by printing a selection of the epithets used against Lincoln, among them *ape, gorilla, fool, despot, liar, tyrant, fiend*, and *butcher*.[48]

Still another device Lincoln employed was the portrait photograph. Mathew Brady, the iconic Civil War photographer, took many of the finest and most memorable pictures of the president, images that remain with Americans today on their currency and served as the models for the most famous statues honoring him. In their own time, small copies of such photos were prized possessions in homes all across the country, inexpensive little treasures that represented a new and inspiring art form.

Photographic sittings were difficult to work into Lincoln's schedule partly because of the long exposure times needed, with a sitter being required to remain motionless for lengthy periods, sometimes with his or her head pressed against an iron brace to ensure that exposures weren't blurred. Notably, in many of Lincoln's likenesses true humanity unmistakably came through, a quality missing in so many mid-nineteenth-century photographic portraits. One suspects Lincoln knew his character would be judged by the expression in his pictures, and that he took special care to try to reflect a kindliness and calm. An odd element in the story of Lincoln and photography was that he was never photographed with his entire family, nor even alone with his wife. Mary was supposedly reluctant to see her short and squat frame emphasized beside that of her tall and thin husband, though surely this could have been avoided with bust- or head-only portraits. Such pictures might have popularized the first family, especially a widely disliked first lady regarded by many as a political liability.

Despite the auguries in Lincoln's favor after Atlanta's capture, that fall the president nonetheless never entirely overcame his fear that the election might still be lost. The Democrats remained a force to be reckoned with during the Civil War, as evidenced by their gains in the midterm elections of 1862. Even though the party had lost a huge part of its membership with the secession of the Southern states, and still more with those who had gone over to the Republicans in the latter's recent "National Union Party" configuration, the Democrats still formed a large and formidable—though generally loyal—opposition in the North, one composed of people sick of the war, people who had opposed the war, sympathizers with the Southern cause, and Northerners not the least interested in black emancipation and who were opposed to any further social gains or advancement of a race still widely and deeply despised even outside the South. Even so, the Democrats strongly appealed to the notion of national "union," though the party may well have eventually settled for an armistice and a peace treaty allowing the Southern states' departure and thus leaving a far smaller "union" than the one President Lincoln had in mind.

Election Day—November 8, 1864, a gray, rainy Tuesday—had just seen the Lincolns move back into the White House from their much loved summer home. According to Noah Brooks, Lincoln's assistant, the president seemed uneasy, aware that in national elections there was no such thing as a sure thing. The family passed a relatively quiet day, gratefully receiving no horrendous news from any of the battlefronts. The president began his workday routine by recognizing one Teodoro Manara as the Guatemalan consul in New York City, a matter that like so many others called for the chief executive's imprimatur. The youngest Lincoln happily learned that the soldiers guarding the family and who were bivouacked on the White House grounds were that day planning to vote for his father. In the afternoon a wire from John Nicolay, traveling in Illinois, informed the president that Springfield was reporting a majority of twenty votes for its native son, which exceedingly slim home-town margin might well have caused the president some consternation.

As darkness fell, Lincoln was drawn to the telegraph machine in the War Department next door to the White House. At seven, he and Hay walked in a heavy rainstorm over to Stanton's headquarters, where the national returns would soon start arriving. On entering the second-floor office, an attendant immediately handed Lincoln a dispatch from Philadelphia, where a ten-thousand-vote Republican majority was being reported. The president kept sending the evening's largely good election news to his wife in the White House, explaining to those gathered around him, "She is more anxious than I." He probably didn't realize how right he was; Mary had indeed spent the evening highly anxious, fearing that her husband would lose the presidency. The evening's wild weather caused many telegraph wires to be out of commission, so the president passed some of the waiting time telling jokes. The starchy Secretary Stanton, unable to fully appreciate that Lincoln's bantering helped him keep an even keel in trying circumstances, didn't find the yarns all that amusing, perhaps especially because Stanton was sick with chills and fever.

By midnight, sufficient returns had been received to persuade Lincoln that a Republican electoral vote victory was all but a certainty. In the still dark hours of Wednesday morning, supper was brought to the wire office courtesy of Major Thomas T. Eckert, and the president himself cheerfully served up plates of fried oysters to the men gathered around him. Sometime after one in the morning, revelers who had congregated in the street serenaded Lincoln, accompanied by a brass band. Though he disliked extemporaneous speaking, the crowd persuaded the president to deliver a few words. In the now clear night Lincoln told the onlookers, "It is no pleasure to me to triumph over anyone, but I give thanks to the Almighty for this evidence of the people's resolution to stand by free government and the rights of humanity."[49] His top general, Grant, wired the president from his Virginia encampment, "The victory is worth more to the country than a battle won." In truth, the great Union commander summed up the real importance of the election's outcome far too lightly.

The decisive electoral vote victory ensured that Lincoln would remain in the White House for four more years. Every state but Kentucky, Delaware, and New Jersey went Republican (there was, of course, no vote from the eleven seceded states), the 212–21 electoral vote margin a major triumph for a president who only that summer had privately all but concluded that he would lose the race. In the popular vote, the results didn't look quite so overwhelming, a not uncommon feature of American presidential contests. The president received just over 55 percent of the total cast, McClellan just under 45 percent. The result was convincing to be sure, even though nine out of every twenty voters had cast their ballot to turn Abraham Lincoln out of office. (Had women possessed the franchise in 1864, the results may well have gone against the incumbent, given that the fighting had cost so many wives their husbands and so many mothers their sons.)

As for McClellan, he immediately resigned his major general's commission. The man who would always be called "the little general" then took sail for Europe, travel that would see him away from the United States and its war for many months. He would eventually win moderately high political office, becoming governor of New Jersey—one of three states whose vote he carried.

Anyone might have thought Mary Lincoln would breathe a sigh of relief at her husband's victory and be cured from the shopping mania that had so worried her over the past months. But such would not be the case. No sooner had her husband safely secured the White House for another term than Mary began ordering ornaments for both body and home from the beckoning shops and department stores of New York and Washington. As continuing first lady, she expected and was duly rewarded with enough credit to purchase whatever she needed to keep herself looking like a queen and her home like a palace.

Mary's new purchases included a 508-piece set of White House china meant to substitute for the dishes she had acquired in her first year as mistress of the White House. So that she would be appropriately dressed for the upcoming inaugural ball, she spent $2,000 for her gown and almost $3,000 on pearl, amethyst, and diamond jewelry from Washington's Galt Brothers Jewelers.[50] While such purchases remained within the realm of comprehension, her three hundred newly acquired pairs of kid gloves did not.

Mary's excessive shopping and increasingly bizarre behavior probably did not intrude much on her husband's consciousness. Notwithstanding the Union's huge boost in prospects in the few weeks since the summer's bad tidings, the war was by no means yet won. Jefferson Davis had, like most of his generals and much of the Confederate population, been hoping for a McClellan victory in the Yankee elections and the peace negotiations that Southerners widely expected to follow a Democratic success. But Davis continued no less militant even after Lincoln's electoral victory, declaring that the Confederacy would fight on until it won its independence. Despite Davis's bravado, the South's morale took a nosedive. Even if Davis continued to hold firm against the Northern tidal wave, most thinking Southerners now realized that the South's "glorious cause" had become a lost cause.

A week after the voting, General Sherman began his demonstration to the nation—and to the watching world—of the rebellion's hopelessness. Instead of turning westward from Atlanta so as to destroy the rebel armies remaining on his flank, Sherman and the bulk of his forces headed southeast, toward Savannah and the sea. In destroying just about everything inside a sixty-mile-wide swath between Atlanta and the Atlantic Ocean, the federal army's true mission was to make obvious to a South on its knees the futility of further resistance. It is hard today to understand the depth of this savagery in the federal army's month-long drive and how thorough the destruction it caused to Georgia: As the blue-clad army passed eastward, virtually every structure and every human possession it touched was put to the torch, blown up, or taken away by Sherman's hardened warriors. One outraged Georgia farmer caught in the Yankee firestorm sarcastically asked the general, "Why don't you go over to South Carolina and serve them this way? They started it."[51]

With simultaneous and decisive Union victories in the West—the Confederate Army of Tennessee was virtually annihilated in these weeks—Lincoln was sensing greater hope than at any time since Fort

Sumter's martyrdom nearly four years earlier. The South now retained only a single port—Wilmington, North Carolina, which sat behind the protection of its seemingly impenetrable Fort Fisher—through which blockade runners were able to land supplies, perhaps most critically European medicines, but a trickle that came nowhere near meeting the dying Confederacy's desperate needs. Only Grant was still held back—by Lee, in front of Petersburg, where the Confederates were making their last great stand and the federals were waiting to fall upon Richmond, the grand and long-sought prize that lay a few miles to the north.

SEVEN

———

AN UNFINISHED WORK

T HE USUAL MIXED MULTITUDE OF BOTH THE CELE-
brated and the anonymous presented themselves for the 1865 New
Year's reception—the Lincolns' fourth in the Executive Mansion and the
biggest one yet—all impatient to shake the president's hand and nod
courteously at the first lady. At noon on January 2 (the Sabbath had delayed the event for a day this year) members of the diplomatic corps and
the president's cabinet got the annual affair started, their rank giving
them the right to be the first to congratulate the Lincolns on the
prospect of a victorious year. General officers and Supreme Court justices, next in the order of protocol, arrived thirty minutes later. At one
o'clock, ushers finally threw the doors open to everyone else. Some in
Congress had been heard grumbling that the legislative body hadn't
been given its own special precedence, though any senator or representative was, of course, welcome to join the estimated five thousand ordinary people who formed the line snaking back out from the mansion's
portico and down Pennsylvania Avenue. In the distinctive style of the
American republic, the attendees produced a memorably democratic
throng in the White House's jam-packed rooms.

Gathered that morning outside the mansion gates was a part of the
public that had never before been welcome in this house. These were
the black Washingtonians, men and women who felt far from certain of

admittance to the reception, let alone of receiving a welcoming hand-shake from the president himself. These "other" Americans varied from those of financial substance who looked indistinguishable from the white guests save only for the color of their skin, all the way down the social ladder to indigents, many likely as not ex-slaves, who had been fortunate just to find presentable garments in which to pay their respects to the liberator president. After some two hours of watching white people stream into the great building, at around two o'clock the city's colored people gingerly advanced toward the mansion's door, finally walking together into this mighty symbol of nationhood. Amazingly, no one resisted their entrance. Indeed, Lincoln appeared happy to see and greet the least advantaged of the day's visitors. Many of the Negroes were heard calling down God's blessing on the great president as they passed through the line. A reporter for the New York *Independent* wrote, "Those who witnessed the scene will not soon forget it. For a long distance down the Avenue, on my way home, I heard fast young men cursing the President for this act; but all the way the refrain rang in my ears, 'God bless Abraham Lincoln!'"[1]

CAPTAIN LINCOLN

Early in the new year, the long-simmering issue of the eldest Lincoln son's military "situation" finally reached an agreeable end. In the prior fall Robert had left the Harvard law school, having been enrolled for only a short while. The circumstances surrounding his departure aren't entirely clear, but Robert became ill and his parents wanted him with them in the White House, the president wiring his son saying, "[We are] a little uneasy about your health. . . . If you think it would help you, make us a visit."[2] In the last days of 1864, the young man likely discussed his future at Harvard while with his parents. He remained at the White House through New Year's and joined the president and first lady for their annual reception. He then returned to Cambridge and attended a January law lecture given by Professor Joel Parker, notable for his constructionist views on the Constitution and for his condemnation of the president's use of his office's war powers. Parker was undoubtedly aware that Lincoln's son was sitting in the classroom listening to his anti-Lincoln views. The incident may have prompted or at least contributed to Robert's decision to leave the law school. In any case, Robert was all too aware of widely held public opinion that it was unbefitting for the commander in chief's son not to participate in the war and risk his life just as were the thousands of sons of less powerful parentage.

Robert was eager to end this criticism, and probably, at long last, a sympathetic president persuaded his wife that their son's enlistment was the proper course, especially as he did not wish to remain any longer at Harvard. A few days after the beginning of the year Lincoln wrote to Grant, "Please read and answer this letter as though I was not President, but only a friend." He *was* president, and he *wasn't* a "friend" to General Grant, but such was Lincoln's consummate sense of courtesy and of not wishing to literally command Grant in what Lincoln held to be a private matter, an issue he believed should if at all possible be decided by his top commander without inference of coercion. "My son, now in his twenty-second year, having graduated at Harvard, wishes to see something of the war before it ends. I do not wish to put him in the ranks, [nor] yet to give him a commission, to which those who have already served long, are better entitled, and better qualified to hold. Could he, without embarrassment to you, or detriment to the service, go into your Military family with some nominal rank, I, and not the public, furnishing his necessary means? If no, say so without the least hesitation, because I am anxious, and as deeply interested, that you shall not be encumbered as you can be yourself."

Grant's answer to the president arrived two days later: "I will be most happy to have him in my Military family in the manner you propose. The nominal rank given him is immaterial, but I would suggest that of Capt. as I have three staff officers now, of considerable service, in no higher grade. Indeed I have one officer with only the rank of Lieut. who has been in the service from the beginning of the war. This however will make no difference and I would still say give the rank of Capt. Please excuse my writing on a half sheet, I had no resource but to take the blank half of your letter."[3] The busy commander thus graciously and with subtle courtesy consented to his commander in chief's request while at the same time gently but plainly informing him of the complications it raised in respect of his own loyal and long-serving aides.

Undoubtedly Grant understood the president's public relations difficulties regarding Robert's military service, and he intelligently put aside any notion on the president's part that Robert should be paid privately, explaining to Lincoln that to do so would place his son on something less than an equal footing with his other officers. As for Robert, he was pleased to be asked to serve under the nation's most famous general and promptly wired Grant with his grateful acceptance of a commission as an assistant adjutant general.

Among the new captain's first tasks on receiving his commission was to buy a horse. The president ordered one brought to the White House, where the seller requested $200. Robert's father possessed considerable knowledge of horses, having bought many during his long career as a circuit-riding lawyer and judge in Illinois. Lincoln estimated this horse was not worth $200, in fact, no more than $150. The sale was promptly concluded for the lesser amount.

On February 22, 1865, Robert reported for duty to his new posting, the field headquarters of the federal army's commanding officer. But an anxious-sounding wire from Lincoln arrived at the command post two days later, the president stating that he hadn't yet heard whether his son had arrived safely. Grant immediately responded yes, putting the president's mind at ease.

Though Grant assigned Robert duties that kept the young officer in something as near to "perfect safety" as could be conjured on an active war front, the general did so not to keep the commander in chief's son from harm for his own sake or that of his mother. Instead, Grant considered the consequences of the president's son being captured alive by the Confederates as too high to be risked. So Captain Lincoln passed his military days—which amounted to only the last few weeks of the war—performing largely perfunctory although sometimes high-profile tasks. In March the nationally famous financier Jay Cooke and his family visited the headquarters, and Grant had the young captain personally escort Cooke on a tour of the front. Only days before the war's end, when two women arrived in camp on a flag-of-truce boat, Robert was detailed to escort them to the Confederate lines near Petersburg (in this case Grant evidently discounted the danger of Robert being recognized by desperate Confederates). To Robert's surprise, one of the women turned out to be his aunt Emilie, now sadly but permanently estranged from the first lady. At this unexpected meeting, the president's son and the general's widow exchanged family news from both sides of the battle lines.

GETTING A SECOND TERM UNDER WAY

For Lincoln, the late winter and early spring of 1865 happily turned out to be considerably less stressful than most of the rest of his presidency. In the new year it became obvious that the war was irreversibly leading toward a Union victory, even though the fighting remained widespread and deadly. A week after the New Year's reception, the first lady started off the White House social season with a lavish party at which the president, dressed in his usual black suit and wearing the white kid gloves that Mary insisted on, dutifully greeted his guests while standing just inside the Blue Room door; exhausted from the socializing, he left his company at eleven o'clock and strolled over to the War Department's telegraph room to catch up on the news from his troops in the field. The first couple also managed to occasionally get out to the theater for some much needed relaxation for the president, as when they attended a performance of *Leah* that starred Avonia Jones in the title role and to which they brought an excited Tad with them. A few days after the reception, Mary presided as hostess at still another White House party, greeting her guests while proudly standing between her husband and her eldest son; after the introductions and formalities were observed, the evening's company promenaded through the state rooms, accompanied by the music of the Marine Band.

All through these days of lifted spirits, more favorable news continued to pour in from the war fronts. On the fifteenth of January, the same day on which Edward Everett—Lincoln's cospeaker at Gettysburg—died in Boston, a message arrived from Admiral Porter reporting that North Carolina's Fort Fisher was finally taken, a victory that closed the last major Confederate port through which the rebellion was being supplied from abroad. Confederate vice president Alexander Stephens called the loss of the fort "one of the greatest disasters which has befallen our Cause," and the stronghold's demise at last prompted President Davis toward peace feelers with the North.

But the unending avalanche of responsibility threatening to bury Lincoln was the one burden no one could lift from the president. Even with news from the battlefronts improving, the commander in chief remained worryingly exhausted through the first weeks of 1865. Perhaps some of his unshakable weariness was just part of the emotional weight that accompanied the scent of victory in the air, but whatever the case Lincoln found himself too tired to want to do much of anything. Mary tried, often fruitlessly, to get him to accompany her on carriage rides around the city, a treat that had always lifted his spirits, though one obviously incapable of providing him with any real exercise. The president's clearly visible exhaustion finally began to alarm his wife. "Poor Mr. Lincoln is looking so brokenhearted, so completely worn-out," Mary told Lizzy Keckly, "I fear he will not get through the next four years."[4] The emotional and physical toll on his mind and body over the four horror-filled years since he'd entered the White House indeed strongly suggests that Lincoln would not have lived through his second four-year term. Photographs of the president from 1860 reveal a vigorous-looking man in the height of his middle years, while those taken in the spring of 1865 portray a prematurely aged specter of the earlier man, incredibly still only fifty-six years old but bearing a deeply rutted face, sunken eyes, sallow complexion, and an expression of nearly inhuman weariness.

For what turned out to be the last time, Joshua Speed visited his old friend late that winter, and as always, the president was lifted by his presence. Lincoln's own physical ailments worried him though, and he likely needed a little sympathy from the Kentuckian. The president, too, was anxious about surviving another four years of the kind of pounding his office imposed. "Speed, I am a little alarmed about myself; just feel my hand," he confided. The younger man wrote that the president's hand was "cold and clammy," and he went on to describe Lincoln putting his feet close to the fire, causing steam to rise from them, a sign—to Speed, at any rate—that the famously large feet were probably just as cold and clammy as were his hands. A modern doctor might judge that Lincoln's circulation was impaired, or that the president had been afflicted by one of a dozen other debilitating medical problems. Certainly, for a man his age, Lincoln's health had sunk to appalling straits: He was overworked, underexercised, relentlessly subjected to near superhuman stress, and even inadequately nourished thanks to the preponderance of the fatty and fried foods of the times and his own indifference to eating regularly and well.

Given all that, Lincoln could now at least spend his working day in a more socially agreeable atmosphere. His biggest cabinet headache was at last gone, the ever contentious and self-serving former treasury secretary Chase now sworn in as chief justice. Likely an even more pleasant change in his official family, certainly in personal terms, was the man who in December had stepped into the shoes of the retiring attorney general, Edward Bates. For the post the president had nominated Joshua Speed's brother James, who since Lincoln's arrival in Washington had become the beneficiary of a large share of the president's friendship for Joshua. Though a Democrat, the Kentuckian supported Lincoln's war aims, was a committed abolitionist, and had represented an important voice in holding Kentucky in the Union after the war started.[5] Lincoln openly spoke of his need for a Southerner in his cabinet to serve his own political purposes, colorfully characterizing this factor in Speed's appointment as "the shrieks of locality having to be heeded."[6]

Another welcome appointment to the cabinet introduced a bridge between the president's official and actual families. Interior Secretary John P. Usher, whom Lincoln had not found particularly satisfactory,[7] resigned that late winter, and Lincoln was happy for the chance to replace him. He chose Iowa's Senator James Harlan. The senator had been one of the president's strongest supporters at the Capitol end of Pennsylvania Avenue, an asset that Lincoln was losing and that must have caused him pain when he chose him for his cabinet. But a plus for the president was the reality that the new second-term cabinet bore not a single member jockeying for a future presidency of his own. (Confirmed by the Senate but not yet sworn in at the time of the assassination, Harlan finally became Secretary of the Interior a few weeks after Johnson, who renominated him, became president.)

Harlan would soon be connected to the Lincoln family in another way. Robert Lincoln had for some time been courting the senator's daughter, Mary Eunice Harlan, a young woman three years his junior and much admired in the capital's society. Washingtonians regarded her as extraordinarily poised, and took her being an accomplished harpist as a considerable accomplishment. No engagement had yet been announced, but the president was aware of the depth of the couple's attachment to each other.

Other important second-term changes were in the making even nearer to home. In a momentous development, the two men closest to Lincoln for the last four years both decided to leave their White House jobs. John Nicolay's shaky health had seriously been weakened by the demanding service he had devotedly rendered Lincoln and the presidency. Though Nicolay was criticized in Washington for a taciturnity that sometimes shaded into conceit, Lincoln himself had never for a moment doubted his private secretary's loyalty and over the years had come to instinctively depend on him for his political skills. Nicolay's post–White House reward was to be appointment as American consul in Paris. John Hay was worn-out as well, but was convinced that he had given Lincoln his best and thus now deserved a quieter job. Hay was slated to become secretary of the American legation in France.

The principal replacement for the two men was Noah Brooks, whom Lincoln had befriended in the mid-1850s; more lately Brooks had worked as a reporter for the *Sacramento Union* and openly used his position to support Lincoln's causes. A novel quality Brooks would have brought to the White House was his and Mary Lincoln's liking for each other; indeed, both Lincolns enjoyed Brooks's presence in the Executive Mansion. During his tenure as Lincoln's private secretary during a second administration, Brooks's writing talents would likely have stood him in good stead as a presidential spokesman and as an alter ego to a man whose views he understood and shared.

Congress's towering achievement in the winter of 1865 was its passage of the Thirteenth Amendment, outlawing slavery. The accomplishment might have been even more towering had Congress come up with an amendment mandating that all laws require total legal indifference to skin color, which provision would have represented a genuinely color-blind amendment. But Congress knew any such effort would have represented an impossible goal, its implications simply too great for nineteenth-century politicians to consider; such would have meant, among other revolutionary notions, that states could no longer forbid interracial marriage. Instead, what Congress did pass simply banned the institution of chattel slavery. On January 31, 1865, by a margin of 119 to 56, the House of Representatives passed a bill joining one already approved a year earlier by the Senate. Lincoln lobbied hard to persuade as many House Democrats as possible to vote with the Republicans, and in the end he was deeply gratified to have the legislative branch pass a measure that would, assuming its ratification by the states, protect the substance of his Emancipation Proclamation from subversion by a court or a future Congress. He was further pleased when Illinois became one of the first states to ratify the amendment. Sixteen more states joined Illinois during February, but declining were the border states of Delaware and Kentucky, where slavery had remained legal throughout the war. The latter development meant that votes of at least some of the Confederate states would be required to put the amendment into the Constitution, a road that could only be taken after the war was over and when Congress would again acknowledge the seceded states' official acts.

In an effort to finish a war all knew the Confederacy had now virtually lost but which nonetheless continued to drag murderously along, Lincoln agreed to lend the prestige of his office and of his person to a negotiated peace effort. Though he rarely left Washington, he did so in the first week of February. At Hampton Roads, Virginia, the president received three representatives sent by Jefferson Davis to a conference aboard the private paddle-wheel steamer *River Queen*. The Southerners in attendance had to agree to one condition at the outset: They could not speak of "two separate nations," given that Lincoln refused to participate in any discussions based on that unlawful status.

With Secretary of State Seward at his side, Lincoln sat down with the Southern delegates in the yacht's comfortably appointed salon. One of the Confederates, a man who had before the war spent many years in Washington, began the meeting by asking Seward, "How is the Capitol? Is it finished?" The secretary of state courteously described the now completed building's splendor. When more substantive concerns were then raised, Lincoln opened by stating that as an absolute minimum for peace the Southern states must agree to remain in the Union and must also forsake slavery. Lincoln promised that once the rebels laid down their arms and rejoined the Union, the Southern states would be "immediately restored to their practical relations to the Union." He also informed the Southerners that Congress had just passed an amendment abolishing slavery, which bill was being sent to the states for ratification, information that appeared to shock the three Southerners. The meeting ended, deadlocked, when the Confederates concluded that further discussion was "fruitless" given Lincoln's unconditional demands on the Union and slavery. With the Confederate representatives having disembarked, the yacht departed Hampton Roads for Washington that evening. On his return to the capital, Lincoln reported to Congress that the encounter—the only

real peace talks between the warring sides during the entire war—
"ended without result."

ANOTHER INAUGURATION

Saturday, March 4, 1865, was a typical late-winter day in Washington.
Rain drenched the city in the gloomy light, and cold winds gusted across
the city. Thanks to the steady downpour, the pedestrian paths along
Pennsylvania Avenue were covered in a slimy, muddy paste that clung
to every pedestrian's boots and befouled skirts no matter how diligently
women tried to keep them above the muck. The sidewalks were, however, marginally cleaner than the streets themselves, the latter splotched
with mounds of animal manure ground into sludge by the wagon wheels
and horse hooves crowding the avenue, traffic that was especially dense
given that the second of Abraham Lincoln's inaugurations was being carried out today.

Hours before the noontime ceremonies got under way at the Capitol's
east front, a great multitude had begun gathering in the plaza that
·emerged out of East Capitol Street and ended at the majestic flight of
steps rising to the great building's entrance. Workers had erected a
speaker's stand on those steps, though it was crude-looking compared to
the later tabernacles under which later presidents would be shielded on
their inaugural day. Little effort seemed to have been exerted to control
the spread of the crowd, which meant knots of spectators claimed the
best viewing spots right on the steps and parapets surrounding the
speaker's stand. No matter where the attendees stationed themselves,
though, by the time the ceremony got under way everyone was dripping
wet and the crush of the animated but generally good-tempered throng
had long since ruined many a female spectator's elaborate toilette.

The man at the center of the day's ceremonies rode uncovered up
Pennsylvania Avenue from the White House to the Capitol, presumably
getting just as wet as any of the spectators who lined what was then and
is still the city's great ceremonial thoroughfare. Still feeling unwell with
the ailment he complained about to Joshua Speed, Lincoln appeared
startlingly skeletal to the spectators; a thirty-pound weight loss in recent
months looked to have collapsed the flanks of his face, with dark and
blotchy skin swagged over protruding cheekbones.

Both the arrangement and location of the swearing-in ceremonies were somewhat different from later inaugurals. When he arrived at the Capitol, Lincoln found a few new bills awaiting his signature. After he disposed of this paperwork, the first part of the official agenda began with the swearing in of the vice president. This segment of the day's ceremonies was carried out distinctly separately from the president's, being conducted not on the Capitol steps but inside the Senate chamber. At exactly noon, officials escorted the vice president–elect, Johnson, into the crowded room, whose overhanging galleries were filled with seated ladies whom Noah Brooks patronizingly described as "chatting and clattering like zephyrs among the reeds of a waterside." After Johnson's introduction to the seated greats of the nation—the cabinet and Supreme Court, legislators, every rank of general and admiral, Mary Lincoln upstairs in the diplomatic gallery and being personally attended by Senator Henry Anthony of Rhode Island—the former tailor from Tennessee rose to speak, his hands bereft of any prepared text.

Johnson had recently suffered a bout with typhoid fever. Probably because he was still suffering the illness's aftereffects, he had felt it necessary to take a number of strong drinks that morning to help him get out of his sickbed and show up for the most important occasion in his life. But the alcohol left his face noticeably reddened, and it was apparent from his first words to his audience that an embarrassing display was about to follow. Johnson didn't disappoint. "Humble as I am, plebeian as I may be deemed," he began, "permit me in the presence of this brilliant assemblage to enunciate the truth that courts and cabinets, the President and his advisers, derive their power and greatness from the people." Lincoln arrived just as his new vice president was beginning to ramble and, from his seat in the middle of the front row, winced as the maudlin Johnson reminded and re-reminded the assemblage of his own low origins. The about-to-be-ex-vice president, Hannibal Hamlin, started to grab at Johnson's coattail to get him to sit down when it became apparent that the inebriated man had nothing to say that was worthy of the occasion. The Senate clerk then joined Hamlin in the effort, but both failed. Many senators, putatively friends of the new vice president's, bowed their heads so as not to look at Johnson. At last he stopped, and the oath of office was administered to him. When finished, Johnson dramatically took into his hands the Bible on which he had just sworn, wetly pressed his lips to its pages, and blubbered in a loud and theatrical voice, "I kiss this Book in the face of my nation of the United States." Senator John Henderson of Missouri, seated next to the president-elect, noticed that Lincoln leaned over to a nearby marshal and quietly ordered, "Do not let Johnson speak outside."

After the former tailor's unseemly performance, the swearing in of new senators took place. With that done, everyone rose and processed through the Capitol's corridors to the open-air temporary stand from which the president would address the waiting throng and finally take his own oath. During the passage, Senator Harlan escorted the first lady, while Robert bore Harlan's daughter on his own arm, the latter pair drawing knowing smiles from many of those privy to the young woman's connection with the president's son. Literally standing out with his great height in the parade of dignitaries, Lincoln received a mighty fanfare of applause from the crowd as he appeared. Just as he neared the small iron table that served as the lectern, a solitary glass of water sitting on it, the struggling sun broke out from behind the clouds and happily brightened the gloomy scene as if a giant and comforting lamp had been lit.

Lincoln's speech, surprisingly brief by the standard of inaugural addresses but still taking the significance of the war into sharp account, bestowed on the entire nation (the oration was telegraphed out to newspapers only moments after the crowd at the Capitol was hearing it) the most humane address ever uttered by an American president. Its 703 words were few enough so that they could be set on a single sheet of paper, the type divided for clarity in two broad columns. Most today remember it for the president's generously directing the American people to bear "malice toward none" but instead "charity for all." But Lincoln's oratory also spoke trenchantly of the war having been the price the nation was forced to pay for the sin of slavery, which all surely knew was the cause for the conflict. He spoke of how the conflict had come, saying that one side had decided to go to war rather than let the Union live on, while the other took up arms rather than let it perish. He spoke of the immorality of slavery's supporters in asking God's aid in maintaining that institution. And he prayed that the war might end quickly. But in the address's most profound words, he said that if "God wills that [the war] continue, until all the wealth piled by the bondman's two hundred and fifty years of unrequited toil shall be sunk, and until every drop of blood drawn with the lash shall be paid by another drawn with the sword, as was said three thousand years ago, so still it must be said, 'The judgments of the Lord are true and righteous altogether.' "

In Lincoln's audience that day was one man for whom we know that such words of national reconciliation and of just deserts for America's transgressions were unbearable. Just above the president on the balustrade of the Capitol's steps stood a young actor named John Wilkes Booth, rural Maryland bred but accustomed to the sophistication of great cities of both the North and the South and to the adulation of their theater audiences for his stage skills *and* (probably even more so) for his astonishingly handsome face. Booth was the younger son of what was then the nation's most famous stage family, comparable in their day to the Barrymores of the next century. The president and first lady had in fact once seen Booth in a play called *The Marble Heart*, a drama presented not long before at Grove's Theatre in downtown Washington. The actor was attending the inaugural ceremony not to hear the president's address, but to sneer at the man he hated more than anyone else in the world. Booth had long been monomaniacally fixated on doing harm to Lincoln, whom he held responsible for the chaos now choking to death his supposedly beloved South. What no one else knew that day was that the young Marylander hoped to kidnap Lincoln and take him to Richmond. And if he could not, he would then kill him.

As Lincoln concluded the speech, pocketed his copy, and accepted the audience's enthusiastic applause, Chief Justice Salmon Chase stepped forward to administer the oath of the presidency. Lincoln put his hand on an open Bible that a Supreme Court clerk had passed to Chase, echoed the justice's words that conferred on him the highest office in the nation for a second term, and bent forward after stating "so help me God" to conclude by kissing the proffered book. The ceremony ended when a battery fired a salvo of salute, the report of the exploding shells carried by the wind up and over the newly completed dome crowned by its luminous bronze statue of Freedom. When afterward Chase presented the swearing-in Bible to Mary, he showed her the page on which Lincoln had touched his lips. It was at the fifth chapter of Isaiah, where it says, "None shall be weary nor stumble among them; none shall slumber nor sleep; neither shall the girdle of their loins be loosed, nor the latchet of their shoes be broken: Whose arrows are sharp, and all their bows bent, their horses' hooves shall be counted like flint, and their wheels like a whirlwind."[8] Perhaps by that choice Lincoln was promising that he would hold steady the course of his governance.

Before the couple's day ended, that evening they were obliged to host a public reception in the White House. The papers reported that some six thousand persons—though some said no more than two thousand—passed by the president and shook his hand; whatever the tally, Lincoln likely sustained the usual painfully swollen right hand that he got from such events. Mary complemented the white silk gown she wore with an ermine-and-silver-spangled fan and purple violets and with white jasmine adorning her lavish headdress; the first lady clung to the conviction that more was better than less. At midevening, Frederick Douglass arrived to join the white people congratulating Lincoln. Two policemen at the door started to whisk away this Negro with the temerity to attempt to socialize with whites, but Lincoln saw the commotion and quickly told an aide that Mr. Douglass should be brought to him. Their warm chat was full of mutual admiration, but the unprecedented liberty on Douglass's part predictably displeased many of the white guests who underwent the extraordinary experience of being made to wait behind a black man.

The major inaugural social event came two days later, on Monday night, in the Patent Office building. Each ball ticket admitted one gentleman and two ladies and in addition gained the buyer admittance to the ball's three elegant suppers, where guests were served such delicacies (delicacies they really were, given the reality of wartime shortages) as terrapin, oysters, smoked meats, ice creams, tarts, and chocolate. All monies left over after expenses from the $10 inaugural ball tickets were pigeonholed for soldiers' families' relief. Recalling the Lincolns' first such ball, the city's finest confectioners created a gigantic sugar model of the Capitol, a replica complete with tiny copies of each of the building's statues, not to mention small working gas lamps that mimicked the real thing. As per the standard social practice of the time, tickets were not sold to black persons.

At the gala Mary presented herself in as grand a manner as possible, what with her $2,000 silk ball gown. Just before leaving for the ball, while Lizzy was getting Mary into her dress and making final arrangements to her coiffure, the president came into the bedroom. The seamstress seized the opportunity to offer Mr. Lincoln congratulations on entering a second term. Lincoln hesitated for a moment, then grasped her hand and said, "Well, Madame Elizabeth," his customary manner of addressing Mrs. Keckly, "I don't know whether I should feel thankful or not. The position brings with it many trials." Choosing not to treat the congratulatory remark as merely a polite exchange, he gravely added, "We do not know what we are destined to pass through. But God will be with us all. I put my trust in God."[9] When Lizzy finished making Mary look as beautiful as the seamstress's considerable skills would permit, the president and the first lady, their arms entwined, left the White House for their carriage drive to the Patent Office and its awaiting throng of well-wishers.

The couple arrived at about half past ten, well after a huge crowd had already gathered and the evening's merriment had gotten under way. The building was packed with the city's highest society, outstanding among them the gentlemen of the cabinet, whose wives were turned out in elaborately skirted dresses with high, tight bodices, outfits tinted in the creamy pastels that marked 1865's latest fashion. The diplomatic corps, the top ranks of the army and navy, and the members of Congress, most accompanied by splendidly bejeweled wives, were happily swirling away to the graceful waltzes and perky polkas directed by Professor Withers, for which long evening's work the popular conductor and his forty musicians were paid a generous $1,000. In accordance with protocol, for the Grand March the first lady did not circle the dance floor on the arm of the president but was instead led by the patrician Senator Charles Sumner of Massachusetts. The presidential couple remained chatting with admirers until near one o'clock in the morning, when their carriage finally returned them, surely exhausted, to the White House and bed. The great ball closed Washington's official season, and except for a theater visit a month later, it was the last evening occasion at which the Lincolns would appear together socially outside the White House.

RICHMOND

Though physically spent in the days after the inauguration, Lincoln must have derived some relief, as did most of the nation, from the war's seeming to be near its end. Four years of destruction and death had come down to confrontation between Grant and Lee over the fate of Richmond, with Grant showing every sign of winning. Other pockets of fighting admittedly remained in the still heavily armed and partly unsubdued South, but if Grant triumphed in Richmond, most believed he would be writing the Confederacy's obituary.

As a matter of necessity, Lincoln's attention was beginning to center on the nation's journey from war to peace, from how to defeat the rebellion to how to return the seceded states to the Union. On March 15, following the bed rest that helped him to recuperate from his illness, the president held a long meeting with a delegation from Louisiana to discuss the nature of that state's postwar government. Lincoln knew it would be the first of many such deliberations in his second term. But also filtering in to him were critical issues unrelated to the war, as when on March 17 he proposed the prosecution of anyone caught furnishing hostile Indians with arms, a serious and growing offense on the Western frontier. Unsurprisingly, though, it was the military action in Virginia—Grant's siege against Richmond and Petersburg—that held the president spellbound since its beginning and most of his waking hours had been given over to the war.

On March 20, Grant invited Lincoln—the invitation was actually suggested by the general's wife, Julia Grant—to visit his command headquarters at City Point, Virginia, the town that formed the mouth of the gigantic funnel through which was fed the federal army's supplies for its push on Richmond. Grant assumed that an absence from Washington would be good medicine for the worn-out president, and Lincoln jumped at the offer. What was more, he decided to take Mary and Tad with him and to have Robert join them there for a full-fledged family reunion.

Lincoln again traveled on the *River Queen,* the side-wheel steamer on which he had hosted his floating conference a few weeks earlier; a Navy vessel could as easily have met his own requirements, but the president judged the facilities on the *River Queen* would be better suited for the first lady's more complicated personal needs. After they left Washington on March 23 in a nasty rainstorm, shipboard conditions went further downhill when contaminated Potomac River drinking water caused the entire family to become ill before the first night was out. But the trip— down the Potomac, into Chesapeake Bay and the James River, and finally up to City Point—ended without further annoyance, the little steamer settling snugly under the protecting guns ringing Grant's enormous entrepôt.

Though Grant's hope that the commander in chief might find a measure of rest was not realized—from the very beginning of the visit every moment of the family's time was filled with activities ranging from troop inspections to group dinners—Lincoln probably was happier and more relaxed during his City Point stay than at any time since he became president. Having escaped Washington's backbiting for a spell, Mary, too, began the visit in high spirits, happily regarding herself as "presidentess" to the troops, a term she liked and which was taken up by the *New York Herald* after her husband's reelection. But because great numbers of soldiers constantly monopolized the president, Mary was largely left on her own, which turned out not to be a good idea. Common sense should have suggested that as a matter of the basic courtesy due the first lady far more attention be paid Mary. In an omen of worse to come, on the first day a trifling indiscretion regarding another lady's precedence badly angered Mary, filling her with a sense of injury of the kind that almost always festered if not quickly resolved.

And matters involving the first lady did rapidly worsen. A massive and complicated troop review was held the following day, for which occasion Mary Lincoln believed she would be accorded an important and honored role. But badly mishandled logistics led to disaster. Joining Major General Edward Ord, commander of the Army of the James, Lincoln left for the review without the first lady. Ominously though, Ord's wife did accompany the two men. Separated from her husband, the first lady was being transported to the review in a covered ambulance along with Julia Grant, the latter staying with her husband on board a ship in the James River. Unfortunately, the ground almost everywhere in City Point was deeply rutted, and the makeshift corduroy road covering—a surface fashioned from lashed-together striplings—did little to level it. Already far behind the president and the Ords, the first lady urged the ambulance driver to speed up the horses, but when the rig hit a particularly bad patch, the resulting jolt threw the two women upward, with Mary's head slamming against one of the iron rungs over which the ambulance's canvas hood was stretched. The painful shock to Mary's skull inflamed what was already a seriously sour state of mind.

But the match that lit the day's real fireworks was struck when Mrs. Grant and Mrs. Lincoln finally arrived at the review. Unaware that another woman would be included in the military exercise, the already aggravated first lady was stunned to see Mary Ord. Mrs. Ord was not only a handsome woman but also an accomplished equestrienne, looking elegant as she rode a horse directly between the president and her husband. Making Mary even angrier was that the general's wife was fashionably turned out in a feathered Robin Hood's hat then all the rage in France, making for an unfortunate contrast between the two women's appearances. Perpetually jealous of other women entering her husband's orbit, extremely sensitive regarding her status as first lady, deeply offended at being relegated to what she considered second place among the women attending this great triumphal gathering, and absolutely certain that the assembled troops mistook Mrs. Ord for herself, the first lady erupted into a fury never to be forgotten by those who witnessed it.

In a hurried bid to meet and courteously welcome the first lady, Mary Ord immediately rode over to Mary Lincoln. The latter had just stepped down from the ramshackle ambulance, which vehicle contrasted extremely poorly with Mrs. Ord's handsome mount. Mary immediately started to loudly berate the general's wife, screaming, "What does this woman mean by riding by the side of the president and ahead of me? Does she suppose that *he* wants *her* by the side of *him*?" Mary even snapped at the now benumbed Julia Grant, who was diplomatically trying to persuade Mrs. Lincoln that Mrs. Ord had done nothing purposely wrong. "I suppose," the first lady spit at Mrs. Grant, "you think you'll get to the White House yourself, don't you?"[10] The latter's eyes welled with embarrassed tears, after which Mary turned her wrath directly on her husband. Lincoln tried to mollify his wife by addressing her endearingly as "Mother," as he often did in private. Many of the men gathered on the field could hear, if not the words, certainly the anger in the explosion, and those closest to the president avoided his eyes in embarrassment. One officer remembered years later that Lincoln "bore it as

Christ might have done with an expression of pain and sadness that cut one to the heart."[11]

At dinner aboard the *River Queen* that evening, the president and the first lady were obligated to entertain the Grants, an occasion that must have been near to choking with tension. Still, though, Mary Lincoln wasn't finished with the confrontation. Loudly and in front of the entire company, the president's wife expressed her extreme displeasure with General Ord, ordering her husband to fire him immediately and calling him "unfit for his place." Grant staunchly rejected the affront as unwarranted.

The aftermath was all mortification and regret. Ill, or feigning illness, Mary spent the next several days in her cabin, seldom leaving the steamer except to walk down to the riverbank with Tad or Robert. This went on for six days, when finally she realized her ongoing presence was burdening her husband. The first lady finally returned to Washington, her absurd excuse an urge to see whether the White House had burned down—a scenario that she said had come to her in a dream. Tad stayed to share a few days with his father in a historic experience that doubtless remained a cherished memory for the rest of the boy's life.

On her trip back up the Potomac to the capital, the mercurial nature of Mary's personality is apparent in the recorded memory of a fellow passenger. Traveling with her was Congressman Carl Schurz, who so greatly enjoyed her company and her graciousness that he wrote his wife of the experience, saying, "The Mother of the Country is extremely kind. She is an astonishing woman—in just a few hours I learned more state secrets than I ever would."[12]

The president stayed with the troops at the front for another nine days—until April 9—his lengthy absence from Washington unprecedented for his entire presidency. It is easy to imagine he enjoyed being away from a White House that had given him little pleasure and a wife who gave him a great deal of pain and embarrassment. On Sunday, April 2, the day after Mary left, Lincoln went ashore to look over the entrenchments and to watch—from a distance—the ongoing fighting, preparation for what he knew was going to be Grant's climactic push on Petersburg. Thoughtful as usual to Mary, he made sure his wife remained informed of the events leading to the end of the war by wiring the first lady early that Sunday morning with the news from Grant that "all now looks highly favorable," and adding that federal forces had enveloped the one remaining stronghold in front of Richmond. He ended with "Tad and I are well." Later that same day he also sent his regards to his triumphant general: "Allow me to tender to you, and all with you, the nation's grateful thanks for this additional, and magnificent success. At your kind suggestion, I think I will visit you to-morrow."[13] One cloud—although a dark one—dimmed Lincoln's sunniness: Lee and his Army of Northern Virginia, Grant's ultimate objective, had escaped westward from Richmond and were most likely preparing to carry on their desperate fight against the Yankees.

That Sunday morning was the last the people of Richmond would experience their city as still whole. By the time the Sabbath sun set, the Confederate capital was a charnel house, exploding factories and ammunition dumps having turned the upper South's most sophisticated and elegant metropolis into a burnt-out shell in which survivors drifted like wraiths through its wrecked blocks. For the first time in their lives the city's slaves had taken to the ruined streets as free human beings, and the sight of them terrified many of the white citizens cowering in their homes or fleeing before the Union troops. When these blue-clad soldiers began to pour into the town, their regimental bands triumphantly blared out "The Star-Spangled Banner" and the hated "Yankee Doodle."

Two days later, Lincoln experienced one of the most memorable events of his presidency. Accompanied by his young son and guarded by a small party of soldiers, on Tuesday the president left City Point on a danger-fraught exploration of Richmond. Nothing else so much embodied the Confederacy and the war it fought against the Union as did the South's capital, and Lincoln was determined to have a look at it the moment it became possible.

Written impressions of Lincoln walking calmly through the city's ruins quickly became a staple of Civil War iconography. All describe the many African-Americans who approached the president, a man whose trademark stovepipe hat made him unmistakably recognizable. It was for the freedom of those slaves in Richmond that day, and millions of others like them, that Lincoln had paid so great a price. The South's untouchables knelt in front of him, as if to a king, with twelve-year-old Tad at his side. The president was embarrassed by these supplications and told one genuflecting slave-now-free, "Don't kneel to me. That is not right. You must kneel to God only, and thank Him for the liberty you will enjoy hereafter." If this memory of the president's words perhaps slightly formalizes what had probably been far more homespun words, the response is nonetheless pure Lincolnian in its humility and allusion to how humans should relate to one another.

Lincoln took a great risk to his life—even though he was surrounded by troops eyeing the surrounding buildings for snipers, he was in danger in a city where white hatred for the president was boundless—to visit the just abandoned residence of his Southern counterpart. Already the city's conquerors had appropriated the South's executive mansion to serve as a federal military headquarters, only slightly less than forty-eight hours after the Davis family had fled the city. When Lincoln entered the house, he made straight for the Confederate president's study on the first floor. There he sat down and asked for a glass of water—the day was sweltering and made worse by the heat radiating from the many still burning buildings. Finally he said, "Thank God I have lived to see this." Lincoln would see to it that Richmond was not treated the way Sherman had treated Atlanta: The president wanted this city released from what he called its "nightmare," and he took immediate steps to try to ensure that it was not further harmed.

After leaving the Davis mansion, the president and his son climbed aboard an ambulance to be driven randomly around the streets of the city. The vehicle made but a single stop. At the Capitol, Lincoln got down and walked about the building, a wonderfully proportioned Greek-style temple designed by Thomas Jefferson to serve as the statehouse for the commonwealth of Virginia and now standing in heartbreaking if picturesque ruins. After the day's extraordinary sightseeing ended, father and son finally bedded down for the night on the *Malvern*, the navy ship that had brought them upriver from City Point.

In a letter written the next day to his secretary of state, the president invited Seward to come and join him in City Point. But the reply from Washington late in the afternoon informed Lincoln that Seward had just been involved in a carriage accident in which he was thrown to the ground, sustaining a broken arm and a broken jaw. Doctors had fitted a steel brace on the secretary's wounded head to keep it from moving. In little more than a week, the brace would literally save his life.

As for Lincoln's health and physical well-being, the notional reason for his long visit in Virginia, the stay with the army at City Point and the surprise visit to Richmond seemed to have miraculously rejuvenated the president. The center of attention, indeed of adulation, from the troops, hundreds of whose hands he happily shook, appeared to be relieved of the exhaustion that had been close to overtaking him just prior to his departure from Washington. The unplanned five-day respite he had from Mary came, unfortunately, to an end on April 6, when the first lady rejoined him at City Point. Mary brought a traveling party this time, people certain to be a good deal more congenial to her than had been Julia Grant. Joining her were senators Sumner and Harlan, the latter accompanied by his wife and daughter, young Mary Harlan, now betrothed to Robert. With typical generosity, Mary also allowed Lizzy Keckly to come along as a passenger, thus giving the seamstress a chance to visit her old home in the newly liberated Petersburg.

A single day after the first lady and her guests joined the president at City Point, General Sheridan gave Lincoln cause to be reasonably certain that Lee was on the brink of surrender. The president telegraphed Grant with the portentous news: "General Sheridan says 'If the thing is pressed, I think Lee will surrender.' Let the *thing* be pressed."[14] Sheridan did indeed press, commanding his troops to "Go through them! They're demoralized as hell."[15] With Lee now deprived of the food necessary to keep his army from starving, the Confederate commander finally accepted that resistance to the federals' strength was futile; as he retreated ahead of the pursuing Grant, Lee's real goal had now become one of feeding his men rather than of giving them victories. Still, both Lincoln's and Grant's greatest nightmare remained the vision of Lee keeping his army in the western-Virginia wilds and from there pursuing a guerrilla war, a fight the starving but still courageous rebel army might have carried on indefinitely.

Leaving Robert in Virginia, the Lincolns departed City Point on April 8. On that same day the family visited Petersburg, the president wishing to meet his wounded troops in the town's hospitals (the first lady had the day before gone to Richmond and seen for herself the Davis home, though Mary was irritated that her husband and Tad had already visited the site without her). On the slow river trip on the *River Queen* back to Washington, Lincoln worried aloud about Seward's condition, but tried to get his mind off the war and his secretary of state by reading aloud to his assembled guests. He chose long passages from Shakespeare, largely of the tragic king, Macbeth.

PEACE

Late in the afternoon of April 9—Palm Sunday—the *River Queen* docked in Washington. After a little more than two weeks away from the White House, the president had returned home in good spirits. He found War Secretary Stanton waiting for him at the dock, the cabinet officer having just heard that Lee had agreed to surrender to Grant, news Stanton was eager to share with the commander in chief. Senator Sumner joined the men for the drive to the White House in the president's official black barouche, each undoubtedly eager to discuss the consequences of the news from army headquarters. Immediately after arrival at the mansion, the president took leave of the pair. Tired but benefiting from tolerably good health—only headaches and insomnia were troubling him at the moment—he walked across Pennsylvania Avenue to visit his wounded secretary of state. Entering the first-floor foyer of the house on Lafayette Square, Lincoln climbed the stairs and was shown into Seward's bedroom, where he found the cabinet's ranking member flat on his back, his upper body encased in a bulky steel frame that held his head and broken jaw immobile.

Wanting to be certain Seward would understand the news he was bringing, Lincoln did something typical of his self-confidence that few other men would even have considered: He hauled his long frame onto Seward's sickbed and stretched himself alongside the supine patient. Then, with his mouth close up against the secretary's face, the president told him of the magnificent news from City Point. "I think we are near the end at last," Lincoln murmured. In a low voice, Seward advised the president to hold off proclaiming a day of thanksgiving until Confederate general Johnston surrendered, then drifted into sleep. Lincoln quietly left the house.

That same evening, confirmation of the news from the Army of the Potomac reached Lincoln at the White House. After forty-eight hours of personal written communication between Grant and Lee, the latter had at last accepted the Union commander's surrender terms. The capitulation had taken place that Palm Sunday at a little Virginia crossroads village called Appomattox Courthouse, ninety-five miles west of Richmond. Though we don't know if Grant specifically meant it as a historical gesture, he thoughtfully bid his adjutant Captain Robert Lincoln to accompany him when he went to meet Lee, an act that resonates as a nod to the president whose dedication to saving the Union had led to this day's events.

The city of Washington quickly transformed itself in light of the stunning news. Lee had surrendered the powerful Army of Northern Virginia, but a complete end to the war hadn't yet been delivered: Confederate commanders were still left at the head of some 175,000 men in the field, most notably General Johnston's unbowed army in North Carolina. But the people of the North regarded the capitulation of the Confederacy's foremost general as all but the same as war's end, as indeed did at least the more rational citizens of the dying Confederacy. To celebrate the best news Washington had heard in four years, its citizens set bonfires ablaze all over the city, and throughout that early-spring night thousands of jubilant people jammed the streets in ecstatic celebration.

The next morning, an enthusiastic crowd surrounded the White House, where scores of merrymakers packed themselves into the mansion's north driveway and under the portico. Though Tad appeared in a second-story window roguishly waving a captured rebel banner, their pleas for the president himself seemed as if they would go unanswered. But Lincoln did finally come into view just behind his son, and the sight of the chief executive caused hats to be spontaneously raised by every man present. Never a comfortable extemporaneous orator, and understandably wanting his words at so momentous a time to be polished and carefully considered, Lincoln declined to speak other than to say that his comments would come soon. To placate people who nonetheless rightfully expected their president to say *something*, he smilingly asked the band that was present to play "Dixie," a piece little performed in public in Washington in recent years. But the president called it "one of the best tunes I have ever heard," and lightheartedly said that the attorney general had told him the song was now "a lawful prize" and could be played at will.

The president's schedule remained busy. Lincoln spent a good part of that day composing the remarks he wished to deliver the following day.

On returning to the White House after a visit to the Navy Yard, he heard serenading him outside the gates yet another boisterous and grateful crowd. In the afternoon, the president stopped for a session at Gardner's photography studio, where he sat for several portraits to be made. Following a late cabinet meeting, he found time to jot a note to Secretary Stanton requesting some flags for which Tad was pleading. "Can he be accommodated?" Lincoln politely asked. It was followed by another note to Navy Secretary Welles, asking to "let Master Tad have a Navy sword."[16]

The following day, Tuesday, April 11, the city laid on an elaborately decorated and illuminated victory celebration. Above the Capitol's western pediment, an enormous gaslit transparency was raised, announcing, "This is the Lord's doing. It is marvelous in our eyes."[17] Also splendidly lit up was General Lee's old home, Arlington House, high on the bluff above the Potomac's Virginia shore. Homeowners all over Washington and many government office workers rigged out their houses and office buildings with every degree of decoration in displays both modest and lavish to mark the victory. Even the dour Secretary of War Stanton had decorations installed at his home, an arrangement of gas jets over his portico spelling out PEACE.[18]

Mary wrote to Senator Sumner, her traveling companion on the recent trip to City Point, asking him to view the evening's spectacle with the president and herself—she specified "about 8½ o'clock." Not unusual for Washington though, politics frustrated any such get-together. The Radical Sumner declined on the grounds that his presence at even a purely social White House gathering might be seen as approval of what many expected to be Lincoln's overly lenient treatment of the defeated Confederacy.

Lincoln passed his typically hectic office routine on this Tuesday, attending to many small bits of war business. He issued a proclamation closing Southern ports, stipulating that all foreign ships entering such harbors with dutiable cargoes "shall be forfeited to the United States." A related decree barred foreign military vessels use of American ports where such ships' home countries refused equal treatment to U.S. warships. With the federal government ending its debilitating war, Lincoln clearly felt justified in putting other nations on notice not to challenge American sovereignty at home or abroad.[19] The president

met with General Benjamin Butler to talk about the difficulties surrounding the South's newly freed slaves, an issue Lincoln well knew
would consume a great deal more of his time. And he chaired a regular
cabinet meeting.

Having spent the best part of the day working on his evening's
speech, by the time the day's regular schedule of tasks had been cleared
he was finally ready to deliver his homily marking the war's conclusion.
But contrary to what many Washingtonians expected, Lincoln had no intention of using the occasion to mundanely boast of victory or of how the
war had been won. He would instead talk about his plans for winning
the peace. The setting for the speech was his own home grounds—the
north front of the White House, specifically the room in the center of
the mansion's second floor and whose window overlooked Pennsylvania
Avenue.

Long before the announced time for Lincoln to begin his address,
the north grounds had been crowded with an expectant and cheerful
crowd. When the window sash finally rose and the president appeared,
an enormous wave of applause greeted him, causing his wife, clearly
visible to the audience, to beam happily from the adjacent window. Unfortunately, the window from which the president was to speak had not
been designed as a speaker's platform: No balcony existed on which to
step outside to enable him to be better seen, nor was the room's dim interior light strong enough for him to clearly make out his text. But
given his anxiety to ensure that his carefully prepared words were understood, the president was determined to read them exactly as he
wrote them. He first tried grasping a lantern with one hand and using
the other to hold the speech, but it quickly became apparent that this
approach didn't allow for page turning. He finally asked Noah Brooks,
standing next to him but hidden by window draperies, to hold a lantern
over the page from which he was reading. That worked, and as he finished a page, he would drop it to Tad, who was sitting, legs akimbo, at
his father's feet. As Lincoln dropped each sheet, the excited boy eagerly scooped it up.

Regrettably, the speech didn't really suit the occasion—not, at least, in
the view of the audience filling the White House's north front. Little
sense of exhilaration came from a crowd expecting verbal fireworks. But
Lincoln was, of course, speaking to the nation and, in a sense, to the entire

civilized world, and he wanted people to know his views on the "re-inauguration of the national authority." After graciously first noting that the week's victory belonged to "General Grant, his skillful officers, and brave men," the president almost immediately turned to a closely reasoned argument in respect to Louisiana's future place in the Union, particularly given the ambiguous wartime role of that state's people. He warned about the future nature of African-Americans' lives unless the country made wise choices for postwar rebuilding, cautioning that the "cup of liberty" that the war endowed to former slaves could, in the absence of wisdom, be taken away with disastrous consequences. He furthermore restated his long-held attitude regarding black suffrage, stating, "It is unsatisfactory to some that the elective franchise is not given to the colored man. I would myself prefer that it were now conferred on the very intelligent, and on those who serve our cause as soldiers."[20] It was a remarkable comment insofar as no American president had ever before publicly spoken in favor of *any* measure of voting rights for African-Americans.

Part of the crowd—including some of the newspaper reporters sprinkled among the throng—were simply lost by the president's ponderous policy presentation. The influential *New York Tribune* would write the speech "fell dead, wholly without effect on the audience." Obviously trying for some humor after what he himself likely realized was a misfire given the occasion and his immediate audience, Lincoln lamely remarked to Brooks, who had vigilantly held the lantern over him throughout, "That was a pretty fair speech, I think, but you threw some light on it."[21]

Standing in the crowd that night was the same young actor who had a few weeks earlier watched with fury and loathing as Lincoln swore for the second time his oath as president. On this occasion two associates named Lewis Powell and David Herold accompanied John Booth, men whom the actor had persuaded to conspire with him to harm the Yankee president. Up to this point, Booth still envisioned a nonlethal option. But as he listened to the man whom he held responsible for the humiliation of the Southern people and destruction of their way of life, the bile of hatred rose in the actor's throat and his plans took on a murderous form. That the president of the United States would propose that Negroes should vote, that *any* white man would allow so disgusting a travesty, consumed Booth with loathing. When Lincoln finished talking, the handsome but hard-eyed matinee idol turned to his partners and exclaimed, "That means nigger citizenship. That will be the last speech he will ever make."[22] Almost incoherent with rage, he spoke directly to the youthfully muscular Powell, demanding that the younger man take out his pistol and shoot the president then and there. When the frightened Powell refused, Booth hissed, "By God, *I'll* put him through."[23]

LAST TASKS

Wednesday and Thursday, April 12 and 13, found the president busy trying to figure out how to bring order to the crushed Confederacy. Though still exhausted, on Wednesday Lincoln met privately with Stanton and with James Speed, his new attorney general. Facing these cabinet officers could not have been pleasant for Lincoln since both came to complain about the president's tolerant reconstruction ideas for Virginia, views the two men considered overly lenient. A second meeting with Stanton that day resulted in much the same issues being rehashed, namely that Lincoln's wish to quickly bring the seceded states back into the Union had the effect of treating traitorous rebels far more gently than they deserved. Furthermore, the president wanted to directly deal with Confederate legislatures as the best means for seeing to it that necessary tasks were accomplished; not least on Lincoln's mind was the sitting Confederate legislatures' authority to immediately withdraw troops, thereby halting the ongoing fighting. Much of Lincoln's cabinet viewed this approach as politically unwise: The majority of its members, as well as many congressional Radicals, wanted the former Confederate states governed from Washington, contravening Lincoln's view that the states' own governing bodies must somehow lead themselves back into full membership in the Union. The president backed down from his plan, but he remained determined to fully restore the former Confederate states with all the speed and consideration he could command.

That night the president wrote a note to his wife, a sweet little message probably intended to help her forgive him and thus make up for the terrible scene at the City Point review. She later divulged that it was "playfully and tenderly worded, notifying the hour of the day he would drive with me."

Thursday saw more of the same grinding routine. Lincoln met with his navy secretary to discuss reestablishment of authority in the defeated states, Welles taking the Radicals' harsher views on the issue. On a morning visit to the telegraph office in the War Department, the president first greeted the operator and then continued on to Secretary Stanton's office. This cabinet officer's opinion of Lincoln had risen astronomically since Stanton took office early in the first administration, and now at war's end Stanton had become an extraordinarily close adviser to the commander in chief. Leaving the War Department, the president indulged himself with a horseback ride out to the Soldiers' Home, likely as much to escape the White House and its pressures as to gain a small measure of exercise. While on the road between the White House and the first family's summer residence, Lincoln passed alongside a coach carrying the assistant secretary of the treasury, Maunsell B. Field, who later commented that the chief executive had looked weary and sad. No formal social events were scheduled for the evening, nothing for which the president would have to get himself dressed up and shake countless proffered hands. This spring day was neither extraordinary nor entirely without incident, instead just another of the busy days that Lincoln would bear through the next four years, during which he knew he would in all probability find little rest as he directed the traumatized nation's reconstruction.

GOOD FRIDAY

On Good Friday, the day marking the most awe-inspiring phenomenon in Christian belief, the people of Washington were amply justified in believing themselves delivered of their own miracle. Despite an overnight downpour spoiling what had been fine spring weather, citizens of the District and the thousands of military personnel who still crowded it remained buoyant in the happy glow created by Lee's surrender. But making the day even more electrifying was the news that the general who had done so much to bring the war to a triumphant close had come to town. Ulysses Grant was due this morning to join the president and the cabinet at the White House to discuss the future of the peace. Most people in the city figured Lincoln was going to have a fine time over the next few days, especially by showing off his magnificent fighting general.

In the White House, the Lincolns saw their day started in the best way possible: Robert had just returned to Washington as a part of General Grant's entourage and would join his family at breakfast. The president, who awakened at seven o'clock that morning, was elated that his son had arrived home. Knowing the memento he had brought home would interest his father, Captain Lincoln showed the president a new photograph of Lee. Looking at it pensively, Lincoln said, "It is a good face, the face of a noble, noble brave man," adding, "I am glad that the war is over at last."[24] Robert recounted for his unusually spirited family his impressions of the historic surrender scene at Appomattox Courthouse, to which Grant had so considerately asked the young man to attend on him. It is thought that the first lady then invited her son to join her and his father at the theater that evening. Such entertainment was just the kind of outing that the president liked best, and Robert's parents were to see a comedy called *Our American Cousin,* and Mary probably believed it would also serve her son as a pleasurable antidote to his harried days in Virginia. If she did indeed ask him, the son declined, likely wishing to join his close friend John Hay in catching up on the latest news of their lives (John Nicolay was out of town on a presidential mission). Moreover, Robert was fatigued, the journey from Appomattox having been a hard slog through country torn to pieces by the war and in which the railroads remained out of commission. As for Tad, the family's youngest member was expecting an excursion later that morning with one of the White House doormen and was doubly excited at the prospect of the evening's planned trip with his tutor to see a production of *Aladdin* at the National Theater.

Routine appointments consumed most of the president's postbreakfast morning. He met first with Indiana congressman Schuyler Colfax, the Speaker of the House, who was preparing to leave on a trip to the West Coast; ebullient with the Speaker, Lincoln told him that he believed America was about to become "the treasury of the world" and that immigration would "land upon our shores hundreds of thousands . . . from overcrowded Europe."[25] Before leaving for a carriage ride with General Grant, Lincoln received New Hampshire senator John Hale, whom he had just named minister to Spain. Sprinkled throughout the rest of the day were congressmen and senators who stopped by the White House to congratulate the president on an apparently successful end to the war. As was his lot almost every working day, a line of supplicants—many of whom merely wanted to shake his hand—waited in the corridor outside his office. Most were allowed a minute or two to lay their wants or their best wishes before the president.

Though presumably an invitation to join the first family at the theater would be seen as a high honor, Lincoln was nonetheless having a terrible time trying to find someone to go with him and Mary that evening to see *Our American Cousin*. Perhaps what was causing some of the numerous invitees to decline was simply Good Friday's religious significance. But even the not-devoutly-religious Stantons turned down the president, most likely because Ellen Stanton's antipathy to Mary just about equaled that of Julia Grant. Lincoln persevered, throughout the day inviting everyone of any note he ran into. Though later in the afternoon Mary would protest that she had a headache and suggested they abandon their evening plans, Lincoln retorted that because the theater had advertised his and his wife's planned attendance, it would be inconsiderate on their part if they failed to show up. Furthermore, he said that if they stayed home, he knew that people would make all kinds of demands on his attention and were thus bound to ruin his evening.

General Grant's presence made the regular noontime cabinet meeting far more special than usual. The conquering hero presented to Lincoln and his highest advisers a report detailing Lee's surrender five days earlier, historic events of keen interest to everyone present. Listening to Grant's report on the surrender were War Secretary Edwin Stanton, Navy Secretary Gideon Welles, Treasury Secretary Hugh McCulloch (who had replaced William Fessenden earlier that year), Interior Secretary John Usher (having replaced Caleb Smith in 1863), Postmaster General William Dennison (who had replaced Montgomery Blair the prior year), Attorney General James Speed, and Acting (for his own father) Secretary of State Frederick Seward. The men in the room found Lincoln unusually upbeat, given the load he had for so long carried, and each politely commented on the commander in chief's seeming good spirits. Lincoln knew "the butchering"—his apt word for the war—was about at an end, and nothing could have been more important to him than that American soldiers were to finally stop dying in mutual slaughter. The general air of euphoria aside, the advisers thrashed out contentious questions dealing with national restoration, with a wide divergence of opinion as to the harshness with which the South should be treated during its reconstruction. Lincoln commented on the central question of restoring the rebel state governments: "We can't take to running state governments in all these Southern states. Their people must do that, although I reckon at first they may do it badly." When someone raised the issue of dealing with rebel leaders, the president said that he himself wished they would simply flee the country. The fate of Jefferson Davis was an especially sensitive topic, since everyone in the room knew that most Northerners wanted to see the Confederate president simply and immediately hanged.

Oddly, the president shared the substance of his prior night's dream with the gathering, relating something about a ship "moving with great rapidity toward a dark and definite shore"; he thought it had been a fine dream, of a type that always presaged good news. Perversely though, he had been plagued for days by troubling dreams, some bordering on nightmares. One had to do with his own funeral in the White House. Lincoln apparently remembered the details of these dreams, episodes that would today likely be associated with depression. Less clear was why he felt compelled to share their contents with friends and guests, as he had done on White House social occasions over the past weeks.

The meeting broke up at about two o'clock, but before Grant could get away the president asked him if he and Mrs. Grant would join him and the first lady at the theater that evening. It must have delighted Lincoln when Grant tentatively accepted the invitation, his only proviso being that his wife consent as well. Unsurprisingly, she didn't consent. Julia Grant's *stated* reason was the couple's commitment to leave that evening for Burlington, New Jersey, to join their children. Probably her real objection was to the prospect of a social occasion with Mary Lincoln, given the recent unpleasantness at City Point. In justice to Julia Grant's innate kindness, though, she did regard the widely known reports of Mrs. Lincoln's outlandish behavior at her husband's headquarters as "embellished" by a staff member, her own view being that Mary Lincoln was simply "fatigued" at the time.

In the hour following the cabinet meeting, Lincoln returned to his office to face more visitors: well-wishers, members of Congress and politicians, and a few people who had come to seek releases of or pardons for prisoners. The president and his wife then had lunch, after which Lincoln met with his new vice president. Among his last tasks that afternoon was putting his signature to a sheaf of pardons. One went to save a doomed Union soldier, a deserter on whose file were written the words "not perfectly sound." Another released a condemned Confederate soldier; as he signed the document that meant life for the latter young man,

Lincoln commented to his secretary John Hay, "I think this boy can do more good aboveground than underground."

Late in the afternoon Lincoln forsook his office and the paperwork that still lay deeply stacked on his desk. He had promised the first lady a carriage ride, it was a nice day, and he intended to get out of the White House and fill his lungs with clean spring air. Today it would be just him and Mary in the barouche—plus, of course, the usual escort of soldiers riding alongside to protect him from, among other dangers, Southern agents thought to still represent a threat to the man who had led the defeat of the Confederacy. The couple's destination was the Navy Yard, in the southeastern quadrant of the city and a considerable distance from the White House. Lincoln clearly enjoyed the place since he had visited it dozens of times in his presidency, more often, in fact, than any other site in the capital except the Soldiers' Home. The president and first lady stepped out of the carriage at the dock where the USS *Montauk* lay tied up, paying a surprise visit to the ironclad's crew. As the couple wandered through the ship, the president likely dispelled some of his curiosity about the naval weapons of war used under his commandership in chief, almost all of which fascinated him. The surgeon on board, Dr. George Todd—not a relation to the first lady—noted that the pair seemed "very happy" that day.[26]

The ride back to the White House has been enshrined in the Lincoln story. Mary wrote about it seven months afterward, the scene she described becoming a part of many Americans' image of the couple's sometimes rocky but nonetheless affectionate and long-lived marriage. Mary noted that her husband seemed "almost boyish" that afternoon, that he was "so gay" that she was "almost startled" by his "great cheerfulness." His words to her, as she remembered them, became legendary: "We must *both*, be more cheerful in the future—between the war & the loss of our darling Willie—we have *both*, been very miserable." It was clear to Mary, and probably to history as well, that Abraham Lincoln was looking forward to a far happier second term than the first had been for the nation and for his own family.

They still had the theater to think about though. After so many turndowns to their invitation, the Lincolns at last recollected a young couple that they thought might like to accompany them to Ford's, and an invitation was dispatched. Henry Rathbone was an army major, and though

not close to the first family he must at some time have entered their social orbit and suitably impressed. His fiancée, Clara Harris, was the
daughter of a senator from New York, and she and Major Rathbone were
not only engaged to be married, but were stepsiblings as well. What
mattered, though, was that they accepted and were apparently highly
honored to have been asked.

So after the Lincolns' seven o'clock dinner—we don't know what was
served at the White House that evening—a carriage left the executive
residence bearing the president of the United States and his wife, going
first to the Harris home to pick up their guests, before heading for Tenth
Street and an anticipated happy and relaxed evening.

FORD'S

It was an unusually late hour for anyone to be rapping on Robert Lincoln's bedroom door. When the twenty-one-year-old army captain arose
to answer the knock, he found White House guard Thomas Pendel
standing in front of him, the blood drained from his face. Only moments
earlier Pendel had heard that the president had been shot at the theater.
The guard, who found Lincoln with a vial of medicine and a spoon in his
hands and assumed he wasn't feeling well, said, "Captain, there has something happened to the President; you had better go down to the theatre
and see what it is."[27] Lincoln asked Pendel to fetch Hay, and he and his
father's secretary immediately left a White House already in the first
stages of turmoil from the various people bursting through its doors.
The weather had turned cold and foggy, threatening to rain. Halfway to
Ford's Theater they passed a roadblock, just having been set out to try
to snare an escaped assassin. Lincoln cried out at the soldier on duty,
"It's my father! My father! I'm Robert Lincoln."[28]

As they neared Ford's, someone told the son and the secretary that the
president had been taken to a boardinghouse directly opposite the theater. In the last hour the house had been transformed from its mundane
function into the nerve center of the American government, there gathered and still gathering many of the most important men in the country.
Stepping in splotches of blood, the pair quickly dashed up the outside
steps of the nondescript little building, which they later learned was
owned by a man named Petersen. Robert Stone, the Lincolns' family

doctor, was standing at the front door. He told Robert as gently as possible that there was no hope that his father could survive the gunshot wound he had sustained less than an hour before.

Ascending the stairs, Lincoln and Hay dashed along one side of the corridor wall. Robert saw that a goodly crowd had already wedged itself inside an ordinary little bedroom at the head of the narrow hall passage. Inside the bedroom door, the president's son was presented with a scene as grotesque as any played out in the nation's history. Sprawled on the bed was a man's long frame, placed at an angle so the legs didn't have to be bent up against the end of the bedstead. The figure was the nearly spent president, and every pair of eyes in the room was looking down at the horror-filled scene. One of the doctors present—Charles Sabin Taft—remembered that in the first moments of Robert's presence, Captain Lincoln was nearly overwhelmed by grief, but that he quickly comported himself into a stoic quietness. Robert saw another agonizing image: His mother was nearly demented with grief, and he instantly understood that the events of the last hour had embodied the collapse of her world.

When the first lady, her husband, and their two enthralled guests had arrived at Ford's Theater earlier that evening, the action on the stage was already well along. Nonetheless, when the presidential party entered its box overlooking the stage, the actors respectfully halted the play and both they and the audience broke into sincere and prolonged applause for a man now regarded as the nation's redeemer.

Mary couldn't have been happier, largely because of the long-missing joy she again saw in her husband's eyes. The headache she had said she was suffering earlier that afternoon was long forgotten. Now the first lady was contentedly basking in the warm glow of an adoring throng as well as in the familiar kindness of a husband of nearly a quarter century, with whom she could look forward to growing gracefully old. As the play progressed to one of its well-known laugh lines—*Our American Cousin* and its old jokes had long since become stale, but the play's humor still found appreciative audiences—the president, stretched out in a comfortable rocking chair specially provided by the theater's management, reached over to his wife and took her hand in his. Mary voiced some soft embarrassment at this public familiarity, whispering to her husband that their guests might be scandalized. The president rejoined that in his view nobody would think a thing about an old married couple sitting hand in hand. Just as he returned his attention to the action onstage, a derringer's half-inch-diameter bullet smashed into the back of his head, penetrating his brain with deadly force. Although he would not die for several more hours, the wound was mortal.

Mary screamed out across the theater and fell in shock over her husband's inert frame, Major Rathbone grabbed at the assassin but in return for his heroic efforts was nearly killed with the slash of Booth's knife, Clara Harris saw herself drenched with her fiancé's blood, the killer jumped over the box's front edge and managed a successful escape into the alley behind the theater, the audience quickly came to understand that the commotion in the presidential box wasn't part of the play but rather an attack on its occupant, onlooker Dr. Charles Leale sized up what had happened and ran to the president's box to give assistance but saw that the wound was fatal, yet another doctor sprinted from the orchestra seats to the stage and was lifted into the box where he began to help Leale, the female star called loudly from the proscenium for calm, soldiers numbly gathered to carry the president away but didn't know where to take him, but once outside the theater and on the street they followed shouted orders to carry their awkward burden into the boardinghouse just across the way. Robert arrived only a little time after these dizzyingly congested events.

For the remainder of the night, the men who ran the United States looked at the president and waited, most surely aware that their vigil was a deathwatch. Mary was in and out of the room, her shrieks reverberating through the black hours holding back the dawn. Secretary Stanton took charge, brusquely but capably directing a search for the assassins, deciding on Vice President Johnson's part in the drama, sending Mary out of the death chamber when her sobs got to be more than he could stand. From time to time, though, the first lady came back to the president's bedside, once pleading that her youngest son be sent for because she thought the boy's presence would cause her husband to speak to Tad "because he loved him so well." Over all this passion Robert watched, pulling himself together from a stunned young son into the new head of the Lincoln family and stroking his mother's hand while murmuring to her that she should put her "trust in God and all will be well." In reality, nothing would ever again be well for Mary Lincoln.

It ended early in the still gray morning hours of the fifteenth, when the president breathed his last shallow breath. One of the doctors folded Lincoln's arms over his body and said simply, "He is gone." The grim and dark-eyed secretary of war—having become, at least by his own lights, the acting president of the United States—stared at the body, tears streaming down his cheeks, and spoke the immortal words that his chief and friend now belonged to the ages. Mary had been out of the room when the end came, which would cause her pain throughout her widowhood. When she was brought into the chamber where the still warm corpse lay, Robert enfolded his nearly paralyzed mother in his arms and then shepherded her down the stairs and out the door to the carriage that through gloomy and sodden Washington streets bore her to a place that was really no longer hers to call home. The city's bells had already started their desolate tolling, a tribute that was soon taken up by nearly every populated place in the North.

DEATH IN THE WHITE HOUSE

Two great tasks fell to the United States in the early hours after the president's death. One was to stage a proper and fitting, which is to say grand, funeral for the slain president. The other was to apprehend the killers, in the plural. There was no notion yet of the breadth of the plot, but to Stanton it was almost certain that the crime had been a conspiracy, with the main assassin assisted by at least one other killer. At the same time that the president was shot, a murderous assault was waged against the secretary of state. At his home across the street from the White House's north entrance, William Seward was attacked and came within a trice of being killed in what appeared to be an attempt to decapitate the federal government. After taking a delivery of a medication to gain entrance to the Seward home, first the assassin nearly fatally wounded Seward's son, Frederick, the acting secretary of state (since his father's injury in a carriage accident a few days earlier), and then assailed Seward himself in his bed, inflicting appalling knife wounds to the secretary's upper torso and head, injuries that would almost certainly have ended his life had his vital arteries not been protected by the heavy neck brace he was wearing as a result of his recent carriage mishap.

As the government began to link rapidly accumulating details surrounding the crimes, evidence of a plot of even greater extent seemed overwhelming. Most seriously, it speedily became clear that the assassins had also pursued the vice president, though for unknown reasons he was not physically attacked. But with the president, vice president, and secretary of state having been targets, conspiracy was a foregone conclusion. Given that the war was not yet entirely won—General Johnston's army still commanded parts of the Confederacy, of which Jefferson Davis remained president—many concluded that the assaults had officially been orchestrated by the enemy, which would likely have meant that Jefferson Davis approved of them. Hours before Johnson was sworn in as the new president, Stanton ordered a gigantic manhunt to find the immediate culprits.

Though these issues consumed a public staggered by the tragedy, inside the White House gloom and sorrow of indescribable proportions filled every corner. Tad was, of course, crushed by his father's death. The boy had been enjoying himself at the National Theater the night before with his tutor when a messenger came down the aisle and whispered into the older man's ear. The tutor, nearly fainting from what he'd been told, immediately returned Tad to the White House. Thomas Pendel, the same messenger who had awakened Robert, tried to comfort Tad, embracing the boy, who was exhausting himself from his weeping. Pendel undressed the president's youngest son, laid him in his bed, and stayed with him until a few hours of sleep briefly removed him from the pain.

After what had been for him a sleepless night, in the morning Robert had to occasionally interrupt the business of directing his family affairs, most urgent of which was wiring the family lawyer, David Davis of Chicago, to come to Washington to "take charge of my father's affairs." Primarily, though, Robert had to see to his mother, whose paroxysms of grief were so profound that she seemed to be nearly asphyxiating from convulsions. Tad came in to join his brother in trying to comfort their mother. "Don't cry so, Mamma," he implored, "don't cry, or you will make me cry, too! You will break my heart."[29] The boy was barely holding himself together. Navy Secretary Welles passed Tad in the White House hall that day of calamitous bewilderment. "Oh, Mr. Welles," he begged, "who killed my father?" Welles could find no answer.

The widow had refused to be placed in her own bedroom, evidently because she didn't want to enter any of the family rooms and be confronted with the memories they held for her. Instead, she was put in a small room sometimes used by the president during the summer when the family lived at the Soldiers' Home. Robert tried to tend a mother still shrieking in agony, but Lizzy Keckly eventually took over and did her best to calm the ravaged woman, who for four years had been her friend and benefactor. It was the beginning of a nearly six-week-long ordeal, with Mary remaining in the White House, in bed, her sanity hanging by a thread, while the world moved around her without her caring about a single thing but the loss of her husband. Throughout, Lizzy unwaveringly stayed at Mary's side.

Those most intimately connected to the late president decided to hold the funeral on the following Wednesday. Robert and Stanton likely bore the principal voices in the matter; the widow was far too distraught to be approached about such issues. In fact, on the day of the funeral Mary was still too unwell to transport herself anywhere, let alone to appear in public. As workmen downstairs in the East Room were finishing the funeral's catafalque, they had to be told to muffle their hammering because Mrs. Lincoln protested that each blow sounded like the gunshot made by the assassin.

Beautiful spring weather in Washington greeted the mourners on the day of the funeral, the sky sunny and a gentle breeze blowing across the city. Of course, the Executive Mansion represented the complete opposite of the day's lovely brightness: The outside of the house had nearly been obscured with black crepe, the inside turned into a shrine of mourning. Black cloth wound around the mirrors and chandeliers and even covered some of the floor. A flower-covered catafalque dominated the center of the East Room, the mansion's largest chamber. Lying serenely inside the coffin was Lincoln's body, a white pillow supporting the corpse's head. A bed of roses crossed the foot of the coffin. Some six hundred people crowded into the room. The leading mourner was the president of the United States, who was standing midpoint at the side of the coffin, the benumbed Andrew Johnson periodically crossing and uncrossing his hands on his chest. Robert and Tad stood, equally benumbed, at their father's feet. A weeping Grant stood alone at the head.

Four ministers spoke at the service, after which the coffin was closed and carried outside into the sunlight and to a funeral car waiting to bear its treasure up Pennsylvania Avenue. Along the march, it was guarded by black troops at its head, with some four thousand more African-Americans marching along in its wake. Among the sixty thousand people who saw the parade that day was Secretary of State Seward, who watched from his bedroom window, still in severe pain from the wounds he had received from one of Booth's assassins. The procession ended at the Capitol, where the slain president's bearers placed their burden under the rotunda. There it rested on another catafalque for twenty-four hours while thousands of ordinary citizens filed by for one final moment in the emancipator's presence. The next day the body was taken to the Washington train station to start a fourteen-day journey through America to burial in Illinois. The route was the reverse of that which the president-elect had traveled some fifty months earlier when he'd come to Washington to preside over the government of a nation in its last days of peace.

John Hay acted as Mary's go-between in planning for the vacating of what was now Andrew Johnson's White House, though the new president did not in any way importune Abraham Lincoln's widow. Hay understood that Mrs. Lincoln would not be able to coherently consider her future for some considerable time. Immediately following her husband's murder, Mary was incapacitated as she alternated between screaming and near-catatonia. Out of her mind with grief, she had no choice but to leave many personal matters in the hands of her eldest son, and to his credit Robert moved with remarkable skill in directing the affairs now affecting his gravely wounded family. Observing Robert on the day following the assassination, presidential assistant Edward D. Neill commented, "His manly bearing on that trying occasion made me feel that he was a worthy son of a worthy father."[30]

Throughout the following weeks in the White House, Mary refused to see all but a few of the members of official Washington society who came to offer their condolences. Her behavior was greatly resented and did much to cement the negative feelings Washingtonians held for her throughout the remainder of her life. She did consent to see Senator Sumner, Secretary Stanton, and a few senatorial wives—all of whom were subjected to a horrendous scene. One described her as "more dead than alive, broken by the horrors of that dreadful night as well as worn down by bodily sickness."[31] Lizzy Keckly remembered Mary's unending grief as manifested in "the wails of a broken heart, the unearthly shrieks, the terrible convulsion."

Meanwhile, President Johnson was obliged to conduct the office he had so brutally inherited from a small room in the Treasury building, next door to the White House. He sent no sympathy note nor paid even a single call on the widow in the White House, believing, rightly, that Mary Lincoln disliked him—in fact, she had not forgiven his embarrassing behavior at her husband's second inauguration—and would thus be upset by any contact from him. Robert wrote to the president in late April, "My mother and I are aware of the great inconvenience to which you are subjected by the transaction of business in your present quarters but my mother is so prostrated that I must beg your indulgence. Mother tells me that she cannot possibly be ready to leave here for 2½ weeks." But because Mary had no intention of returning to the Springfield house that had been her and her husband's only home before his presidency, she didn't know where to go. That her prolonged stay in the White House inconvenienced the current president of the United States seems not to have made the slightest impression on her broken mind.

While upstairs all was mourning and desolation, downstairs streams of sightseers roamed through what was essentially an open and unguarded building. Almost everything that wasn't nailed down was stolen, including crystal and china and silver, with dishonest staff members taking part. After Mary's departure, the story spread through the country that Mrs. Lincoln had taken these stolen things with her when she'd departed, another unfair and long-uncorrected blemish on her reputation and legacy.

Mary was aroused from her torpor of grief when Robert returned to the White House from having attended his father's burial in Springfield. He told his mother that the municipal fathers there had begun a campaign to raise funds for a memorial and a burial place in the center of the city, whose current prominence was now due more to Lincoln's worldwide fame than it was to simply being the capital of Illinois. But Mary believed her husband wished to be interred in a quiet spot and had already decided on Springfield's Oak Ridge Cemetery. The shock of Robert's news raised Mary's temper to fever pitch to stop what she thought was the contravening of her husband's express wishes—which automatically became *her* wishes.

Since the funeral, the timing of Mary's departure from the White House had been of intense interest in Washington and, for that matter, throughout the nation. Though in mid-May it appeared that she would leave "soon," the expected time came and went when she lapsed into uncontrollable depression. Robert probably persuaded his mother that she had overstayed her welcome in the White House, as her remaining there had become an embarrassment. Sadly, her leave-taking date, May 22, was but a single day before an immense victory celebration for the Union armies. Instead of her husband—and herself—presiding over the eve of this historic celebration, Mary Lincoln, shrouded from head to foot in the heaviest and most somber mourning weeds obtainable, quietly left her home of slightly more than four years. There was no pomp whatsoever. There were no friends to say good-bye. Nor was there even any real attention paid that Abraham Lincoln's widow was departing the capital of the nation he had saved.

EPILOGUE

———

THE FLYING DUTCHMAN

DESPITE BEING THE WIDOW OF THE MOST FAMOUS MAN in the world, Mary Lincoln went off into what was left of her life little noticed and largely unlamented. She would find few days of happiness in her remaining seventeen years. Some of her days would simply be sad, a few catastrophic. During the worst of times, she wished she were dead. Adding to all the misery she had borne, at the end of her life yet a final calamity would come, one that caused her to die with an uncompromising hatred for the only son who would survive her.

From the White House that day in May 1865, Mary, her sons Robert and Tad, and her loyal friend/dressmaker/servant Lizzy Keckly traveled by train to Chicago, the city in which she had decided to live out her widowhood. Her traveling party also comprised a physician and two White House guards; one of the latter, William Crook, later recalled that Mrs. Lincoln passed the entire trip in a daze, almost in a stupor, and wrote, "She hardly spoke . . . no one could get near enough to her grief to comfort her."[1]

After a short stay in an expensive Chicago hotel called the Tremont House, the money-conscious Mary felt constrained to find cheaper lodgings, settling on a three-room hotel apartment in the lakeside community of Hyde Park, seven miles south of Chicago, which was in the middle of nowhere. Both Mary and Robert hated the depressing accommodations, Robert because of the isolation—he was forced to take a long streetcar ride into Chicago every morning to continue his apprenticeship in a law firm—and Mary because no conceivable place could have made her happy. As for the home she owned a day's journey away in Springfield, she leased the house to renters and never considered moving into it herself, convinced she could find no joy as a widow in the city where all her memories revolved around being the wife of Abraham Lincoln.

When Lincoln was assassinated, widows of presidents received no government pension. Her husband left Mary his personal estate of around $85,000, including the value of the Springfield house. Since Lincoln died intestate (no one knows why this lawyer had failed to write a will), the law required that this total be evenly divided among his direct heirs, his widow and his two surviving sons. The interest on the capital of Mary's portion amounted to about $1,800 a year, while Tad's share was put in trust pending his twenty-first birthday. Her interest gave her just enough income to live comfortably if modestly if she had returned to her home in Springfield, where the cost of living was lower than in Chicago. But Mary had persuaded herself that she was destitute, a false perception that nonetheless directed many of the decisions she made after the death of her husband. Some part of her fear undoubtedly initially came from the sizable debt she had accumulated in her role as first lady. That burden had long terrified her and she believed that as a widow she had little hope of seeing it settled.

From being a first lady who could, when she wanted, demonstrate such sophistication even as to make charming conversation in French, Mary quickly metamorphosed into a sickly, reclusive, and, above all, deeply depressed woman whose contentedness lay almost wholly in the companionship of her two sons. Her weeping became so constant that it eventually injured her eyes, the swelling around them nearly blinding her. So as not to be spied on and risk pity from strangers, Mary craved anonymity—yet, paradoxically, she quickly took offense when deference wasn't accorded her for being Abraham Lincoln's widow.

One of the worst shocks of her post–White House life came in 1866, when her husband's old law partner, the prickly William Herndon, finally found the ammunition to use against Mary to repay her haughtiness toward him in the Springfield years. In a lecture Herndon delivered in November of that year, he hypothesized that Ann Rutledge had been the sole true love of Lincoln's life and that his marriage to Mary Todd had been passionless, simply a rebound from his loss of Rutledge. Hurt beyond measure by Herndon's supposition, Mary naturally believed it caused irreversible damage to her public standing, her status being based solely on her relationship to the nation's greatest president.

Mary suffered another wounding incident a year later. In an attempt to pay off the creditors who were pressing her to reimburse the debts she had incurred as first lady—they totaled perhaps $20,000, a substantial sum in late-nineteenth-century dollars—in 1867 she decided to sell her old and now unneeded clothing. The venture turned into a double misfortune. First, Mary made little money off the scheme; though the curious came to paw through the former first lady's belongings, few bought any of the dresses and other personal items on offer, many of the spectators simply being incredulous that the martyred president's widow could truly be in need of money. And second, the project was widely perceived as indecorous for a president's widow, further diminishing her reputation and inviting press ridicule. The outcome came close to robbing her of what little spirit she still possessed.

From the beginning of her widowhood, one of Mary's abiding campaigns was to persuade Congress to legislate a pension for her. She naturally deemed the lack of such a stipend a grave injustice to the widow of the nation's savior, as such she (and millions of her fellow citizens) regarded her husband. At the end of 1865, Congress did vote a onetime gift to Mrs. Lincoln. The amount came to one year of her husband's $25,000 annual salary, minus the portion he had been paid from the day of his second inaugural to the day of his murder. With the deduction, Mary received $22,025.34, which enabled her to buy a Chicago home. But the house she chose was so costly that she could barely afford to furnish it (properly, at least); eventually, she couldn't even maintain it. In 1870, Congress again came to her rescue—however grudgingly and by no means unanimously. That body approved for her an annual pension of $3,000, which twelve years later it raised to $5,000, with a $15,000 onetime "donation" tacked onto the latter amount. One other substantial cash addition increased her total worth: On Tad's death in 1871 she inherited half of his estate, which had amounted to a third of his father's estate; the remaining half went to Robert. Though the circumstances aren't known for certain, her outstanding debt of around $20,000 to merchants on her purchases as first lady was eventually cleared, probably mostly by Robert, and some, so it is thought, when the bills were written off by the creditors themselves.

Feeling hounded and unloved, in 1868 Mary left the United States. Less than a week after attending Robert's wedding to Mary Harlan in September of that year, she sailed with Tad to Europe. There she took up residence, mainly in Frankfurt, Germany, where she put her son into school. On school holidays the pair traveled all over Europe on sightseeing trips and on visits to medicinal spas where Mary sought relief from her many ills, the worst being her nearly crippling back pain. Tad performed well in school, discrediting the notions of mental retardation that were at one time widely circulated and believed because of his early speech impediment. In fact, while accompanying his mother on her wanderings, Tad was growing into a balanced, good-looking, and well-mannered young man, though his health remained problematic. Probably the worst aspect of European life for Tad was that he missed his one surviving brother, and he was clearly eager to return to the United States to be nearer to Robert.

In March 1871—two and a half years after leaving the United States—Mary returned to her native country, likely impelled to do so because of Tad's increasing homesickness. Mary herself would probably have been content to remain in Europe, where she lived in extraordinarily modest circumstances considering her status as Lincoln's widow. In reality, she likely went overboard with her thrift, believing herself on the brink of destitution when such was not the case. Yet she genuinely and deeply feared poverty, probably more than any other circumstance, and in light of that fear usually spent as little money as possible. Back in America with Tad she considered herself homeless and thus accepted Robert's invitation to live with him and his wife, Mary, in Chicago, where his law practice was beginning to provide a comfortable income and the accoutrements of an upper-middle-class lifestyle.

Any chance that Mary might contentedly have settled in Chicago, where Robert would likely have eased if not eliminated her money problems, quickly evaporated. Tad had evidently picked up a cold on the ocean voyage home from Europe, and his fragile constitution was unable to shake it. By the time the illness became serious, mother and younger son were no longer living with Robert and his wife but in a Chicago hotel, the former first lady's combative and prickly nature having already caused a dispute between her and her daughter-in-law that had ended with Mary leaving her elder son's Wabash Avenue house. Despite the services of three Chicago doctors who attended the boy in his and his mother's hotel room, Tad grew sicker daily. The cold weakened the eighteen-year-old, and pleurisy set in, probably caused by either pneumonia or tuberculosis. In a pre-antibiotic age, only his own self-curing strength could have saved him. Unfortunately, there wasn't enough strength left. As water filled Tad's lungs, the boy had to be kept strapped upright to keep him from drowning, his mother having bought a special chair to hold him in that position when he nodded off. Ever weaker, he thus precariously subsisted for weeks. But serum and pus from the bacterial infection were relentlessly filling his lungs. Finally, on the morning of July 15, 1871, Tad turned blue, slumped forward in the chair, and died. The newspapers gave the cause of death as "compression of the heart." Traumatized for a second time in six years, Mary wrote to a friend, "As grievous as other bereavements have been, not one great sorrow ever approached the agony to this."[2]

After this disaster, Mary's behavior began to flow into ever more eccentric channels. What is thought to be the last picture of her was taken in 1872, when the photographer captured a squat little woman, cloaked in her habitual mourning and appearing far older than her actual age of fifty-four. Though the photo of the former first lady wasn't particularly unusual except for the grief that was unmistakably reflected in her eyes, the studio had superimposed on it a ghostlike image of her husband, seemingly looking at Mary and with his hands placed on her shoulders. Mary was delighted with and, apparently, comforted by the doctored portrait.

Her travels resumed, but this time she roamed North America instead of Europe to escape the devils that she believed were pursuing her. In 1875 she reverted to the manic buying that had characterized her White House behavior—only now, of course, she was obliged to pay cash for the things she wanted. Back in Chicago that year, the bent-over little lady in black weeds became a familiar character along the city's main shopping courses, engaging in conversation with anyone who offered his or her ear, the stranger often being refreshed on the details of this sorrowful woman's life story. In the best stores on State Street, Mary bought bagfuls of things she didn't need, couldn't afford, and had no permanent home in which to store: dozens of pairs of gloves, endless panels of draperies for windows that existed only in her imagination, skeins of ribbon that would never decorate a frock or a hat, expensive jewelry, countless bottles of toiletries. In her skirts she hid $57,000 in securities, the larger portion of her capital. All these things mystified and perplexed the one person who still watched over her, albeit ever less sympathetically. But she would not stay with Robert—the younger Mrs. Lincoln did not wish her to stay in her home and the elder woman did not want to be where she believed she was not wanted. Instead she put up at a hotel called the Grand Pacific, an elegant new building meant to symbolize the city's recovery from the disastrous fire of four years earlier. Mary's room was modest, however, one without a sitting area or a bath, again chosen for economy when she could have afforded something more comfortable and fitting to her station in life.

Given his wife's reluctance to share her home with Mary, Robert also took a room at the same hotel to be close at hand to a mother he believed could no longer be trusted to safeguard herself or manage her affairs. Her behavior at the Grand Pacific was probably most responsible for Robert's subsequent actions. Mary appeared in the hotel's hallway in her nightclothes, and when Robert asked an employee to help him lead his mother back to her room, she screamed that her son was trying to kill her. After that shocking scene he believed she was mentally unable to keep herself from grave physical or financial harm. In short, her son was certain she was insane, and Robert petitioned a court to have his mother so declared and thus in need of confinement.

This chapter in the lives of the former first lady and her last remaining son represents one of the most controversial episodes in the long Lincoln story. Some historians believe Mary was incarcerated on evidence fabricated by Robert, his motive being that he either wanted to ensure that his mother's estate not be squandered or that he abhorred the embarrassment she was causing him and his ever-quickening reputation as an important lawyer. But other historians think that Robert's motives were selfless, that he believed his mother had placed her own life in danger because of her unbalanced mental state. Ironically, at the time of these events Illinois possessed probably the strongest laws of any state in the country safeguarding the rights of persons whom other persons (often husbands) were attempting to have declared mentally incompetent. As a result of the Illinois protective law, Mary received a formal trial in which Robert was required to prove his assertions to the satisfaction of the court.

The case went to trial in Chicago in May 1875. After hearing the testimony of Robert and other witnesses regarding Mary's behavior, the jury found itself "satisfied that the said Mary Lincoln [was] insane and [was] a fit person to be sent to the State Hospital."[3] The episode's effect on the relationship between mother and son was lethal. From that time forward, Mary considered herself childless, her relationship with Robert and his wife becoming nonexistent except for the unremitting hatred she bore for the injury her son had done to her *and* to the legacy of Abraham Lincoln.

Mary Lincoln did not go to a "State Hospital." Instead, Robert had her taken to an expensive sanatorium in Batavia, thirty-five miles west of Chicago. Bellevue Place was a private women's mental institution, and in it Mary was cared for in a well-appointed suite of rooms far removed from the *Snake Pit* image of premodern psychiatric care. She enjoyed the liberty of the grounds and even dined with the director and his family. There were, of course, some deeply ill inmates at Bellevue—for example, the anorexic Miss Minnie Judd, who had to be force-fed, and a Mrs. Wheeler, who "raved in the mornings"[4]—but apparently Mary was treated with the respect due to her unique status. Yet however gentle her incarceration relative to nineteenth-century norms, the one unbearable reality for Mary resulting from Robert's actions was the loss of her freedom.

Mary's confinement didn't last long. Before the end of that summer of 1875, the once again articulate former first lady was released from Bellevue, thanks to the testimony of friends who took up her cause and to a judge who, believing she no longer required confinement, signed a limited-release order. Helpfully, Robert acquiesced and also supported his mother's freedom from incarceration. From the sanatorium in Batavia, Mary went to Springfield and her sister Elizabeth's house, the big one on the hill in the best part of town, where Mary and Abraham had been married thirty-three years earlier. A year later she was officially and fully released from the court's custody when, on her own petition, a jury formally found her once again compos mentis.

Immediately after her success Mary wrote her son a letter, one that strains credulity in that Robert allowed it to come to history's notice. In it Mary didn't even address her tormentor as "Dear Robert," but started the letter with the brutally curt "Robert T. Lincoln." It included a demand that he and his wife return everything that she had ever given them—*immediately*. More shockingly, she informed him that "two prominent clergymen have written me, since I saw you—and mention in their letters, that they think it advisable to offer up prayers for you in Church, on account of your wickedness against me and High Heaven." She ended by informing her son that "you have injured yourself, not me, by your wicked conduct." She signed herself "Mrs. A. Lincoln."[5]

The freed "Mrs. A. Lincoln" now had no intention of remaining in Springfield, certainly not on her sister's benevolent hospitality. Instead, Mary moved back to Europe and for the next four years lived in Pau, France, a small city in the southwestern part of the country, hard against the Pyrenees, which separate France from Spain. The town's temperate climate and its reputation as a health spa drew her to this obscure corner of Europe, Pau's main claim to prominence being its robust English expatriate colony drawn to it for the same therapeutic qualities that attracted Mary. Even though the former first lady was still a relatively young fifty-eight, Mary was plagued with a wide range of illnesses—eye problems, boils, colds, excruciating headaches, and a painful back. She hoped that Pau's highly regarded mineral baths would relieve the whole array of what was ailing her.

Aside from concerns about health, Mary principally occupied herself in Pau by carefully looking after her finances. Greatly helping her in this regard was a Springfield banker, who kept and passed on to history some ninety-two of the letters he received from her, correspondence that exhibited her remarkably sophisticated knowledge of her investments and financial standing.

By late 1880, Mary's health had so sunk that she could no longer physically take care of herself. She made what must have been for her a difficult decision to return to the United States, again to Springfield and to the Edwardses, the closest family she still had. Robert, in her view, no longer counted as a part of her family, though she did display a warm regard for the elder of his two daughters, even as she did not for the younger one or for her one grandson, who was named Abraham, for his grandfather.

Ensconced in one of the Edwardses' upstairs bedrooms, she kept the chamber perpetually darkened because any light hurt her eyes. She refused to let in any visitors, barring even well-wishers from among her own family, and she rarely stepped a foot outside the tightly curtained room. Mary turned herself into a virtual recluse, which went down poorly with her family and led to constant arguments with Elizabeth, who remarked that her sister's "enjoyment of a darkened room, does not accord with my ideas of enjoying life." What made Mary's life, if not enjoyable, at least bearable was her unceasing rummaging through the sixty-four trunks she'd brought with her to Springfield, all of which were kept in a spare room across the hall from her own. The family, understandably, worried that their massive weight might splinter the floor and send the entire heap crashing through to the parlor below.

Mary saw Robert only once more. In May 1881, Robert, now President Garfield's secretary of war—the son was unquestionably rising in the world—came to Springfield to visit his mother, bringing with him the granddaughter he knew she would be pleased to see. This visit did not work any genuine family reconciliation. However, a different kind of happy tidings did come a few months later when Congress took up the question of raising her pension from $3,000 a year to $5,000. The real impetus for the legislative body's concern was the fate of the assassinated President Garfield's widow, who was left with children and for whom $3,000 would clearly be inadequate; Mary was brought into the equation only to keep all former first ladies' pensions on an equal footing. Early in 1882, the measure passed both houses of Congress. Regrettably, Congress's largesse came too late to do much for Mary.

In the fading hours of a scorching Sunday evening—July 16, 1882—Mary Lincoln's final struggle began. For the prior week her body—she now weighed only one hundred pounds—had been aggravated by pain from boils, and the intensely hot and dry summer weather only worsened her distress. Though her family said she was unconscious throughout most of her last day, the nearly blind (she could hardly blink because her eyelids were so painful) and partially paralyzed Mary had long been ready to go and was doubtless looking ahead to a place she knew would be better than life.

Death released her at a quarter after eight that evening. Dr. Dresser, the attending physician, wrote down the cause simply as "paralysis," though her final illness was probably underlain by diabetes and, most immediately, by apoplexy, which is to say a cerebral stroke. In reality, she had simply worn down. The family placed Mary's body in a coffin, and someone neatly entwined her fingers across her breast. Taken downstairs to the front parlor, she was positioned in front of the fireplace, on almost the exact same spot where forty years earlier she and her Abraham had married. Standing on the mantelpiece were the garnet-colored whale-oil lamps that had illuminated that long-ago matrimonial service. Mary's ring finger was still encircled with the wedding band she had received that day, though nearly worn away were the words inscribed on the golden ring's inner surface: "Love is eternal."

Three days later the remains were memorialized in a simple funeral service, the gathering having been held up pending the arrival from Washington of Mary's long-estranged son. In the same church she and her husband had attended before the presidency called them away from Springfield, the Reverend Reed alluded in his homily to the bond between Abraham and Mary Lincoln. He told a story about intertwined trees. He said that when one of the trees had been blown down, its mate appeared still to live—but that in reality the other hadn't survived at all. The preacher suggested the still standing tree's fate, exemplified by Mary Lincoln, had been merely a living death.

Mary's coffin was taken to Oak Ridge Cemetery, there to rest for eternity next to Abraham and Eddie and Willie and Tad. The mayor of Springfield, understanding that respect had to be paid, made the day an official holiday.

For a woman who thought she was nearly destitute, she left the world pretty well-off. Her estate came to $84,035. Like her husband, though, she died intestate, and the entire sum thus went to the man she no longer considered her son.

Robert lived until 1926. In fact, he lived well. He was immensely successful in his Chicago law practice, and his magic name eventually led him high into Republican politics. After his tenure as secretary of war he became minister to the Court of St. James's in London. In industry, he achieved one of the highest corporate positions in the America of his era. As counsel to the Pullman Corporation, the company that manufactured the railroad sleeping cars whose name became eponymous with the firm's founder, Robert was elected its president by the corporation's board shortly after founder George Pullman's death. Later, Robert served as the company's board chairman, a position he held until four years before his own death.

By sad coincidence, Robert was closely associated with the deaths of the first three assassinated American presidents. After his own father's murder, he was present at the 1881 assassination of President James Garfield in the Washington, D.C., train station. Twenty years later, he was standing close to William McKinley when that president was shot in Buffalo.

Robert and Mary Lincoln were, as mentioned, the parents of three children. Their son, Abraham II, who was called Jack in the family, died at the age of sixteen in the winter of 1890, evidently from the effects of blood poisoning; his death ended the presidential Lincolns' name. Both of Robert's daughters went on to have families of their own. The older, Mary—called Mamie—married Charles Isham, and the couple had one son, Lincoln Isham; Lincoln would marry but have no children. The younger, Jessie, would marry Warren Beckwith and have a son and a daughter; after divorcing Beckwith, Jessie married twice again, but neither marriage produced children. The children from the Beckwith marriage were named Robert "Bud" Beckwith and Mary "Peggy" Lincoln Beckwith. Peggy never married. Bud did but, like the marriage of his cousin Lincoln Isham, his marriage was also childless. Bud, the longest-living great-grandchild of Abraham and Mary Lincoln, died in 1985 and with his death ended the Abraham Lincoln family lineage.

Robert Lincoln's last major public appearance came in 1922, when he was the honored guest at the dedication of the Lincoln Memorial in the nation's capital. He was said to have received the greatest ovation that day of any of the many and famous guests who attended the inauguration of the great marble temple honoring the sixteenth president's memory and deeds. By this time, Robert had for many years been living in Vermont, close to the village of Manchester. His home was near where he and his mother had visited to escape the trials of wartime Washington, and evidently the memory of his happiness there called him back in the days of his own great successes in life. In a spectacular setting just outside Manchester, he built a splendid mansion, which he named Hildene, after the hills and valley on which the house and its grounds were set. In the last years of his life, the by then famously private, nearly reclusive son of Abraham Lincoln disliked ever leaving what he had built as a summer residence but which in his last years became his sole home.

Having lived a life more than a little apart from those of his parents and his brothers, so did he choose to stay apart even in death, abjuring Springfield as the site for his own burial. Instead, he chose Arlington National Cemetery. His grave in the nation's premier resting ground looks out beyond the Potomac to the city of Washington, across a river that would have been a national boundary but for the courage of his father.

NOTES

1: MARCH 4, 1861 — WASHINGTON CITY

1. Federal Writers' Project, 39.
2. Klingaman, 32.
3. Whitcomb, 130.
4. Randall, *Mary Lincoln*, 209.
5. Leech, 46.
6. Boller, 226.
7. Internet, Mr.Lincoln'sWhiteHouse.org.
8. Leech, 11.
9. Theodore Roosevelt would in 1901 officially change the building's name from Executive Mansion to White House.
10. Baker, 182.
11. Kunhardt, 276.
12. Marx, 176.
13. Helm, 55.
14. Evans, 287.
15. Helm, 81.
16. Randall, *Lincoln's Sons*, 23.
17. Fleischner, 169.
18. Randall, *Mary Lincoln*, 141.
19. Ibid., 147.
20. Fleischner, 206.
21. Zimmerman, 43.
22. Internet, from Lincoln Institute (Brooks).
23. Seale, 380.

24. Burlingame, *With Lincoln*, 64.
25. Ibid., 156.
26. Leech, 47.
27. Miers, 1861, 27.

2: SETTLING IN

1. Hatfield.
2. Barton, 20.
3. Wilson and Davis, 166.
4. Barton, 23.
5. Klingaman, 15.
6. Sandburg, *Abraham Lincoln*, 217.
7. Klingaman, 18.
8. Helm, 183.
9. Ibid., 187.
10. Kunhardt, 151.
11. Ibid., 244.
12. Randall, *Ellsworth*, ix.
13. Ibid., 263.
14. Whitcomb and Whitcomb, 137.
15. Turner and Turner, 82.
16. Leech, 288.
17. Baker, 187.
18. Donald, *Lincoln*, 301.
19. Leech, 101.
20. Donald, *Lincoln*, 307.
21. Davis, *Brother*, 83.
22. Leech, 105.
23. Thomas, 125–26 (Internet printout).
24. Ibid., 388.
25. Randall, *Lincoln's Sons*, 89.
26. Ibid., 97.
27. Goff, 44.
28. Baker, 199.
29. Ibid.
30. Miers, 1861, 58.
31. Baker, 200.
32. Leech, 289.

3: CALAMITY IN WAR, CALAMITY AT HOME

1. Hertz, 176–77.
2. Boritt, 51.
3. Randall, *Lincoln's Sons*, 71.
4. Bayne, 49.
5. Randall, *Lincoln's Sons*, 82.
6. Ross, 165.

7. Davis, *Brother*, 101.
8. Fleischner, 222–23.
9. Ross, 123.
10. Ibid., 143.
11. Leech, 291.
12. Donald, *Lincoln*, 312–13.
13. Oates, *With Malice*, 275.
14. Pratt, 130.
15. Turner and Turner, 99.
16. Randall, *Mary Lincoln*, 310.
17. Thomas, 265.
18. Chadwick, 18.
19. Sandburg, *Lincoln Collector*, 114.
20. Katz, 5.
21. Sandburg, *Abraham Lincoln*, 185.
22. Miers, 1861, 80.
23. Thomas, 282.
24. Klingaman, 89.

4: DEATH IN THE WHITE HOUSE

1. Oates, *With Malice*, 276.
2. Ibid., 277.
3. Klingaman, 95.
4. Baker, 206.
5. Ibid., 209.
6. Bayne, 82.
7. Ross, 170–71.
8. Baker, 207.
9. Ibid., 209.
10. Kunhardt, 291.
11. Randall, *Lincoln's Sons*, 101.
12. Kunhardt, 291.
13. Baker, 214.
14. Jones, 90.
15. Ross, 175.
16. Ibid., 176.
17. McPherson, 64.
18. Fleischner, 247.
19. Ibid.
20. Klingaman, 118.
21. Ibid., 179.
22. Ibid., 180.

5: SHADOWS EVERYWHERE

1. Seale, 353.
2. Pinsker, 56.

3. Baker, 217.

4. Pinsker, 58.

5. Ibid., 60–61.

6. Ibid., 83.

7. Leech, 303.

8. Baker, 215.

9. Leech, 305.

10. Randall, *Mary Lincoln*, 293.

11. Leech, 272.

12. Hubbard, 104.

13. Ibid., 113.

14. Donald, *Lincoln*, 392–95.

15. Wilson and Davis, 166.

16. Davis, *Lincoln's Men*, 177.

17. Ibid.

18. Goff, 46.

19. Randall, *Lincoln's Sons*, 115.

20. Ibid., 112.

21. McPherson, 95.

22. Marx, 175.

23. Internet, Abraham Lincoln's Research Site.

24. Marx, 179.

25. Ibid., 183.

26. Ibid., 184.

27. Randall, *Mary Lincoln*, 320.

28. Goff, 52.

29. Ibid.

30. Pinsker, 106.

31. Ross, 195.

32. Helm, 216–17.

33. Baker, 223.

34. Helm, 221–22.

35. Ibid., 226–27.

36. Baker, 225.

37. Donald, *Lincoln*, 463.

6: VICTORIES

1. Turner and Turner, 194, 196.

2. Ibid., 163.

3. Ibid., 162.

4. Ross, 210.

5. Evans, 233 ff.

6. Helm, 204–5.

7. Turner and Turner, 141.

8. Randall, *Mary Lincoln*, 221.

9. Ibid., 222.

10. Ibid., 243.
11. Ibid., 254.
12. Gienapp, 161.
13. Kunhardt, 242.
14. Miller and Pohanka, 313.
15. Chadwick, 238–39.
16. Ibid., 239.
17. Miers, 249.
18. Ibid., 276.
19. Ibid., 239.
20. Ibid.
21. Seale, 411.
22. Pinsker, 127–28.
23. Goff, 60.
24. Ibid., 62.
25. Pinsker, 136.
26. Leech, 337.
27. Ibid., 340.
28. Lee, 9.
29. Gienapp, 156.
30. Leech, 317.
31. Donald, *Lincoln*, 508.
32. Donald, *We Are Lincoln Men*, 203.
33. McPherson, 172.
34. Donald, *We Are Lincoln Men*, 190–91.
35. Kincaid, 27–28.
36. Donald, *Lincoln*, 514.
37. Ibid., 515.
38. Turner and Turner, 163.
39. Keckley, 127.
40. Donald, *Lincoln*, 530.
41. Pinsker, 177.
42. Ibid., 163.
43. Ibid., 181.
44. Neely, 172.
45. Thomas, 451.
46. Sandburg, *Abraham Lincoln*, 612.
47. Ibid., 594.
48. Ibid.
49. Ibid., 611.
50. Fleischner, 279.
51. McPherson, 198.

7: AN UNFINISHED WORK

1. Sandburg, *Abraham Lincoln*, 643.
2. Goff, 63.

3. Ibid., 64.

4. Donald, *Lincoln*, 568.

5. Thomas, 493.

6. Lamon, 135.

7. Donald, *Lincoln*, 550.

8. Sandburg, *Abraham Lincoln*, 665.

9. Keckley, 147–48.

10. Sandburg, *Abraham Lincoln*, 677.

11. Baker, 239.

12. Ibid., 240.

13. Miers, 324.

14. Ibid., 326.

15. Winik, 135.

16. Miers, 327.

17. Baker, 241–42.

18. Hubbard, 150.

19. Sandburg, *Abraham Lincoln*, 692.

20. Steers, 91.

21. Sandburg, *Abraham Lincoln*, 694.

22. Steers, 91.

23. Donald, *Lincoln*, 588.

24. Goff, 68.

25. Kunhardt, 348.

26. Steers, 101.

27. Goff, 69.

28. Ibid., 70.

29. Randall, *Lincoln's Sons*, 165.

30. Goff, 72.

31. Baker, 249.

EPILOGUE: THE FLYING DUTCHMAN

1. Fleischner, 293.

2. Baker, 309.

3. Turner and Turner, 611.

4. Baker, 333.

5. Turner and Turner, 617.

BIBLIOGRAPHY

Angle, Paul M., ed. *The Lincoln Reader.* New Brunswick, NJ: Rutgers University Press, 1947.

Baker, Jean H. *Mary Todd Lincoln: A Biography.* New York: W. W. Norton, 1989.

Barton, William E. *The Life of Abraham Lincoln.* Indianapolis: Bobbs-Merrill, 1925.

Bayne, Julia Taft. *Tad Lincoln's Father.* Lincoln: University of Nebraska Press, 2001.

Bishop, Jim. *The Day Lincoln Was Shot.* New York: Scholastic Book Services, 1955.

Boller, Paul. *Presidential Anecdotes.* New York: Oxford University Press, 1996.

Boritt, Gabor S., ed. *The Historian's Lincoln: Pseudohistory, Psychohistory, and History.* Urbana: University of Illinois Press, 1993.

Burlingame, Michael, ed. *Lincoln Observed: Civil War Dispatches of Noah Brooks.* Baltimore: The Johns Hopkins University Press, 1998.

———. *With Lincoln in the White House: Letters, Memoranda, and Other Writings of John G. Nicolay, 1860–1865.* Carbondale: Southern Illinois University Press, 2000.

Carpenter, F. B. *The Inner Life of Abraham Lincoln: Six Months at the White House.* Lincoln: University of Nebraska Press, 1995.

Chadwick, Bruce. *The Two American Presidents: A Dual Biography of Abraham Lincoln & Jefferson Davis*. Secaucus, NJ: Birch Lane, 1999.

Davis, William C. *Brother Against Brother: The War Begins*. Alexandria, VA: Time-Life Books, 1983.

———. *Lincoln's Men: How President Lincoln Became Father to an Army and a Nation*. New York: The Free Press, 1999.

Denney, Robert E. *The Civil War Years: A Day-by-Day Chronicle of the Life of a Nation*. New York: Sterling, 1992.

Donald, David Herbert. *Lincoln*. New York: Simon & Schuster, 1995.

———. *Lincoln at Home: Two Glimpses of Abraham Lincoln's Family Life*. New York: Simon & Schuster, 1999.

———. *Lincoln's Herndon: A Biography*. New York: Da Capo Press, 1989.

———. *We Are Lincoln Men: Abraham Lincoln and His Friends*. New York: Simon & Schuster, 2003.

Eaton, Clement. *A History of the Southern Confederacy*. New York: The Free Press, 1954.

Evans, W. A. *Mrs. Abraham Lincoln: A Study of Her Personality and Her Influence on Lincoln*. New York: Alfred A. Knopf, 1932.

Federal Writers' Project. *Washington: City and Capital*. Washington, DC: U.S. Government Printing Office, 1937.

Findley, Paul. *A. Lincoln: The Crucible of Congress*. New York: Crown Publishers, 1979.

Fleischner, Jennifer. *Mrs. Lincoln and Mrs. Keckly*. New York: Broadway, 2003.

Gienapp, William E. *Abraham Lincoln and Civil War America*. New York: Oxford University Press, 2002.

Goff, John S. *Robert Todd Lincoln: A Man in His Own Right*. Manchester, VT: Friends of Hildene, 1969.

Guelzo, Allen C. *Abraham Lincoln: Redeemer President*. Grand Rapids, MI: William B. Eerdmans Publishing, 1999.

Gwynne-Thomas, E. H. *The Presidential Families*. New York: Hypocrine Books, 1989.

Harris, William. *Lincoln's Last Months*. Cambridge: Belknap Press of Harvard University Press, 2004.

Hatfield, Mark O. *Vice Presidents of the United States, 1789–1993*. Washington, DC: U.S. Government Printing Office, 1997.

Helm, Katherine. *The True Story of Mary, Wife of Lincoln*. New York: Harper & Brothers, 1928.

Henig, Gerald S., and Eric Niderost. *Civil War Firsts: The Legacies of America's Bloodiest Conflict*. Mechanicsburg, PA: Stackpole Books, 2001.

Hertz, Emanuel. *The Hidden Lincoln*. New York: Blue Ribbon Books, 1940.

Hibbard, Charles M., ed. *Lincoln Reshapes the Presidency*. Macon, GA: Mercer University Press, 2003.

Holzer, Harold, ed. *Lincoln as I Knew Him*. Chapel Hill, NC: Algonquin Books, 1999.

Hubbard, Charles M., ed. *Lincoln & His Contemporaries*. Macon, GA: Mercer University Press, 1999.

Johnson, Paul. *A History of the American People*. New York: Harper-Collins, 1997.

Jones, Dorothea. *Washington Is Wonderful*. New York: Harper & Brothers, 1956.

Katz, Johnathan Ned. *Love Stories: Sex Between Men Before Homosexuality*. Chicago: The University of Chicago Press, 2001.

Keckley, Elizabeth. *Behind the Scenes*. Chicago: R. R. Donnelley & Sons, 1998.

Keelan, Donald B. *Robert Todd Lincoln's Hildene and How It Was Saved, 1975–1978*. Arlington, VT: The Keelan Family Foundation, 2001.

Kincaid, Robert. *Joshua Fry Speed: Lincoln's Most Intimate Friend*. Harrogate, TN: Department of Lincolniana, Lincoln Memorial University, 1943.

Klingaman, William A. *Abraham Lincoln and the Road to Emancipation: 1861–1865*. New York: Viking, 2001.

Kunhardt, Philip B., Jr., Philip B. Kunhardt III, and Peter W. Kunhardt. *Lincoln: An Illustrated Biography*. New York: Gramercy, 1992.

Lamon, Ward Hill. *Recollections of Abraham Lincoln: 1847–1865*. Lincoln: University of Nebraska Press, 1994.

Lee, Richard M. *Mr. Lincoln's City: An Illustrated Guide to the Civil War Sites of Washington*. McLean, VA: EPM Publications, 1981.

Leech, Margaret. *Reveille in Washington, 1860–1865*. New York: Harper & Brothers, 1941.

Luthin, Reinhard H. *The Real Abraham Lincoln*. Englewood Cliffs, NJ: Prentice Hall, 1960.

Martin, Edgar W. *The Standard of Living in 1860*. Chicago: The University of Chicago Press, 1942.

Marx, Rudolph, M.D. *The Health of the Presidents*. New York: G. P. Putnam's Sons, 1960.

McPherson, James M. *The Atlas of the Civil War.* New York: Macmillan, 1994.

Meredith, Roy. *Mr. Lincoln's Contemporaries.* New York: Scribner's, 1951.

Miers, Earl Schenck. *Lincoln Day by Day: A Chronology, 1809–1865.* Dayton, OH: Morningside, 1991.

Miller, Iris. *Washington in Maps, 1606–2000.* New York: Rizzoli, 2002.

Miller, Willam J., and Brian Pohanka. *An Illustrated History of the Civil War: Images of an American Tragedy.* Alexandria, VA: Time-Life Books, 2000.

Miller, William Lee. *Lincoln's Virtues.* New York: Knopf, 2002.

Neely, Mark E. *The Last Best Hope of Earth: Abraham Lincoln and the Promise of America.* Cambridge: Harvard University Press, 1993.

Neely, Mark E., and Harold Holzer. *The Lincoln Family Album.* New York: Doubleday, 1990.

Neely, Mark E., Jr., and R. Gerald McMurtry. *The Insanity File: The Case of Mary Todd Lincoln.* Carbondale: Southern Illinois University Press, 1986.

Nicolay, Helen. *Lincoln's Secretary: A Biography of John G. Nicolay.* New York: Longman, Green, 1971.

———. *Personal Traits of Abraham Lincoln.* New York: The Century, 1912.

Oates, Stephen B. *The Man Behind the Myths.* New York: Harper & Row, 1984.

———. *The Whirlwind of War.* New York: HarperCollins, 1998.

———. *With Malice Toward None: A Life of Abraham Lincoln.* New York: HarperCollins, 1977.

Pinsker, Matthew. *Lincoln's Sanctuary: Abraham Lincoln and the Soldiers' Home.* New York: Oxford University Press, 2003.

Pratt, Harry E. *The Personal Finances of Abraham Lincoln.* Springfield, IL: The Abraham Lincoln Association, 1943.

Randall, J. G. *Mr. Lincoln.* Ed. Richard N. Current. New York: Dodd, Mead, 1957.

Randall, Ruth Painter. *Colonel Elmer Ellsworth: A Biography of Lincoln's Friend and First Hero of the Civil War.* Boston: Little Brown, 1960.

———. *Lincoln's Sons.* Boston: Little Brown, 1955.

———. *Mary Lincoln: Biography of a Marriage.* Boston: Little Brown, 1953.

Ross, Ishbel. *The President's Wife: Mary Todd Lincoln.* New York: G. P. Putnam's Sons, 1973.

Sandburg, Carl. *Abraham Lincoln (The Prairie Years & The War Years)*. New York: Harcourt, Brace, 1954.

———. *Lincoln Collector.* New York: Bonanza, 1960.

———. *Mary Lincoln: Wife and Widow.* New York: Harcourt, Brace, 1932.

Schreiner, Samuel A., Jr. *The Trials of Mrs. Lincoln.* New York: Donald I. Fine, 1987.

Seale, William. *The President's House.* Washington, DC: White House Historical Association, 1986.

Seward, Frederick Whittlesey, Jr. *Obadiah Seward of Long Island, New York, and His Descendants.* Goshen, NY: Private Paper of Author, 1948.

Simon, John Y., and Harold Holzer, eds. *Rediscovering Abraham Lincoln.* New York: Fordham University Press, 2002.

Steers, Edward, Jr. *Blood on the Moon: The Assassination of Abraham Lincoln.* Lexington: The University Press of Kentucky, 2001.

Stoddard, William O. *Inside the White House in War Times: Memoirs and Reports of Lincoln's Secretary.* Ed. Michael Burlingame. Lincoln: University of Nebraska Press, 2000.

Strozier, Charles B. *Lincoln's Quest for Union: A Psychological Portrait.* Philadelphia: Paul Dry Books, 2001.

Temple, Wayne C. *By Squares & Compass: Saga of the Lincoln Home.* Mahomet, IL: Mayhaven Publishing, 2002.

Thomas, Benjamin P. *Abraham Lincoln: A Biography.* New York: Alfred A. Knopf, 1952.

Truman, Margaret. *First Ladies.* New York: Random House, 1995.

Turner, Justin G., and Linda Levitt Turner. *Mary Todd Lincoln: Her Life and Letters.* New York: Alfred A. Knopf, 1972.

Varhola, Michael J. *Everyday Life During the Civil War: A Guide for Writers, Students and Historians.* Cincinnati: Writer's Digest Books, 1999.

Wagner, Margaret E., Gary W. Gallagher, and Paul Finkleman, eds. *Civil War Desk Reference.* New York: Grand Central Press, 2002.

Whipple, Wayne. *The Story-Life of Lincoln.* Philadelphia: The John C. Winston Co., 1908.

Whitcomb, John, and Claire Whitcomb. *Real Life at the White House: Two Hundred Years of Daily Life at America's Most Famous Residence.* New York: Routledge, 2000.

Williams, James A. *Abraham Lincoln: Attorney and Counselor at Law.* Barrington, IL: Barrington Publishing, 2000.

Wills, Garry. *Lincoln at Gettysburg: The Words That Remade America.* New York: Touchstone, 1992.

Wilson, Douglas L., and Rodney O. Davis, eds. *Herndon's Informants: Letters, Interviews, and Statements About Abraham Lincoln.* Urbana: University of Illinois Press, 1998.

Winik, Jay. *April 1865: The Month That Saved America.* New York: Harper-Collins, 2001.

Zimmerman, Warren. *First Great Triumph: How Five Americans Made Their Country a World Power.* New York: Farrar, Straus & Giroux, 2002.

INDEX

A. Y. Ellis and Company, 96
Abolitionist Party, 2
abolitionists, 128, 130
"Ach, du lieber Augustin," 59
administration, different from
    today's, 13–14
Agassiz, Louis, 150
Aladdin, 241
Albert (prince), 114, 117
    actions in *Trent* Affair by, 105–6
Alexander T. Stewart, 53
"All About the Domestic Economy
    of the White House," 177
American consul in Paris. *See*
    Nicolay, John
American legation secretary in
    France. *See* Hay, John
Ames, Mary Clemmer, 124
Anacostia River, 7. *See also* Eastern
    Branch
Anderson Cottage, p6. *See also*
    Soldiers' Home
Anderson, Major Robert, 13, 41, 43
Anthony, Senator Henry, 222
Antietam Creek, 134, 147
Antonie (princess), 189
Arkansas, 44
Arlington National Cemetery, 265,
    p6
Army of Northern Virginia, 182, 235

Army of the Potomac, 234
assassination
    conspiracy of, 248
    of Garfield/McKinley, 264
    as honorable war measure, 138
    of Lincoln, 246–48
    possible attempt of, 161
Atlanta, fall of, 199
Attorney General. *See* Bates,
    Edward; Speed, James

Baker, Edward Dickinson, 18, 83–84
Baker, Jean, 119, 167
Ball's Bluff battle, 83
Barnum, P. T., 161
Barrymores, 224
Bates, Edward, 36, 39–40, 218
Beadle Dime Library, 206
Beauregard, General P. G. T., 41, 57,
    58
    Manassas battle of, 58–61
Beckwith, Jessie Lincoln, 264
Beckwith, Mary "Peggy" Lincoln,
    264
Beckwith, Robert "Bud," 264
Beckwith, Warren, 264
Bellevue Place, Mary's release from,
    260
Ben-Hur, 193
Berret, Major James G., 6

black persons
  attitudes about, 128
  changes in lives of, 238
  colonization of, 129
  at funeral, 250
  inaugural tickets unavailable to, 225
  integration of, 129
  Mary's attitude toward, 179
  at New Year's reception, 212–13
  post-slavery ideas for, 127
  suffrage for, 238
  Union military employment for, 82, 132
  war riot over, 160
black/white intermarriage, 205
Blair, Montgomery, 36, 40
blockage. See federal blockade
blue mass, mercury in, 155
Bonaparte, Clothilde, 71
Bonaparte, Eugenie, 87
Booth, John Wilkes, 250, p1
  assassination by, 246–47
  background of, 224
  kidnapping plan of, 224
  threats of, 238–39
border slave states
  emancipation not applicable to, 134
  placating of, 131
Brady, Mathew, 206, p8
British Foreign Office, 7
Brooks, Noah, 26, 143–44, 193, 208, 222, 237, 238
  Mary's approval of, 219
  as new aide, 219
Browning, Senator Orville and Mrs., 107, 121
Buchanan, James, 2, 4, 10, 13, 33, 43, 47, 70, 77, 95, 137
Bucktail Brigade
  duties of, 140
  Lincoln's relationship with, 141–42
Bull Run, 103, 133, 137
  battle at, 58–61
  eye witness account of, 60
Burnside, General Ambrose, 153
Butler, General Benjamin, 237
Butler, William, 96

cabinet, presidential, 13, 107, p3
  as antagonists, 31–32
  Fort Sumter solution of, 41–42

  improvements in, 218
  Lincoln's attitude toward, 32
  selection of, 35–36
Cameron, Simon, 36, 39, 42, 91
  irregularities in department of, 111
Canada, 105
Capitol
  dome on, 3, p1
  traditions of, 4
Carpenter, Francis, 181
Chain Bridge, 193
Charles XV of Sweden and Norway (king), 189
Chase, Kate, 38, 117, p3
Chase, Salmon P., 36, 37–38, 39, 42, 181, 218, 224, p3
  chief justice appointment of, 197
  firing of, 197
  presidential ambitions of, 184, 195–96
  resignation of, 196–97
"the Chicago Surrender," 204
Chickamauga battle, 163
chloroform, 157
Cincinnati Commercial Gazette, 85
Civil War, 104
  beginning of, 44–45
  British economic view of, 130
  emancipation as reason for, 130
  favorable news of, 216
  Lincoln's religious views changed by, 201–2
  military units in, 139–40
  pessimism over, 153
  poor showing in, 125
  popular government testing for, 201
  as race war, 132
  requirements for ending, 55
  slavery as concern of, 127
  Union army executions during, 148
  Union army murders during, 148
Colchester, Lord, 143–44
Cold Harbor battle, 183–84, 189
Colfax, Schuyler, 241
Confederate Army of Tennessee, 210–11
Confederates, 2. See also seceded slave states
  destruction of armies of, 110
  diplomatic recognition of, 104
  failing economic foundations of, 187

Confederates (*continued*)
  at Fort Sumter, 42
  government of, 55
  Lincoln's removal hoped for by, 186
Conscription Act, 153
Cooke, Jay, 215
Copperheads, 91, 177
  newspaper control by, 109, 186
Corps of Engineers, 80
Court of St. James's, 263
Crook, William, 254
Cuba, 104

Davis, Eliza, 101
Davis, Jefferson, 22, 33, 55, 58, 92,
    126, 181, 186, 199, 243, 249
  attempt on life of, 187
  emissaries to Europe sent by, 104
  facing disintegration, 187–88
  fleeing Richmond, 232
  on Fort Sumter, 42
  Lincoln's similarities/differences
    with, 93
  McClellan victory hoped for by,
    210
  peace conference representatives
    sent by, 220
  peace feelers of, 216
  poor health of, 93–94
  presidential skills of, 93
  on slavery, 94
  on son's death, 187–88
  on war, 95
Davis, Joe, death of, 188
Davis, Judge David, 40, 249
Davis, Varina Howell, 22, 23, 94,
    187–88
Davis, Winnie, 188
Dawson, Elodie, 45
Declaration of Independence, 134
Defense Department, 39
Delaware, 45, 220
Democrats, 32, 91
  election attacks of, 205
  election chances of, 207
  McClellan's nomination by, 203
  platform of, 203–4
  press made of, 109
  as pro-slavery, 33
Dennison, William, 242
Derickson, Captain David V.
  background of, 139–40
  description of, 142
  Mary helped by, 142

reminiscences of, 140
  transfer of, 160
Derickson, Charles, 140
diplomatic corps, 107
Dix, Dorothea, 117
"Dixie," 235
Donald, David, 130, 201
Douglas, Stephen, 3–4, 6
Douglass, Frederick, 225
draft, 181, 205–6
Dred Scott, 2, 107
Dresser, Dr., 262

Early, General Jubal, Washington
    attack of, 192–94
Eastern Branch, 7
Eckert, Major Thomas T., 208
Edwards, Elizabeth Todd, 16, 22, 29,
    123, 151, 260, 261–62
election returns, 208–9
Ellsworth, Elmer Ephraim, 46–49,
    79
emancipation
  abolitionists demanding, 129–30,
    132
  Chase upholding, 198
  Civil War fought for, 130
  enforceability of, 132
  by executive decree, 131, 133
  military decision of, 133
  military victory justifying,
    133–34
  in Washington, 133
Emancipation Proclamation, 134–35,
    160, 219
  border slave states excluded from,
    134
  Northerners unwilling to fight for,
    153
Equinox Hotel, 200
Evans, Dr. W. A., 17, 178
evening ball, (1862), p4
  events of, 116–18
  plans/motivation for, 114
  political cost of, 113–14
evening levee, first, 28–29
  calamity at, 28–29
  protocol at, 28
  as success, 29–30
Everett, Edward, 167
  death of, 216
  Gettysburg speech of, 168
Executive Mansion. *See* White
    House

Fair Oaks, 126
Farmington, 97
federal blockade, 56, 104
  of cotton to Britain, 130
  South's resupplies stopped by, 187
federal departments, 31
Federal Union of the States, 203–4
Fessenden, Senator William P., 197
Field, Maunsell B., 240
Fifty-eighth Virginia Infantry, 195
Fire Zouaves, 48
First Missouri Volunteers, 82
Ford's Theater, 244, 245, p3
Fort Barrancas, 106
Fort Donelson, 125
Fort Fisher, 211, 216
Fort Pickens, 106
Fort Stevens, 194
Fort Sumter, 12–13, 57, 118, 137,
    210–11
  cabinet views on, 35
  dilemma of, 40–41
  Lincoln's actions on, 42–43
  as military/political catastrophe, 13
  unprepared for crisis in, 13–14
Fort Warren, 105–6
Fortress Monroe, Virginia, 164
Fox, Augustus, 193
France, 159
Francis Joseph I of Austria
    (emperor), 189
Fredericksburg battle, 153, 179
Frémont, John C., 184
French, Benjamin, 88, 89
Frontier Guard, 45
funeral, Abraham Lincoln, 250–51

Galt Brothers Jewelers, 210
Gardner, Alexander, p8
Garfield, James Abram, 262, 264
Georgetown Pike, 193
Georgia, peace movement in, 187
Gettysburg address, 168–69
Gettysburg battle, 159, 167
the Globe, 18
Godey's Lady Book, 206
government credit, 205
government pension
  Congress gifts of, 256
  for Garfield's widow, 262
  for Mary, 255, 256, 262
Grand Pacific, 259
Grant, Julia, 227, 228–29, 233, 242,
    243

Grant, Ulysses, 125, 186, 189, 195,
    209, 238, 242, 243, 250
  first battles of, 182–84
  Lee's surrender to, 234
  Ord defended by, 230
  Petersburg siege by, 198
  reception for, 181–82
  Robert's enlistment accepted by,
    214
  unpopularity of, 188
  Washington visit by, 240
Grant's Sixth and Nineteenth corps,
    194
Great Britain, 104–6, 159
  Confederacy as "belligerent" for,
    104
  economic view of South, 130
Greeley, Horace, 154
greenbacks, 125, 196
Greenhow, Rose O'Neal, 58
Grimsley, Elizabeth, 29, 53, 72
Grover Theatre, 171
Gurley, Dr. Phineas D., 121

habeas corpus, suspension of, 44–45,
    109, 148
"Hail, Columbia," 6
Hale, Senator John, 241
Halleck, General Henry, 140–41
Halstead, Murat, 85
Hamlin, Cyrus, 33
Hamlin, Hannibal, 222
  background of, 33–34
  as president, 170
  as replaced, 185–86
Harlan, James, 218, 223, 233
Harlan, Mary Eunice, 218, 223, 233
  descendants of, 264
  wedding of, 257
Harper's Weekly, 206
Harris, Clara, 244–45, 247
Harris, Ira, 165–66
Harvard College, 68–69, 167
  grading at, 150
  studies at, 149
Haughwout & Company, 53
Hay, Dr. Charles, 25
Hay, John, 49, 62, 69, 89, 110, 115,
    138, 149, 189, 193, 241, 243, 251,
    p2
  at assassination, 245–46
  background of, 25–26
  loyalty of, 200–201
  Mary's relationship with, 26, 201

Hay, John (*continued*)
    military rank of, 200
    president's thoughts noted by, 201
    resigning, 219
    Robert's relationship with, 152
Helm, Emilie, 45–46, 179, 215
    anger toward Lincolns of, 166–67
    argument of, 165–66
    Mary's kindness to, 164–65
    request of, 166
    travel permission for, 164
    as widowed, 163
Helm, General Ben Hardin, 45–46,
        163, 164
Helm, Governor, 164
Henderson, Senator John, 223
Henning, Fanny, 101–2
Herndon, William, 75, 83, 97, 154–56
Herold, David, 238
Hildegarde, archduchess 189
Hildene, 264
HMS *Rinaldo*, 106
Hollywood Cemetery, 188
Holmes, Oliver Wendell, 150, 194
Holt, General, 148–49
homosexuality, 97–100
hospitals, military, 2, p2
Hutchinson family, 107
Hyde Park, 254–55

Illinois State Register, 177
inaugural ball (1861), 5–6
inaugural ball (1865), 225–26
inauguration, first, 1, 2–3, 9
    address at, 3–4
    security at, 2–3, p1
inauguration, second, 221–25
    address at, 223–24
    security at, p1
Independent, 213
Indians, furnishing with arms, 227.
        See also Minnesota Sioux
        Indians
inflationary crisis, 196, 205
Irish, war riot by, 160
Isabella of Spain (queen), 87
Isham, Charles, 264
Isham, Lincoln, 264
Isham, Mary Lincoln, 264

Jackson, Andrew, 8
Jackson, General, 106
Jackson, James W., 48
Jackson, Rachel, 85

Jefferson, Thomas, 9, 232
"John Brown's Body," 59
Johnson, Andrew, 203, 222, 247, 249,
        250, 251
    Mary's relationship with, 251
    unfortunate speech of, 222–23
    as vice president, 185–86
Johnston, General Joseph, 57, 126,
        198, 234, 235, 249
    Manassas battle of, 58–61
Joint Committee on the Conduct of
        the War, 91
Jones, Avonia, 216
Judd, Miss Minnie, 260
judge advocate general, 146

Keckly, Elizabeth, 22–24, 28–29,
        82–83, 114, 118, 119, 120–21,
        123, 143, 179, 203, 217, 226, 233,
        249–50, 251
Keckly, George, 83–84
Kennesaw Mountain battle, 198–99
Kentucky, 45, 220
Key, Philip Barton, 165
Kitty, 48

Ladies' Soldiers' Relief Association,
        171
Lamon, Ward, 204
Lane, Harriet, 4, 5, 47, 50
Lane, Senator James, 45
Leah, 216
Leale, Dr. Charles, 247
Lee, General Robert E., 44, 57, 59,
        92, 133–34, 182, 198
    Confederate forces commanded
        by, 126
    Grant's first battles with, 182–84
    losses of, 159–60
    possibility of guerrilla war by, 233
    president complimenting, 241
    Richmond escape of, 231
    surrender of, 234, 242
L'Enfant, Pierre-Charles,
        Washington plan of, 6
Leopold of Belgium (king), 189
Leslie's Weekly, 206
Liberator, 124
Lincoln, Abraham, 208–9, p1, p5, p7,
        p8
    abolitionists lacking support from,
        130
    administrative choices of, 112
    answer to Emilie's request, 166

Lincoln, Abraham (*continued*)
  assassination of, 246–48
  attempted shooting of, 204
  attitude of, toward cabinet, 32
  belief in law, 130–31
  beloved by soldiers, 148–49
  black suffrage supported by, 238
  Bucktail Brigade's relationship
    with, 141–42
  characteristics of, 149
  Chase and generosity of, 197
  Chase's firing by, 197
  as churchgoer, 202
  City Point visit by, 227–33
  companionship from aides with,
    200
  Confederate states, restoration of,
    and, 239
  as Congress representative, 18
  Davis's similarities/differences
    with, 93
  demands on, 30, 43, 56–57, 61–63,
    91–92, 139, 141, 153–54, 181
  dental problems of, 156–57
  depression of, 154–55, 198
  Derickson's bond with, 141–42
  "Dixie" requested by, 235
  election returns for, 208–9
  as father, 18, 20–21, 74–76
  fatigue of, 216–17
  at Fort Stevens, 194–95
  frayed marriage of, 200
  funeral of, 250–51
  Gettysburg address by, 168–69
  Gettysburg address, composing,
    167–68
  Gettysburg battle rebuked by, 159
  grief from Ellsworth's death, 49
  grief from Willy's death, 120, 121,
    122
  health of, 155–57, 221
  horse bought by, 215
  humanity of, 145
  illness of, 169–70
  on immigration, 241
  on Indians as inferior, 147
  intellect of, 21
  just decisions for military crimes
    by, 148
  last photo of, p8
  Lee complimented by, 241
  lonely summer for, 162–63
  loyalty from aides to, 200–201
  marriage, fear of, 99–100

  marriage to Mary by, 102
  Mary's courtship of, 100–102, 155
  Mary's spending ignored by, 176
  Mary's spiritualism and, 143
  Mary's treatment by, 158
  Mary's wrath tolerated by, 229–30
  as nation's savior, 256
  no written will of, 255
  pardon for Minnesota Sioux
    Indians by, 147–48
  peace conference of, 220
  personal prejudice of, 35
  pessimism over war by, 153
  on post-slavery blacks, 127
  on preserving the Union, 128–29
  reaction of, to Bull Run, 60
  reconstruction ideas of, 239
  reelection activities of, 206–7
  relations with youngest sons, 70,
    76, 189–90
  reprieve/pardon authority of,
    144–45, 148–49
  Robert confided in by, 162
  Robert's enlistment request by,
    214
  Robert's relationship with, 67,
    69–70, 191–92
  saving habits of, 89
  sharing dreams of, 243
  slavery and achieving presidency,
    127
  slavery, ending plans of, 131
  slavery's animosity of, 127–28
  slavery's spread stopped by, 131
  social obligations of, 189
  soldiers able to see, 145–46
  Speed, Joshua, relationship with,
    97–103
  summer clothing of, 64
  Trent Affair reaction of, 105
  understanding of fighting war by,
    81–82, 109–10
  vice president, relationship with,
    34, 185–86
  war changing religious views of,
    201–2
  weaknesses of, 32
  wife's note by, 239
  winning peace speech of, 237–38
Lincoln, Abraham II, 264
Lincoln, Edward Baker, 18, 67
  death of, 19
Lincoln, Mary Todd, 3, 114, 222,
  243, 250

Lincoln, Mary Todd (*continued*)
  accident of, 161–62
  as accused of theft, 252
  attraction of, 17
  Bellevue release of, 260
  on black persons, 179
  Chase, Kate, relationship with, 39
  City Point accident of, 228–29
  City Point tantrum of, 228–30
  City Point visit by, 227–33
  as confined by Robert, 260
  courtship of, 100–102, 155
  death of, 262–63
  debt pressure of, 177, 203, 256–57
  Derickson's help to, 142
  on destitution, 255, 257
  dress of, 6, 117
  early life of, 15–16
  eccentric behavior of, 157–58,
    258–59
  education of, 16
  escaping from Washington, 162
  estate left to, 255
  estate of, 263
  European life of, 257
  family fragmentation by war of, 45
  frayed marriage of, 200
  gifts to, 177
  government pension desired by,
    256
  grief over Lincoln's assassination
    of, 246, 247–84, 249–50, 251, 254
  grief over Edward's death, 19, 20
  grief over family deaths, 163–64
  grief over Willy's death, 119–20,
    121, 122–23
  health/financial concerns of, 261
  hospital visitations of, 178–79
  husband and expectations of,
    17–18
  husband's concern by, 217
  ignoring war, 103, 113–14
  injuring eyes, 255
  kindness to injured child by, 165
  leaving the White House, 251–53
  in Lincoln's early career, 157
  as "Madam President," 1, 15
  marriage to Lincoln, 102
  mental/emotional problems of,
    157, 158
  mercy appeal by, 180–81
  as mother, 20–21, 74–76
  moving to Chicago by, 254–55
  moving to France by, 261

  nervous breakdown of, 125
  North/South sentiments of, 84
  Ord criticized by, 230
  overspending by, 54, 88–89,
    176–78
  parties of, 216
  perceived weaknesses of, 158
  personality of, 16–17, 21, 174–75,
    178, 180, 230
  physical description of, 23
  political damage by, 176–77
  portraits of, 207, 258, p2, p5, p7
  presidential aides' relationship
    with, 26, 86
  press censure for, 110–11, 122,
    124, 177
  pressures on, 176
  recovering at Soldiers' Home by,
    139
  redecorating White House by,
    50–54
  reelection reaction of, 209–10
  Robert and angry letter by, 260–61
  Robert, living with, 257
  Robert's relationship with, 70–71,
    259–61
  rules broken by, 84–85
  satisfactions of, 92
  selling her clothes, 256
  Seward, William, relationship
    with, 37
  shopping/traveling addictions of,
    86, 100, 162–63, 173–74
  slavery experience of, 15–16
  social status concerns of, 174, 175
  spiritualism, beliefs of, 142–43,
    165
  Stanton's relationship with,
    112–13
  summer clothing of, 63–64
  suspicions of loyalty of, 90–91, 124
  thwarted position of, 86
  trial of, 260
  understanding for, 66
Lincoln Memorial, 264
Lincoln, Nancy, 97
Lincoln, Robert Todd, 19–20, 66–71,
    75–76, 99, 117, 121, 123, 139,
    161, 162, 172, 193, 218, 223, 227,
    233, 241, 247–48, 249, 250, 251,
    252, 256, p4, p6, p7
  after assassination, 245–46
  associated with assassinations, 264
  avoiding publicity by, 149, 150–51

Lincoln, Robert Todd (*continued*)
  burden of, being father's son, 150
  as Captain, 214–15, 235
  classical knowledge gained by,
    151
  descendants of, 264
  description of, 68
  exemption of, 141, 149, 152,
    191–92
  father confiding in, 162
  father's relationship with, 67,
    69–70, 151–52, 191–92
  future plans of, 191–92
  at Harvard, 68–69, 150
  Hay's relationship with, 27, 152
  last public appearance of, 264
  military service for, 213–15
  mother confined by, 259–60
  mother's care by, 259
  mother's relationship with, 70–71
  mother's release supported by,
    260
  as secretary of war, 262
  success of, 263–64
  war duties of, 215
  wedding of, 257
Lincoln, Thomas, 97
Lincoln, Thomas "Tad," 47, 64, 67,
    71, 103–4, 118–19, 120, 123, 125,
    139, 155–56, 190, 216, 227, 235,
    236, 237, 241, 247, 249, 250, p5,
    p8
  behavior of, 74–79
  City Point visit of, 230–32
  estate of, 256
  European life of, 257
  happiness with father of, 189–90
  last illness of, 257–58
  smallpox for, 167
  typhoid fever for, 114–16, 121
Lincoln, William Wallace (Willy), 20,
    47, 64, 67, 71, 103–4, 108, 156,
    190, p4
  behavior of, 74–79
  funeral of, 121–22
  poem by, 84
  typhoid fever for, 114–16,
    118–20
Lincoln's Tomb, p6
Lives of the Queens of England, 11
London Spectator, 170
Louisiana, 227, 238
Lowell, James Russell, 150
Lyons, Lord, 114

Macbeth, 234
Madison, Dolley, 85, 164, 165
Madison, James, 11
Maillard and Company, 114, 118
malaria, 155
Malvern, 232
Manara, Teodoro, Guatemalan
    consul, 208
Manassas Junction, 57, 58–61, 109.
    See also Bull Run
The Marble Heart, 224
Marine Band, 107, 117, 216
marriage
  between blacks/whites, 205
  between Lincoln, A./Todd, M.,
    102
  between Lincoln R./Harlan, M.,
    257
  Lincoln's fear of, 99–100
  Lincoln's frayed, 200
  between Speed, J./Henning, F.,
    102
"Marseillaise," 72
Mary. *See* Lincoln, Mary Todd
"Mary Lincoln Polka," 117
Maryland, 44–45, 54–55, 134, 137,
    138
Mason and Dixon Line, 187
Mason, James, 104
McClellan, General George B., 103,
    106, 109, 116–17, 121–22, 134,
    137, 141
  as anti-emancipationist, 205
  background of, 80
  caution of, 81–82
  as Democratic candidate, 203–4
  military misconduct of, 110
  as New Jersey governor, 209
  peace plank rejected by, 204
  presidential campaign by, 182
  protection of capital by, 81, 125
  training troops by, 81
  unwillingness of, to fight, 125–26
McCormick Reaper case, 112
McCulloch, Hugh, 242
McDowell, General Irvin, 57, 58,
    79
  Bull Run battle by, 58–61
Meade, General, 159, 168
Mentelle, Madame Charlotte, 16
Mexican War, 57, 80
military crimes, 109, 145
Military Division of the Potomac,
    80

military execution
  disagreement of commanders on,
    146
  Lincoln's decisions on, 146–47
  Lincoln's justice/mercy in, 148–49
military life, hardships of, 106
military/naval grandees, 107
minié balls, 167
Minnesota Sioux Indians
  killing 350 whites, 147
  Lincoln's pardon for, 147
  mass execution of, 147–48
Monocacy River battle, 193, 195
Monroe, President James, 11
Mortimer, William, 177
"Movements of Mrs. Lincoln," 87

Napoleon III (emperor), 71, 87
Napoleon Joseph Charles Paul
    Bonaparte (prince), 71, 72–73
National Theater, 241, 249
National Union Party, 207
negotiated peace, 198, 199
Negroes. See also black persons
  Northerners unwilling to fight for,
    153
  rights of, 2
Neill, Edward D., 251
New Year's reception (1862), 106–8
New Year's reception, (1865), 212–13
New York City Fire Department, 48
New York Herald, 87, 206, 228
New York riots, 160
New York State's Central
    Republican Committee, 203
New York Tribune, 42, 48, 238
Nicolas Auguste (prince), 189
Nicolay, John, 13, 69, 72, 89, 113,
    115, 120, 138, 151, 189, 190, 198,
    208, p2
  background of, 24–25
  on Lincoln's generosity, 197
  loyalty of, 200–201
  Mary's relationship with, 26, 201
  military service for, 200
  resigning, 218–19
  responsibilities of, 27
nomination, Republican, 36
North Ana River battle, 183
North Carolina, 44
  peace movement in, 187
  Wilmington port remaining in,
    211
North Western Railroad, 189

Northern Democrats, wanting to
    split the Union, 131
Northerners
  advantages of, 55–56
  unwilling to fight for Negroes, 153

Oak Hill Cemetery, 122
Oak Ridge Cemetery, 252, 263, p6
office seekers, 5, 26, 37, 65, 154
Old Capitol prison, 195
Old Edward, head usher, 1
Ord, General Edward, 228
Ord, Mary, 228–29
Our American Cousin, 241, 242, 246

Palace of Aladdin, 5
Palmerston, Lord
  "belligerent" status granted by,
    104
  threats by, 105
paper money, 38, 125, 196, 198. See
    also greenbacks
Parker, Joel, 213–14
"Partant pour la Syrie," 72
peace
  celebration of, 235, 236, 237–38
  negotiated, 198, 199
  negotiations, 210
peace conference
  deadlock at, 220–21
  Lincoln's demands at, 220
Pendel, Thomas, 245, 249
Pennsylvania Avenue, 8, 9
Pennsylvania Volunteers, 139
Petersburg, Grant held by Lee at,
    211
Petersen, Mr., 245
Phillips Exeter Academy, 68–69
Pierce, Franklin, 95
Poore, Ben: Perley, 180
popular government, war as test for,
    201
Port Gibson, 159
Porter, Admiral, 216
portrait photograph, 206–7
Postmaster General. See Blair,
    Montgomery; Dennison,
    William
Potomac River, 7
Powell, Lewis, 238–39
presbyopia, 155
presidential vote, (1864), 209
prince of Wales, 70
private stables, fire destroying, 190

proclamations, on ports, 236
Pullman Corporation, 263–64
Pullman, George, 264

Radical Republicans, 184, 239–40
Rathbone, Major Henry, 244–45, 247
reconstruction
    debate over, 242–43
    president's lenient ideas of, 239
Reed, Reverend, 263
Republican Party, 2, 35, 36, 91, 184, 203. *See also* Radical Republicans; Whig Party
reverential biographies, 206
Richmond, Virginia, 126, 183
    Confederate capital of, 57
    destruction of, 231
    Lee/Grant battle over, 227
    Northern attack on, 57
    president protecting, 232
    president's exploration of, 231–32
    slaves freed in, 231–32
    success at, 230–31
    as trophy, 110
Riggs & Company Bank, 89
Riggs, George, 136
River Queen, 220, 227–28, 230, 233, 234
Robert. *See* Lincoln, Robert Todd
Royal Navy, 104
Rutledge, Ann, 256

Sacramento Union, 219
Sally, 15
salmonella typhi, 115–16
San Jacinto, 104–5, 105
Sandburg, Carl, 96, 103
Sanitary Commission, 172
Schurz, Congressman Carl, 230
Scott, Winfield, 3, 5, 14, 34, 41, 51–52, 57, 59, 79, 137
Scott's Nine Hundred, protecting president, 140–41
seceded slave states
    return of, 227
    states joining, 44
"secesh," 194
secession, 32
Secretary of Interior. *See* Harlan, James; Smith, Caleb B.; Usher, John P.
Secretary of Navy. *See* Welles, Gideon

Secretary of State. *See* Seward, William
Secretary of Treasury. *See* Chase, Salmon P.; McCulloch, Hugh
Secretary of War. *See* Cameron, Simon; Stanton, Edwin
sectionalism, 32
security, 189
    Grant's forces for, 193
    presidential, 138–39, 140–41, 192–93, 204–5
Senate, 13
Seward, Frances, 37
Seward, Frederick, 242, 248
Seward, William, 39, 42, 43, 56–57, 105, 110, 168, 220, 233, 250
    accident of, 232
    attack on, 248
    background of, 36–37
    battle report of, 59–60
    entertainment responsibility of, 28, 37
    president's visit with, 234
Shakespeare, 233–34
Sheridan, General Philip, 195, 233
Sherman, General William, 146, 186
    Atlanta campaign of, 198–99, 210
Sickles, General Daniel, 165–66
Sing Sing prison, 180
slavery
    as beggaring the South, 32
    Britain's disgust with, 130
    as causing Civil War, 2, 127
    Confederate government supported by, 55
    Davis, Jefferson, on, 94
    Democrats' support of, 33
    legal problems of, 130–31
    Lincoln's animosity to, 127–28
    Lincoln's plans to end, 131
    Lincoln's presidency propelled by, 127
    people newly freed from, 237
    Southern social order supported by, 131
    Southerners' fear of stopping spread of, 131
    Speed/Lincoln gulf from, 103
    spread of, 33
    Thirteenth Amendment outlawing, 219
    at Todd's, 15–16

Slidell, John, 104
Smith, Caleb B., 36, 40
Smithsonian Institution, 143
Snake Pit, 260
soldiers
    given furloughs to vote, 206
    Lincoln beloved by, 148–49
    pardons for, 144–45, 148–49, 243
    Washington executions of, 145
Soldiers' Home, 6, 61, p1
    Lincoln alone in, 199–200
    Lincolns evacuating from, 193
    Mary recovering at, 139
    refurbishing of, 190–91
    séances at, 143
    second summer at, 160–61
    as summer house, 136–37
South Carolina, militia of, 13
Southern White House, 187–88
Southerners
    damage to society/infrastructure
        of, 186
    fear of stopping slavery's spread,
        131
    low morale of, 210
    loyalties of, 46
    peace movements of, 187
    slavery supporting social order of,
        131
Speed, James, 218, 239, 242
Speed, Joshua, 95, 103, 221
    background of, 96–97
    Lincoln's differences with, 103
    Lincoln's relationship with,
        97–103
    Lincoln's visit with, 100–101
    marriage to Fanny, 102
    visit from, 201–2, 217
Speed, Judge John, 97
Speed, Mrs., 101
spiritualism
    Lincoln's reaction to Mary's,
        143–44
    for Lizzy, 143
    Mary's belief in, 142, 143–44, 165
Spotsylvania battle, 183, 189
St. Paul's Church, 188
Stanton, Edwin, 36, 38, 126, 192,
        204, 208, 234, 236, 239, 242, 247,
        248, 250, 251
    changed view of president of, 240
    incorruptibility of, 112
    Mary's relationship with, 112–13
    rudeness of, 112

Stanton, Ellen, 242
Star of the West, 43
"The Star-Spangled Banner," 165,
    231
State Department, 13
states' rights, 2, 31–32, 94
Stephens, Alexander, 216
Stewart, Alexander T., 54, 177
Stoddard, William O., 27, 180
Stone, Dr. Robert, 119, 245
Stuart, John T., 95
Sumner, Senator Charles, 185, 226,
    233, 234, 236, 251
Swett, Leonard, 35, 148

tableau, 172
Taft, Bud, 77–78, 104, 116, 120, 123
Taft, Dr. Charles Sabin, 246
Taft, Holly, 77–78, 104, 119, 123
Taft, Judge Horatio, 77
Taft, Julia, 77–78, 116
Taney, Chief Justice Roger, 2, 45,
    107
    death of, 197
    decision on *Dred Scott*, 2
    on Negroes' rights, 2
taxes, 205
Taylor, General Daniel, 146
Taylor, Tom, 171
Taylor, Zachary, 94
Tennessee, 44
Therena, 27
Thirteenth Amendment, 219
Thompson, Frank G., 179
Thumb, General Tom, 160–61
Tiber Creek/Canal, 7, 62
The Ticket of Leave Man, 171
Tiffany and Company, 123, 175
Todd, Alexander, 45, 163
Todd, David, 45, 163
Todd, Dr. George, 244
Todd, George, 45
Todd, Levi, 45
Todd, Mrs. Robert, 164
Todd, Robert, 15–16, 67
Todd, Samuel, 45, 124
Treasury building, 45, 62
Treasury Department, 196
Tremont House, 254
Trent Affair, 104–6, 105
Trollope, Anthony, 6–7
Turner, Justin, 89
Turner, Linda, 89
typhoid fever, 115–16

U. S. diplomacy, 104
Union army
  increasing size of, 56
  service of Negroes in, 82
  training of, 79
the Union, 32
  preservation of, 128–29
  splitting of, 2, 131
  victory of, 206
unwritten law, excusing murdering
    husband, 165
Usher, John P., 218, 242
USS *Montauk*, 244

varioloid, 169–70
vice president, 32–33. *See also*
    Hamlin, Hannibal; Johnson,
    Andrew
  Lincoln's relationship with, 34
  replacement of, 184–86
Vicksburg, 159
Victoria (queen), 105, 114
Villard, Henry, 87
Virginia, 44, 47–48, 55, 56, 80, 92

Wade, Senator Ben, letter from,
    113–14
Wakeman, Abram, 202–3
Wallace, Frances, 20
Wallace, General Lew, 193, 195
War Faction, 91
Warren, Lavinia, 161
Washington, D.C. *See also*
    Pennsylvania Avenue
  Bull Run battle confidence of,
    58–59
  danger in, 7–8
  emancipation in, 133
  fear of assault on, 54
  hospitals in, 178
  industry in, 8–9
  light protection for, 192
  as military center, 61, 65–66, 171
  securing from invasion, 44, 45, 125
  size of, 8
  as slave city, 8
  society of, 6, 9
  soldiers' executions in, 145
  Southern sympathizers in, 60
  threat to, 194

unfinished plan of, 6
victory celebration in, 236
water supply of, 7
weather of, 7, 9
Washington Monument, 8
Washington National Republican,
    83–84
Washington, President George, 164,
    181
Washington Star, 118, 172
Watt, John, 88, 90
Welles, Gideon, 36, 39, 236, 240,
    242, 249
Wheeler, Mrs., 260
Whig Party, 32, 35
White House, p6
  accessibility of, 9–10
  condition of, 1, 172–73
  damage during transition of, 252
  germs surrounding, 155–56
  as home, 4–5, 10–12
  last reception at, p7
  during Lincoln's presidency, vi–vii
  privacy in, 11
  public reception at, 225
  redecoration of, 50–54, 87–88, 107
  Seward's responsibility for
    entertainment at, 37
  social season at, 1864, 171
  summer living conditions in, 61,
    64–66
  as tourist attraction, 50–51
  typhoid infection in, 115–16
White, Martha, 45
wife of President, role of, 14–15
Wikoff, Henry, 87
Wilberforce College, 82
Wilderness battle, 182–83, 189
Willard Hotel, 27, 172
William I of Prussia (king), 189
Withers, Professor, 226
Wolf, Dr. G. S., 157
Wood, William, 52–53

Xavier, Francis, 189

"Yankee Doodle," 231

Zouave troop, 47. *See also* Fire
  Zouaves